REPRESENTING FEDERAL EMPLOYEES AND THEIR SPOUSES IN DIVORCE

A PRACTICAL GUIDE

Jessica Markham

ABA
AMERICAN BAR ASSOCIATION
Family Law Section

Cover design by Jill Tedhams/ABA Design

Printed in the United States of America.

25 24 23   5 4 3 2

A catalog record for this book is available from the Library of Congress.

I would like to dedicate this book to my children. To them, I'm gone all day helping other people doing God knows what. But I hope that someday they may pick up this book and understand a little bit more about what I do and why I do it. I've literally written and researched it while changing diapers and breastfeeding and while watching them play. Both my kids accompanied me to my office and watched an iPad while I wrote. I found something I love to do, and I hope someday they do the same. Kids: If Mom can write a book, so can you.

Contents

Chapter Seven

Chapter Eight

Part II: Thrift Savings Plan

Chapter Nine

Forms, samples, and other documents are available for download at https://ambar.org/RepFed

Acknowledgments

I would like to thank my family, but most importantly my mother, who is not only the best mother in the whole world, but the best grandmother, and provides childcare for my two children, who are a handful on a good day. She mostly is paid in hugs and boogers, but sometimes I give her a burrito. Her daily care allows me the unique flexibility to work as much as I need to work, be late and totally undependable, and suffer no consequences. This is a rare and basically unheard-of luxury in this day and age, and I appreciate it daily, even when I don't say it. Knowing my children are taken care of leaves me brain-space to do little things like lawyering, running a law firm, and writing a book.

The whole crew of women who run my family and home extends further to my grandmother Elena, who goes strong at age 90 as chief organizer, laundry doer, wardrobe buyer, child spoiler, and stroller walker; my aunt Maria (Tia Cat), who in addition to being my godmother serves as an "adequate" chauffeur to my daughter and does almost anything and everything else my family needs; and my aunt Lucía, who somehow has energy for us despite having raised seven humans before tackling this crazy crew. This "Bita Crew" has lent me time, love, and labor (including insisting on painting my law firm office), and no thanks could ever be enough. Thank you also to my dad for supporting my education all these years.

I would like to also profusely thank Linda Ravdin, my book project manager, who approached me to write the book; encouraged me; gave me ideas; and provided the most detailed and extensive peer review, editing, and constructive feedback. She also made me believe I could do it and do it well enough to be useful to our peers and meet the standards of the ABA. She refused to accept my first draft or my second and then made the final the best it could be. Her editing skills are beyond compare, but more than that, her confidence in me helped me get the work done when I wasn't sure I could do it. Her knowledge of the content of this book and her attention to detail are an inspiration.

I also deeply thank my colleagues who helped me write this book and research it. They picked up the slack while I was writing, heard me complain constantly and at times stamp my feet (literally), and are generally awesome to be around: Erin Noone, Jillian Morris, Leslie Miller, Samantha Kravitz, Liz Kashmiri, Janelle Walwyn-White, and Lili Lowell. Jillian Morris contributed to the drafting of the domestic violence section and Samantha Kravitz to resources for employees and spouses overseas. Liz Kashmiri extensively helped me organize and type my notes, make charts, and edit. Erin Noone runs my office, most importantly the finances, and basically runs my world, leaving me free to practice law. Lili Lowell contributed to foreign service, HSAs, research, and citations, and Janelle

Walwyn-White contributed her research as well. I would like to also acknowledge my outstanding legal intern Kathleen Huang, who pulled and organized my research, compiled my many binders of materials, read caselaw, wrote summaries, and made many phone calls to government entities (and we all know how fun that is). Thanks also to our former colleague Sydney Montgomery for her contributions.

Leslie Miller deserves a special shout-out as being my QDRO and retirement ride or die and, after working together ten years, chief mind reader. She contributed directly to the drafting of the death benefits and pay scales sections, death benefits having been particularly elusive, difficult, and painstaking. She also read and reread the book, researched all the seemingly contradictory source information, organized, reorganized, edited, and cited again and again. Her hard work and dedication to detail has been critical to the development of this book. Also, if not for her, I might have lost my mind before finishing this book. She has absorbed most of the factoids in this book, which makes her awesome at drafting COAPs but also a great dinner party guest.

The firm's dedication to their work, their joy, and their general coolness are contagious. They say you're an average of the five (or so) people you spend the most time with. In this case, they're my people, and I'm totally satisfied with that fact.

Finally, last but most certainly not least, my husband, Brian, my best friend and biggest cheerleader. For his late-night talks giving management, writing, marketing, and life advice. Believing in me the most. Being an amazing dad to our kids and modeling for the whole family what enthusiasm, relentlessness, and dedication to work really looks like.

About the Author

Jessica Markham is a family attorney in private practice based in Bethesda, Maryland, a suburb of Washington, D.C. Ms. Markham practices all aspects of family law in Maryland and in the district. Ms. Markham and the members of her firm, Markham Law Firm (www.markhamlegal.com), have represented hundreds of parties in divorce cases involving federal employment, have prepared hundreds of retirement court orders, and frequently consult on retirement issues. She has extensive trial experience but advocates settlement over the adversarial process of litigation and is also trained in collaborative law.

Ms. Markham is also frequently engaged by attorneys and parties to prepare their retirement court orders. Finally, Ms. Markham also has an active mediation practice, helping parties to resolve divorce-related disputes as a neutral, and is frequently appointed as a mediator by local courts.

Ms. Markham has been recognized by her peers for her work. In 2018, 2019, and 2020, Ms. Markham was recognized by her peers for inclusion in "The Best Lawyers in America"© in the field of family law for the Washington, D.C., area, and the firm was recognized as a Best Firm in 2019 and 2020. In 2019 and 2020, Ms. Markham was named a Top Divorce Lawyer (Divorce) by *Washingtonian Magazine* and Top Attorney by *Bethesda Magazine* (family law and ADR). Ms. Markham is honored to have been selected by the *Daily Record*, a local legal newspaper, as a 2016 Leading Woman for achievements in her career, and the firm was awarded the "Top Winner" for Best Family Law Firm in 2019 and 2020 and Best Mediation Firm in 2020. Ms. Markham has also received a Martindale-Hubbell Peer Review Rating of AV Preeminent in the field of family law. In addition, Ms. Markham has been selected for inclusion as a "Rising Star" by *Maryland SuperLawyers Magazine* (2011–2020) and *Washington DC SuperLawyers Magazine* (2013–2020).

Ms. Markham and her husband developed an app called AliRecap, which can be found on the iTunes App Store. It calculates alimony recapture and has disappointingly been made largely moot by recent tax law changes.

Ms. Markham is a lifelong Washington area resident and resides in Potomac with her husband and two children. She can be found tweeting at @markhamlegal.

Preface

This book is a deep dive into the world of divorce and the federal employee (current, former, or retiree) or spouse. This book is intended for any family law practitioner who may touch any of these topics in a case involving a current or former federal employee. The information contained in this book is critical to representing the interests of your client no matter what side you're on. By reading this book, you will understand the benefits at stake: retirement, health insurance, life insurance. The fact that this book has never been written is surprising in and of itself. Those of us practicing in this area have been forced for many years to cobble together the information we need from various and sundry sources, mostly 20 years old or more. Now it's all in one place.

I've included the full range of information, so that a recent law school graduate, all the way up to the experienced, partner-level attorney, can find information of critical use in such cases. In most cases, I begin with the elementary aspects of the topics being discussed and work from there to the highest level of detail. I've also included relevant citations so you can delve even deeper into the law should the need arise. I have attempted to make this information easy to digest and understand, and I have included various checklists, glossary terms, and definitions as easy reference. I have also provided samples that you may use in your practice. I hope that less experienced practitioners will use the book to learn the basics they may not yet know or have been too afraid to ask. More experienced practitioners may keep the book on their shelves and be confident that in reaching for it from time to time, they will find what they need.

Beyond the basics, if you understand the nuances, you can help your client negotiate the best possible outcome and divvy up assets in a settlement in the most advantageous way. There are a lot of ways you can add value to your client that are outlined in this book. Perhaps a TSP loan can be used to buy your client a new home or pay off attorney's fees. If your client is the nonemployee spouse and is in fear of losing his or her health insurance, you can help him or her maintain that benefit. This book will help you cover all of the bases.

Introduction

Summary of Topics Covered in This Book

This book will introduce the major features of the largest federal government pension systems—the Federal Employees Retirement System (FERS), the Civil Service Retirement System (CSRS), the Foreign Service Retirement and Disability System (FSRDS), and the Foreign Service Retirement System (FSRS)—and the federal government's defined contribution plans (the largest being the Thrift Savings Plan) and how to divide them in divorce. Specifically, this book primarily addresses how a federal employee and his or her spouse or former spouse may obtain funds from a retirement plan, by distribution, by withdrawal, or by court order.

This book covers each benefit at the three possible points when there could be a federal employee divorce:

a. During active employment
b. After the employee has separated from service but before he or she is eligible for retirement
c. After retirement

This book also addresses issues related to death benefits, including pension survivor annuities, beneficiary designations, life insurance, and insurable interests.

This book discusses issues ancillary to pension division in divorce, such as maintaining health insurance after divorce and the effect of remarriage.

Some federal benefits, such as certain retirement benefits, are available to a former spouse only by court order. Other federal benefits require that a spouse make an election and take specific action within a specified timeframe to avail him- or herself of the benefit, and a court order can neither grant nor deny these benefits, such as Federal Employees Health Benefits continuation coverage.

PRACTICE TIP

Here's a list of information that can be helpful to collect from the client or to request from the other party and that may impact the division of federal benefits:

- History of any federal employment during the marriage or prior, by either party, including dates of service
- Identification of the correct pension system
- Information about any prior military service
- Any breaks in service
- The employing department or agency
- Whether either party has made a deposit to repay a prior refund or for military service
- Whether the employee has been married before;
- Copy of any prenuptial agreement
- A review of the employing agency benefits webpage
- Whether the spouse is on the federal employee's FEHB health insurance

This book also includes information regarding lesser-known protections and benefits offered to federal employees, retirees, and their spouses, such as leave, disability, long-term care insurance, and resources for victims of domestic violence.

This book also briefly reviews litigation considerations such as determining income, garnishment, and obtaining documents from a federal agency.

Who Is the Federal Civilian Workforce?

Federal civilian employment in the United States and U.S. territories as of September 2017 numbered 1,847,469.[1] According to the Office of Personnel Management (OPM), 1,274,956 CSRS or FERS employees retired and became annuitants from fiscal year 2000 to fiscal year 2013.[2]

Various categories of people could have interests in benefits discussed in this book, for example:

- Current federal employees
- Former federal employees with a future entitlement to a pension (deferred annuitant)
- Annuitants (former employees currently retired and in pay status)

1. *Data, Analysis & Documentation*, Off. of Personnel Mgmt. (Sept. 2017), https://www.opm.gov/policy-data-oversight/data-analysis-documentation/federal-employment-reports/reports-publications/federal-civilian-employment/#note1.

2. *Retirement Statistics*, Off. of Personnel Mgmt., https://www.opm.gov/retirement-services/retirement-statistics/ (last visited Nov. 11, 2020).

- Former employees who did not vest in their pensions yet could return to government employment
- Current or former spouses of any of the above
- Minor or dependent adult children of a current or former federal employee

A person with former or current military service may in the future become a civilian employee and could make a deposit to acquire the military service years toward his or her federal pension or could combine a current military pension with a future federal pension.

Due to the expansive nature of the foregoing list, it is important to collect the right information at an initial consultation.

Federal government contractors are not government employees and therefore are not entitled to government retirement benefits or other benefits provided for federal employees.

PRACTICE TIP

Check the employing agency website under "careers" or "benefits" to learn the range of retirement and other benefits that the employee may have available to him or her.

A review of the careers or benefits page of the employing agency website is important. There are many quasigovernmental agencies whose employees do not participate in FERS, CSRS, or the TSP. The lawyer should not assume that an employee of such an entity has a TSP or a FERS pension. Therefore, the lawyer should closely examine the employee's paystub to identify employee and/or employer contributions to a retirement account and the type of account.

There are some governmental agencies that do not participate in FERS or TSP. This may be due to funding reasons. For example, some employees of the Smithsonian Institution are Smithsonian Trust employees, and as such, they receive separate and distinct benefits and do not participate in FERS/CSRS or TSP. Other employees of the Smithsonian Institution fully participate in these federal government retirement benefits. Employees of the FDIC and National Credit Union Administration have retirement savings plans in addition to their pension and TSP entitlements. These are only examples. The attorney will need to make the appropriate inquiries and research what benefits are available to the employee.

What Are the Benefits That Are Divisible in Divorce?

State law defines what is marital or community property and the rules for property division in divorce. Federal law determines whether and how a spouse may get direct access to federal benefits, such as a pension, at divorce. Pursuant to federal law, retirement accounts are generally inalienable, may not be assigned, and are not attachable except in certain limited circumstances.[3] The federal preemption doctrine emanates from the Supremacy Clause, article VI, clause 2, of the United States Constitution, which provides:

> This Constitution, and the Laws of the United States which shall be made in Pursuance thereof; and all Treaties made, or which shall be made, under the Authority of the United States, shall be the Supreme law of the land; and the Judges in every State shall be bound thereby, any Thing in the Constitution or Laws of any State to the Contrary notwithstanding.

3. *See* Chapter 16.

Federal statutes and regulations create the authority for a state court to enter an order directed to the Office of Personnel Management (OPM), or other federal entity, to divide or otherwise allocate federal benefits at divorce. 5 C.F.R. § 838.101 *et seq.* regulates OPM's handling of court orders affecting the CSRS or the FERS, both of which are administered by OPM, and details the effect that terms of such court orders will be given. State courts may enter orders affecting Foreign Service pensions pursuant to 22 U.S.C. § 4060.

In general, for the defined benefit plans, the employee annuity, the survivor annuity, the annuity supplement, and the cost of living adjustments can be divided. A court order can also prohibit or divide a refund of employee contributions.

A court order cannot mandate a continuation of health insurance coverage, but it can make health insurance available as an ancillary benefit, if certain conditions are met.

A court order can require that an employee cover his or her children under his or her health insurance.

A court order regarding a federal employee's life insurance under the Federal Employees' Group Life Insurance (FEGLI) program can (a) assign the life insurance benefit to a former spouse or children or (b) require an employee to name his or her former spouse or children as beneficiaries.

A court order may also garnish retirement benefits for alimony, child support, or an award in a case involving child abuse.

A court order related to a divorce or separation cannot mandate coverage for a divorced spouse for dental or vision benefits under the Federal Employees Dental and Vision Insurance Program (FEDVIP) plan or long-term care insurance.

Overview of Federal Government Pension Systems

31 U.S.C. § 9502 defines the term "government pension plan" to mean a pension, annuity, retirement, or similar plan established or maintained by an agency for any of its officers or employees, regardless of the number of participants.

The plans subject to 31 U.S.C. § 9502 fall into three general categories:

1) Agency plans
2) Nonappropriated fund activity plans
3) Federal reserve and farm credit plans

Agency plans cover employees of executive, legislative, and judicial organizations that are generally recognized as agencies and are generally funded by annual appropriations.

This book covers the two largest and most prominent federal government pension systems for civilian employees under the Civil Service Retirement and Disability Fund (consisting of the CSRS and FERS pensions). This book also covers the Foreign Service Retirement and Disability Fund, which provides benefits to members of the Foreign Service under the FSRDS or the newer FSPS. This book also briefly covers the Federal Reserve Employees' Benefits System.

The above pension systems all fund defined benefit pension plans that provide a monthly annuity to the retired employee for his or her life or a reduced annuity to the employee for life with a survivor annuity to his or her surviving spouse for the spouse's life. The amount of the pension payments made to the retiree, and to the surviving spouse, is determined through a calculation that includes years of service and salary. As governmental plans, federal pensions are exempt from the Employee Retirement and Income

Security Act (ERISA),[4] the federal law that governs the administration of most private employer retirement plans.

According to the Congressional Budget Office,

> [i]n 2016, the federal government spent $91 billion on retirement benefits for most of its civilian employees: $70 billion for CSRS pensions for civilian retirees and their survivors; $13 billion for FERS pensions for civilian retirees and their survivors; and $8 billion for contributions to TSP. Those expenditures were partially offset by $3 billion in revenues from employees' contributions to the CSRS and FERS pension plans.[5]

Nonappropriated fund activity plans cover employees of organizations, such as post exchanges and commissaries, that provide morale, welfare, and recreation services to military components. In large part, these organizations are designed to be self-sufficient and operate with revenues generated from their activities.

The Federal Reserve and farm credit plans cover employees of federal reserve and farm credit system entities, which also operate with revenues generated from their activities.

In addition to the Civil Service Retirement and Disability Fund (CSRS and FERS), Federal Reserve Employees' Benefits System, and Foreign Service Retirement and Disability Fund, which are covered by this book, according to a 1996 General Accounting Office official report,[6] agencies, nonappropriated fund activities, and federal reserve and farm credit entities offered an additional 31 federal defined benefit pension plans.[7] In total, these 34 plans covered more than ten million current employees, separated employees entitled to benefits, and retirees. Fifteen of the 34 defined benefit plans were agency plans. Nonappropriated fund activities, the Federal Reserve, and farm credit entities operated the other 19. Since 1996, it appears that no centralized list of federal pensions has been published by the federal government.

According to the same 1996 General Accounting Office official report, the following federal pension systems existed at that time. Of these 34 systems identified, 97 percent of the participants belonged to FERS, CSRS, or the military pension system:

1. Civil Service Retirement and Disability Fund (CSRS and FERS)
2. Federal Reserve Employees' Benefits System
3. Foreign Service Retirement and Disability Fund
4. Military Retirement System[8]
5. Coast Guard Military Retirement System
6. Public Health Service Commissioned Corps Retirement System
7. National Oceanic and Atmospheric Administration Corps Retirement System
8. Comptrollers' General Retirement Plan

---

4. 29 U.S.C. §§ 1001(23), 1003(b)(1), 1051.

5. *Options for Changing the Retirement System for Federal Civilian Workers*, CONG. BUDGET OFF. (Aug. 29, 2017), https://www.cbo.gov/publication/53003.

6. U.S. GOV'T ACCOUNTABILITY OFF., GAO/AIMD-96-6, PUBLIC PENSIONS: SUMMARY OF FEDERAL PENSION PLAN DATA (1996).

7. Since this report, there appears to be no comprehensive summary of all federal government pensions that includes nonappropriated funds, and it seems that the farm credit plans may have been condensed and combined.

8. The most comprehensive resource for military pensions is MARK E. SULLIVAN, THE MILITARY DIVORCE HANDBOOK: A PRACTICAL GUIDE TO REPRESENTING MILITARY PERSONNEL AND THEIR FAMILIES (3d ed. 2019).

9. Court of Federal Claims Judges' Retirement System
10. U.S. Court of Veterans Appeals Judges' Retirement Plan
11. Judicial Officers' Retirement Fund
12. Judicial Retirement System
13. Judicial Survivors' Annuities System
14. United States Tax Court Retirement Plan
15. United States Tax Court Survivors' Annuity Plan
16. Tennessee Valley Authority Retirement System
17. Retirement Annuity Plan for Employees of Army and Air Force Exchange Service
18. Supplemental Deferred Compensation Plan for Members of the Executive Management Program (Army and Air Force Exchange Service)
19. U.S.A.F. Nonappropriated Fund Retirement Plan for Civilian Employees
20. United States Army Nonappropriated Fund Retirement Plan
21. Retirement Plan for Civilian Employees of United States Marine Corps Morale, Welfare, and Recreation Activities and Miscellaneous Nonappropriated Fund Instrumentalities
22. Navy Exchange Service Command Retirement Plan
23. U.S. Navy Nonappropriated Fund Retirement Plan for Employees of Civilian Morale, Welfare, and Recreation Activities
24. Norfolk Naval Shipyard Pension Plan
25. Western Farm Credit District Employees' Retirement Plan
26. Ninth Farm Credit District Pension Plan
27. Farm Credit District of Springfield Group Retirement Plan
28. Farm Credit District of Baltimore Retirement Plan
29. Seventh Farm Credit District Retirement Plan
30. First South Production Credit Association Retirement Plan
31. Farm Credit District of Columbia, SC Retirement Plan
32. Farm Credit District of Texas Pension Plan
33. Twelfth Farm Credit District Retirement Plan
34. National Bank for Cooperatives Retirement Plan

Part I

Pensions

Chapter One

Civil Service Retirement and Disability Fund Pensions

This chapter covers the two main pension systems for civilian employees, the Civil Service Retirement System (CSRS)[1] and the Federal Employees' Retirement System (FERS).[2] Both CSRS and FERS are technically one pension system and are both funded through the Civil Service Retirement and Disability Fund. This chapter introduces the key elements of these pensions, including calculation of the high-3 salary, minimum retirement ages, refund of employee contributions, special features such as early retirement provisions, and additional payments to which employees may be entitled. The various death benefits associated with the pensions are also introduced.

1.1 Civil Service Retirement System (CSRS)

The Civil Service Retirement System (CSRS) is the older of the two pensions funded through the Civil Service Retirement and Disability Fund. The Civil Service Retirement Act of 1920[3] established a pension system for federal employees in the executive branch of government. Until January 1, 1984, all full-time federal government employees were covered by CSRS; as such, CSRS covers employees who entered United States government civil service on or before December 31, 1983. These federal employees were excluded from Social Security participation, coverage, and taxes.

1.1.1 CSRS Pension—How It Works

CSRS participants generally contribute 7 percent of pay to their future pension benefit, unless they fall into a special category described in Section 1.1.4. The employing agency matches the employee's CSRS contributions. CSRS participants may increase their earned annuity by contributing up to an additional 10 percent of the basic pay to a voluntary contribution account.

CSRS participants do not pay taxes into the Social Security system, except for CSRS Offset participants, discussed in Section 1.2. Thus, they are not entitled to Social Security benefits based on their federal employment. CSRS participants do, however, contribute to Medicare tax (1.45 percent of pay as of December 31, 2019).

CSRS participants may also contribute a portion of their pay to the Thrift Savings Plan (TSP); however, there is no government matching contribution, as there is for FERS participants (see Section 9.1).

CSRS participants are generally entitled to receive an annuity for their lifetime (a single-life annuity, known as the "self-only annuity"). The self-only annuity is a percentage of the employee's high-3 average salary. The high-3 average pay is the highest average basic pay earned in any three consecutive years of service. The Office of Personnel Management (OPM) explains the computation of the high-3 as follows:[4]

1. The provisions of law that govern CSRS benefits are found in 5 U.S. Code chapter 83, subchapter III, Civil Service Retirement. The regulations covering both CSRS and FERS benefits are in part 838 of title 5, Code of Federal Regulations.
2. The provisions of law that govern FERS benefits are found in 5 U.S. Code chapter 84.
3. 5 U.S.C. §§ 8331–8351.
4. *Computation*, Off. of Personnel Mgmt., https://www.opm.gov/retirement-services/fers-information/computation/ (last visited Nov. 11, 2020).

Your "high-3" average pay is the highest average basic pay you earned during any 3 consecutive years of service. These three years are usually your final three years of service, but can be an earlier period, if your basic pay was higher during that period. Your basic pay is the basic salary you earn for your position. It includes increases to your salary for which retirement deductions are withheld, such as shift rates. It does not include payments for overtime, bonuses, etc. (If your total service was less than 3 years, your average salary was figured by averaging your basic pay during all of your periods of creditable Federal service).

CSRS participants accrue percentage points for each year of creditable service, and the cumulative percentage is multiplied by the high-3 average salary. CSRS participants accrue 1.5 points per year for the first five years, 1.75 points for the second five years, and 2 points per year for all years over ten.

The chart below illustrates the accrual of points for CSRS participants:

Years of Service	Percent of High 3-Year Average Earnings	Years of Service	Percent of High 3-Year Average Earnings	Years of Service	Percent of High 3-Year Average Earnings	Years of Service	Percent of High 3-Year Average Earnings
5	7.50%	15	26.25%	25	46.25%	35	66.25%
6	9.25%	16	28.25%	26	48.25%	36	68.25%
7	11.00%	17	30.25%	27	50.25%	37	70.25%
8	12.75%	18	32.35%	28	52.25%	38	72.25%
9	14.50%	19	34.25%	29	54.25%	39	74.25%
10	16.25%	20	36.25%	30	56.25%	40	76.25%
11	18.25%	21	38.25%	31	58.25%	41	78.25%
12	20.25%	22	40.25%	32	60.25%	42	80.00%
13	22.25%	23	42.25%	33	62.25%	43	80.00%
14	24.25%	24	44.25%	34	64.25%		

If the employee's high-3 average pay had been $50,000 and the employee had 20 years of service, the math would work out as follows:

$50,000 × .015 = $750 × 5 years = $3,750
$50,000 × .0175 = $875 × 5 years = $4,375
$50,000 × .02 = $1,000 × 10 years = $10,000

The employee's annual self-only annuity would be $18,125.[5]

5. OPM Publ'n: Information for Disability Annuitants, RI 30-13 (rev. May 2009).

A CSRS participant is vested in the CSRS basic retirement annuity after five years of service. Participants with less than five years of service who separated from service without entitlement to an immediate pension could leave their money in the retirement fund and apply for a deferred annuity if they are reemployed and later meet the age and service requirements, or they could take a refund of employee contributions.

The maximum pension benefit a participant in CSRS can receive is 80 percent of his or her high-3 average pay plus credit for the participant's unused sick leave. This limit generally affects only those who have more than 41 years of service when they retire.

Under CSRS, a participant can retire with full, unreduced benefits under the following conditions: with at least 30 years of service at age 55; with at least 20 years of service at age 60; and with five or more years of service at age 62.[6]

CSRS has various components over which federal law permits the state court at divorce to exercise authority: the employee annuity (paid during the lifetime of the employee), the survivor annuity, cost-of-living adjustments (COLAs), and the refund of employee contributions. For how to divide each of these elements at divorce, see Chapter 2 and Section 5.1.

1.1.2 CSRS Eligibility for Retirement

For CSRS participants, eligibility for retirement is determined with reference to the minimum retirement age (MRA), a combination of the age and years of service of the employee and the type of position. A summary is provided in the following table:

CSRS—Regular	**Age**	**Years of Service**
	62	5
	60	20
	55	30
CSRS Special/Early Optional Requirements: The agency must be undergoing a major reorganization, reduction in force, or transfer of function determined by the OPM. The annuity is reduced if the employee is under age 55.	50	20
	Any Age	25
CSRS Special Requirements: For air traffic controllers or law enforcement and firefighter personnel, nuclear materials couriers, Supreme Court Police, and Capitol Police.	50	20
	Any Age (air traffic controllers)	25
CSRS Discontinued Service: Separation is involuntary and not a removal for misconduct or delinquency.	50	20
	Any Age	25
CSRS Disability: Disabled for useful and efficient service in current position and any other vacant position at the same grade or pay level within commuting area and current agency for which employee is qualified. Must have been disabled prior to retirement, and the disability should be expected to last for more than one year.	Any Age	5

6. Katelin P. Isaacs, Cong. Research Serv., Federal Employees' Retirement System: Benefits & Financing (2015).

1.1.3 CSRS Voluntary Contribution Account and Excess Deductions

An employee covered by the CSRS or the CSRS Offset provisions has the option to establish a Voluntary Contribution Account to purchase additional annuity benefits.[7] The employee may withdraw such voluntary contributions at any time, with interest, before starting to receive the annuity.[8]

A CSRS participant may not receive a pension that exceeds 80 percent of his or her high-3 average salary. When such an employee reaches the years of service that will qualify him or her for a pension that would exceed the 80 percent maximum, his or her retirement deductions thereafter are Excess Deductions. At the retirement or death of the employee, the Excess Deductions are treated in the same way as voluntary contributions.[9]

1.1.4 CSRS Special, Also Known as 6(c) Retirement

Certain employees receive enhanced retirement benefits under CSRS, referred to as "6(c) Retirement"[10] or "CSRS Special." CSRS Special participants are law enforcement officers, firefighters, nuclear materials couriers, or customs and border protection officers. Employees in these positions contribute 7.5 percent of pay, an extra one-half percent over the contribution amount for regular CSRS participants. The employees in this category have more generous retirement benefits and can retire at age 50 and after completing 20 years of service.[11]

The employee's pension is 2.5 percent of the employee's high-3 average pay for each of the first 20 years of law enforcement/firefighter service and 2 percent per year of service thereafter.

The employee must also have been under CSRS coverage for one out of the last two years before retirement. The minimum age and service requirements apply even if the employee retires involuntarily or due to disability. The employee does not need to be in a special 6(c) covered position at the time of his or her retirement.[12] After the employee accumulates 20 years of 6(c) service, he or she can move to a regular position and still receive the 6(c) special retirement computation. Under the special 6(c) provisions, the employee would have been subject to mandatory separation based on age if occupying a law enforcement position at age 57 or firefighter position at age 55, once the employee completed 20 years of service.

The basic annuity of an employee eligible to retire under the special provisions for law enforcement officers and firefighters is expressed in the following chart. Unlike most other federal employees, there is no reduction in the basic annuity for retirement under age 55.

50 percent of the high-3 average salary

plus

2 percent of the high-3 average salary multiplied by years and whole months of service exceeding 20, plus credit for unused sick leave

7. FERS participants do not have this option.
8. OPM Publ'n: Voluntary Contributions under the Civil Service Retirement System, RI 83-10 (rev. Apr. 1998).
9. 5 U.S.C. § 8342(h).
10. 5 U.S.C. § 8336(c).
11. *Id.*
12. OPM Publ'n: Retirement Facts 14, Law Enforcement & Firefighter CSRS Retirement, RI 83-20 (rev. Oct. 1997).

Under CSRS, an Air Traffic Controller ("Controller") can retire at age 50 after 20 years of service or at any age after 25 years as a Controller. While there is no special benefit formula, there is a guaranteed benefit after at least 20 years of Controller service of 50 percent of the employee's high-3 average pay. If the employee retires after 25 years, it works out to earning 2 percent per year. If the employee retires after 27 years, the guarantee provides no more than the regular formula would have. Other than the guaranteed benefit and mandatory retirement, there are no other special CSRS rules for Controllers.

A military reserve technician (also known as a National Guard technician) is a civilian employee who is a member of the Army National Guard of the United States, the Army Reserve, the Naval Reserve, the Marine Corps Reserve, the Air Force Reserve, or the Coast Guard Reserve who is assigned to duties in one of these components and who is required to maintain a specific military grade in order to continue in his or her civilian employment.[13] Under CSRS, a technician is treated the same as any other employee under CSRS. A technician who is involuntarily separated (not for delinquency or misconduct) from his or her position can get a discontinued service annuity at any age with 25 years of service or at age 50 with 20 years of service. The annuity is reduced at a rate of 2 percent for each year the employee is under 55 years of age.

1.2 CSRS Offset

Federal employees hired or rehired on or after January 1, 1984, who were covered by both CSRS and Social Security at the same time are CSRS Offset participants. The legislation that created FERS also created the CSRS Offset plan. Typically, CSRS Offset retirement applies to employees who had a break in service that exceeded one year and ended after 1983 and who had five years of creditable civilian service as of January 1, 1987. Another category of CSRS Offset employee is an employee who was hired before January 1, 1984, acquired CSRS interim coverage between 1984 and 1987, and had at least five years of creditable civilian service by January 1, 1987.[14]

Participants in CSRS Offset earn credit for both their CSRS pension and their Social Security benefits. When they retire, the same rules regarding retirement eligibility and calculation of the pension apply as under the regular CSRS system. However, when the employee becomes eligible for Social Security, the pension annuity is reduced (hence the "offset") by the value of the Social Security benefit earned during the CSRS Offset service. The reduction also applies to the employee's survivor benefit, if there is a Social Security survivor benefit payable.

The age and service requirements for retirement as a CSRS Offset participant are the same as those for a regular CSRS participant. The CSRS Offset participant will receive a full CSRS annuity at retirement that is computed under the CSRS rules, using average salary and years of service.

The CSRS annuity for offset participants will be reduced when the participant becomes eligible for Social Security old-age benefits, usually at age 62. OPM contacts the Social Security Administration (SSA) just before the offset employee is 62 years old to ask how much SSA will pay, figuring the annuitant's benefit with and without the CSRS Offset service. Based on its reply, OPM makes the annuity reduction.

---

13. 10 U.S.C. § 10216, Military technicians (dual status).
14. OPM Publ'n: CSRS Offset Retirement, RI 83-19 (Apr. 1998).

The offset reduction is the lesser of the

1. difference between the SSA monthly benefit amounts with and without CSRS Offset service, or
2. product of the SSA monthly benefit amount with federal earnings multiplied by a fraction where the numerator is the employee's total CSRS Offset service rounded to the nearest whole number of years and the denominator is 40.

$$\text{Social Security benefit} \times \frac{\text{Total Years of Offset Service}}{40}$$

The amount that the employee contributes is likewise reduced by his or her Social Security tax.

- Most U.S. workers contribute 6.2 percent of their pay as Social Security tax (up to the first $128,400 of earnings, as of December 31, 2019).
- CSRS participants pay 7 percent to OPM for their pension coverage.
- However, most CSRS Offset participants pay 0.8 percent of pay for CSRS Offset coverage (7.0 percent minus 6.2 percent for Social Security equals 0.8 percent for offset coverage).[15]

1.3 Federal Employees' Retirement System (FERS)

1.3.1 Who Is Covered

The Federal Employees' Retirement System (FERS) was created by H.R. 2672 (99th Congress), Federal Employees' Retirement System Act of 1986. The bill was introduced on June 5, 1985, and signed June 6, 1986.[16] FERS became effective January 1, 1987. Over 90 percent of current federal employees are covered by FERS. FERS is a three-part retirement program consisting of a defined benefit pension (the FERS pension), a defined contribution account (the TSP), and Social Security.

There were various timing requirements that took effect between 1984 and 1987 that dictated whether an employee would be covered by FERS or CSRS and whether they also participated in the Social Security system. Employees with fewer than five years of nonmilitary experience on December 31, 1986, were covered under interim rules under which they were covered by both CSRS and the Social Security system (CSRS Offset, described in Section 1.2 herein). CSRS Offset participants with more than five years of nonmilitary CSRS service on December 31, 1986, had the option to switch to FERS between July 1, 1986, and December 31, 1987. Employees covered only by CSRS when FERS came into effect remained covered by it unless they opted to switch to FERS.[17]

FERS covers employees of the CIA who are not covered by the CIARDS pension (see Section 1.9) and employees of the State Department who are not covered by one of the Foreign Service pensions (see Chapter 3).

---

15. OPM Publ'n: CSRS Offset Retirement, RI 83-19 (rev. Apr. 1998).
16. 5 U.S.C. § 8402 *et seq.*
17. *New Retirement System for Federal Employees*, Monthly Labor Rev. (1986).

1.3.2 FERS Pension—How It Works

The federal employee is fully vested in the FERS basic retirement annuity after five years of service; there is no partial vesting prior to five years. Employees with less than five years of service who separate from service (i.e., leave federal employment but do not retire) may leave their money in the retirement fund and apply for a deferred annuity, assuming they eventually meet the age and service requirements, or they may take a refund of employee contributions. A refund of employee contributions voids any entitlement to an annuity. If an employee eventually meets the age and service requirements, the employee can go into pay status any time after meeting the requirements, up to the day he or she reaches 62 years of age.

The FERS annuity is calculated and paid as follows:

Age	Formula (FERS)
Under age 62 at separation for retirement, **OR—** Age 62 or older with less than 20 years of service	1 percent of high-3 average salary for each year of service
Age 62 or older at separation with 20 or more years of service	1.1 percent of high-3 average salary for each year of service

Most FERS participants hired before 2013 contribute 0.8 percent of their gross wages toward their future annuity on a per-paycheck basis. Those contributions are withheld from the employee's after-tax income—that is, the contributions are subject to income and payroll taxes. The contribution rates for most employees hired after 2012, however, are much higher, as described below.

FERS participants hired after December 31, 2012, fall into one of two newer categories based on date of hire: FERS-RAE (Federal Employees' Retirement System—Revised Annuity Employee) or FERS-FRAE (Federal Employees' Retirement System—Further Revised Annuity Employee).[18] The applicable abbreviation is typically found on the employee's paystub. With the exception of members of Congress, there is no difference in the FERS basic benefit paid to FERS, FERS-RAE, and FERS-FRAE employees; the only difference is the amount of pay the employee contributes.

FERS-RAE. The Middle Class Tax Relief and Job Creation Act of 2012[19] made a significant change to the FERS by increasing the employee contribution rate from 0.8 percent of gross pretax pay to 3.1 percent for most new employees (as defined in the statute) hired after December 31, 2012.[20] For such employees, their paystub will reflect FERS-RAE as opposed to simply FERS.[21]

FERS-FRAE. Section 401 Bipartisan Budget Act of 2013, signed into law on December 26, 2013, further increased the employee's contribution rate to 4.4 percent for most

18. *See* 5 CFR § 841.403.

19. 47 U.S.C. § 1512.

20. Cong. Budget Off., Options for Reducing the Deficit: 2017 to 2026—Increase Federal Civilian Employees' Contributions to the Federal Employees Retirement System (Dec. 8, 2016).

21. U.S. Off. of Personnel Mgmt. Benefits Admin. Letter No. 12-104 (Oct. 3, 2012) sets forth agency and employee contribution rates for all categories of employees.

employees newly hired after December 31, 2013.[22] For such employees, their paystub will reflect FERS-FRAE.[23]

The following table summarizes FERS retirement employee contribution categories:

Retirement Coverage	Affected Individuals	Employee Contribution Rate
FERS	Employees first hired on/after January 1, 1987 (or rehired after that date with less than five years creditable or potentially creditable service under CSRS)	0.8 percent
FERS-RAE	Employees first hired on/after January 1, 2013 (or rehired after that date with less than five years creditable or potentially creditable service under FERS)	3.1 percent
FERS-FRAE	Employees first hired on/after January 1, 2014 (or rehired after that date with less than five years creditable or potentially creditable service under FERS)	4.4 percent

1.3.3 FERS Eligibility for Retirement

An employee must meet certain age and service requirements to receive an annuity under FERS. Depending on the employee's age and years of service, the employee may be eligible to enter into pay status with an unreduced annuity immediately, may have the option to take a reduced annuity immediately or sooner than age 62, or may have to wait until reaching age 62 before being eligible to go into pay status.

The chart below summarizes the age and service requirements for eligibility for a reduced or an unreduced annuity:[24]

Years of Service	Type of Annuity, Age of Eligibility
Less than five	Not eligible
Five to ten	Unreduced annuity at age 62
At least ten	Unreduced annuity at age 62; OR a reduced annuity at MRA
At least 20	Unreduced annuity at age 60; OR a reduced annuity at MRA
At least 30	Unreduced annuity at any age

22. 5 U.S.C. § 8401(38).

23. U.S. Off. of Personnel Mgmt. Benefits Admin. Letter No. 14-201 (Jan. 30, 2014) sets forth agency and employee contribution rates for all categories of employees.

24. *Voluntary Retirement*, Off. of Personnel Mgmt., https://www.opm.gov/retirement-services/fers-information/types-of-retirement/#url=Voluntary-Retirement (last visited Nov. 12, 2020).

The employee's MRA under FERS is the earliest age on which the employee is eligible to retire and is based on the year of the employee's birth. To determine the employee's MRA, refer to the following table:[25]

Year of birth	MRA is
Before 1948	55
In 1948	55 and 2 months
In 1949	55 and 4 months
In 1950	55 and 6 months
In 1951	55 and 8 months
In 1952	55 and 10 months
In 1953–1964	56
In 1965	56 and 2 months
In 1966	56 and 4 months
In 1967	56 and 6 months
In 1968	56 and 8 months
In 1969	56 and 10 months
In 1970 and after	57

If the employee elects to defer the annuity payment to a date after his or her MRA but before age 62, there are additional implications to be aware of, particularly as they relate to life insurance (see Chapter 12), health insurance (see Chapter 11), and long-term care insurance (see Section 14.3).

If the employee elects to go into pay status prior to age 62 or that employee's specific age on which he or she is eligible to receive an unreduced annuity, then the annuity will be permanently reduced. The reduction amount is 5 percentage points for each year from the date the employee goes into pay status to his or her age 62 or other date on which he or she would otherwise be eligible for an unreduced pension.[26]

For example, if the employee retired at age 56 with at least ten years of service, the employee is eligible as of his or her MRA to go into pay status. Assume the employee's MRA is age 56. That's six years younger than age 62, so the employee's annuity would be reduced by 30 percent if the employee went into pay status as of age 56.[27] However, the employee can elect to defer the annuity until age 62, at which time there would be no reduction, or to a date between age 56 and age 62, in which case there would be a lesser reduction.

25. *Eligibility Information*, Off. of Personnel Mgmt., https://www.opm.gov/retirement-services/fers-information/eligibility/ (last visited Nov. 12, 2020).

26. OPM Publ'n: Information for FERS Annuitants, RI 90-8 (rev. May 2012).

27. Katelin P. Isaacs, Cong. Research Serv., Federal Employees' Retirement System: Benefits & Financing (2015).

1.3.4 FERS Eligibility for Early Retirement and Disability

Employees falling within certain categories may be eligible for early retirement. Regular employees[28] may be eligible for early retirement in certain involuntary separation circumstances, such as a major reorganization or reduction in workforce. In such circumstances, the employee is entitled to an unreduced annuity with at least 25 years of service at any age or an unreduced annuity with at least 20 years of service at age 50.[29]

Employees may receive disability at any age so long as they have completed 18 months of civil service. The employee must have become disabled because of a disease or injury that prevents or limits useful and efficient service in the employee's current position. The disability must be expected to last for at least one year. The employing agency must certify that it is unable to accommodate the disability medical condition in the present position and that it has considered the employee for any vacant positions in the same agency that are at the same grade/pay level and commuting area for which the employee is qualified.

1.3.5 FERS Special

1.3.5.1 Law Enforcement, Firefighting, and Air Traffic Control

FERS provides enhanced benefits for law enforcement and firefighting personnel and air traffic controllers, with some special rules (referred to as FERS Special). First, the FERS definition of a law enforcement or firefighting position includes a requirement that the position be limited to "young and vigorous" personnel. Second, in order to qualify for the special benefits, the employee must have occupied a primary or first-line law enforcement or firefighting position for at least three years before moving to a secondary (administrative or supervisory) position. Agency heads may determine that some supervisory positions are primary because they meet the young and vigorous requirement.[30]

The contribution rate for FERS special law enforcement and firefighting benefits is a half percentage point more pay than for regular coverage, depending on date of hire.

Employees covered by FERS Special accrue 1.7 percent of the high-3 average pay for each of the first 20 covered years of FERS service and 1 percent of the high-3 average pay per year of service thereafter.[31]

Law enforcement officers and firefighters are employees who occupy a position "designated by their employing agency head (or designee) as a law enforcement or firefighter position."[32] Employees in these positions contribute to the pension at a higher rate, the amount of which differs among the categories.[33] Law enforcement officers and firefighters have mandatory separation from service at age 57 and after completing 20 years of service.[34]

---

28. Law enforcement and firefighting personnel and other FERS Special employees have mandatory retirement provisions as well as different rules regarding their regular retirement. See Section 1.3.5 for information specific to these employees.

29. *Voluntary Retirement,* Off. of Personnel Mgmt., https://www.opm.gov/retirement-services/fers-information/types-of-retirement/#url=Voluntary-Retirement (last visited Nov. 12, 2020).

30. There are special rules that apply to Customs and Border Protection officers that this book does not cover. Contact the benefits officer at the employee's agency for additional information. Nuclear materials couriers, Supreme Court police, and Capitol police are also subject to special rules. 5 U.S.C. § 8415(e).

31. *See* 5 U.S.C. § 8415.

32. For precise definitions of law enforcement officers and firefighters, see 5 U.S.C. § 8401.

33. *See* 5 U.S.C.A. § 8422.

34. *See* 5 U.S.C.A. § 8423.

FERS Special law enforcement and firefighter retirees receive cost-of-living adjustments beginning at retirement. By contrast, most other FERS retirees begin to receive cost-of-living adjustments only at age 62.

In addition, FERS Special law enforcement and firefighter retirees will receive the FERS Annuity Supplement (also sometimes referred to as the FERS Special Retirement Supplement) until age 62. The earnings test does not apply to the FERS Annuity Supplement until the employee reaches the MRA. After the employee reaches the MRA, if the employee has earnings from wages or self-employment that exceed the Social Security annual exempt amount, the employee's supplement will be reduced or stopped.

Unlike most other federal employees, for FERS Special employees, there is no reduction in the basic annuity for retirement prior to age 55. Other FERS provisions, including participation in Social Security and the TSP, are the same as for regular employees.

Air traffic controllers are eligible for FERS retirement under the same rules as air traffic controllers covered by CSRS. They receive the same enhanced FERS pension benefits as are provided to law enforcement and firefighting personnel.

1.3.5.2 Military Technicians

A military reserve technician, also known as a National Guard technician, is a civilian employee who is a member of the Army National Guard of the United States, the Army Reserve, the Naval Reserve, the Marine Corps Reserve, the Air Force Reserve, or the Coast Guard Reserve who is assigned to duties in one of these components and who is required to maintain a specific military grade in order to continue in his or her civilian employment.

Under FERS, a technician who is separated from civilian service because he or she no longer qualifies as a member of a military reserve component may retire and receive an unreduced annuity at age 50 if the technician also has 25 years of service. If the technician loses military status due to a disability, FERS disability benefits are payable after 18 months of FERS service. Also, the FERS Annuity Supplement is payable until the employee reaches age 62. The earnings test does not apply to the FERS Annuity Supplement until the employee reaches the MRA. Technicians are not eligible for the 1.1 percent annuity formula under FERS, no matter how long they work or their age at retirement.

1.4 FERS Annuity Supplement

The FERS Annuity Supplement (FAS) provides for a FERS participant who separates from service, and who has met the minimum work and age requirements for early retirement, to receive a supplement to their retirement annuity until age 62.[35] The employee does not have the option of taking FAS until eligible for full unreduced pension benefits.

- Employees at their MRA can retire on an unreduced annuity if they have 30 years of creditable service, which, dependent on year of birth, could occur as early as age 55.[36]
- FERS Special employees (law enforcement, firefighters, air-traffic controllers, and members of Congress (before January 1, 2013)) can retire as early as age 50 with 20 years of service or after 25 years of service at any age.

35. 5 U.S.C. § 8421.
36. 5 U.S.C. §§ 8412, 8414.

The FAS amount is an approximation of what the annuitant's Social Security benefit would have been, if such benefits were payable at the age that the employee retired, and is paid until the annuitant's age 62, at which point he or she can apply for Social Security old-age benefits.[37] The amount is calculated to be the equivalent of the Social Security old-age benefit starting at age 62.[38] The FAS payment can range from $900 to $1,700 per month and can be paid for as many as 12 years, such as for a federal law enforcement officer or firefighter who retires at age 50.

The OPM first estimates what the employee's full-career (40 years) Social Security benefit would be. Then OPM calculates the duration of civilian service under FERS and reduces the estimated Social Security benefit accordingly. For example, if the employee's estimated full-career Social Security benefit would be $1,000 per month and the employee worked 30 years under FERS, OPM would divide 30 by 40, resulting in 0.75, and apply it to the estimated full-career benefit ($1,000 x 0.75 = $750). The result is the employee's FAS, prior to any reductions.

Like Social Security benefits, the employee's FAS is subject to an earnings test.[39] It is reduced if the employee earns more than the exempt amount of earnings (called the minimum level of earnings) in the immediately preceding year. The employee's supplement is reduced by $1.00 for every $2.00 of earnings over the minimum level. It is possible that the employee's FAS could reduce to $0. There is no reduction until after the first calendar year the employee receives the FAS. Then, the employee's earnings during that first calendar year are compared to the Social Security minimum level of earnings for the same year. If the employee earned more than the minimum level of earnings in the previous year, then the current year's FAS will be reduced accordingly. The employee's monthly FAS in the second calendar year is then reduced by 1/12 of the excess earnings. Excess earnings are 50 percent of the amount by which the employee's earnings exceed the Social Security minimum.

The amount the employee may earn without affecting the employee's FAS is determined by the Social Security Administration each year. It will increase with the annual increases in average wages for the national workforce. The employee can obtain the current year's amount on the Social Security Administration website.

The reduction to the FAS for excess earnings does not apply to employees retiring under the special provisions for law enforcement officers, firefighters, air traffic controllers, and military reserve technicians.[40]

The employee's FERS basic benefit is not considered earnings. The employee's earnings for any year will consist of the total sum of wages for service performed in the year, plus all net earnings from self-employment for the year, minus any net loss from self-employment for the year.

37. *See* 5 U.S.C. § 8421; C.F.R. §§ 404.409, 404.310.

38. C.F.R. § 404.312.

39. U.S. Off. of Personnel Mgmt., CSRS & FERS Handbook, ch. 51 (Apr. 1998).

40. *Id.*

1.5 FERS and CSRS—Refund of Employee Contributions

An employee may receive a refund of his or her CSRS or FERS contributions if the employee[41]

1. separates from federal service for at least 31 consecutive days or transfers to a position in which he or she is not subject to CSRS or FERS deductions and remains in such a position for at least 31 consecutive days;
2. files an application with OPM for a refund of his or her retirement contributions;
3. is not reemployed in a position subject to retirement deductions within 31 days;
4. will not become eligible to receive an annuity within 31 days after filing the application;
5. notifies his or her spouse and any former spouse who has rights under a COAP (a court order that grants pension rights to a spouse) that he or she has filed an application for a refund;[42] and
6. does not have a former spouse with the court-ordered right to future pension benefits based on the employee's service.

The receipt of a refund of employee retirement contributions voids any future annuity rights unless the employee is later reemployed and works long enough to earn new retirement rights. In such case, a former CSRS employee would be reemployed as a FERS employee. A refund of employee contributions is irreversible.

Interest is payable on a refund of employee contributions covering service of one to five years. For service under FERS, the interest rate is the same as is paid for government securities for employees who have invested their retirement funds in the G Fund. For service under CSRS, interest will be included in the refund of those contributions if the employee had more than one but less than five years of service. Interest is paid at 3 percent. While the return of employee contributions is not taxable, the interest is taxable.

A former employee may request a refund of FERS or CSRS employee contributions by filing form SF 3106.[43] The form inquires about current and previous federal employment and about marital status. If the employee is married or divorced, the employee must complete Form SF 3106A, "Current/Former Spouse's Notification of Application for Refund of Retirement Deductions." Before the refund can be made, the spouse or former spouse must consent.

The refund can be made by check (subject to 20 percent federal income tax withholding on the taxable portion) or can be payable to an IRA or an eligible employer plan (including the participant's TSP).

1.6 FERS and CSRS—Cost-of-Living Adjustments

Cost-of-living adjustments (COLAs) will increase the amount of the annuity paid to the retiree or to the survivor, as the case may be. COLAs are applied once per year in December, with each monthly payment in the following year increased accordingly.

---

41. OPM Publ'n: Retirement Facts 9: Refunds under the Civil Service Retirement System, RI 83-9 (rev. Oct. 1997).

42. However, a CSRS participant need not notify a former spouse if divorced before May 7, 1985; the marriage to that person lasted less than nine months; or the employee had less than 18 months of CSRS-covered service.

43. A copy of the form is in the downloadable resources provided with this book, available at https://ambar.org/RepFed.

The COLA for CSRS and FERS retirees is calculated based on the Consumer Price Index for Urban Wage Earners and Clerical Workers (CPI-W). However, "if consumer prices as measured by the CPI-W do not increase from the third quarter of the base year to the third quarter of the current calendar year, there is no COLA for annuities paid under CSRS or FERS."[44] OPM releases an annual Benefits Administration Letter announcing the COLA for the coming year. See the following chart for historical COLAs.[45]

Effective Date	CSRS Benefit Increase	FERS Benefit Increase	CPI Change during COLA Measurement Period
December 1992	3.0	2.0	3.0
March 1994	2.6	2.0	2.6
March 1995	2.8	2.0	2.8
March 1996	2.6	2.0	2.6
December 1996	2.9	2.0	2.9
December 1997	2.1	2.0	2.1
December 1998	1.3	1.3	1.3
December 1999	2.4	2.0	2.4
December 2000	3.5	2.5	3.5
December 2001	2.6	2.0	2.6
December 2002	1.4	1.4	1.4
December 2003	2.1	2.0	2.1
December 2004	2.7	2.0	2.7
December 2005	4.1	3.1	4.1
December 2006	3.3	2.3	3.3
December 2007	2.3	2.0	2.3
December 2008	5.8	4.8	5.8
December 2009	0.0	0.0	–2.1
December 2010	0.0	0.0	–0.6
December 2011	3.6	2.6	3.6
December 2012	1.7	1.7	1.7
December 2013	1.5	1.5	1.5
December 2014	1.7	1.7	1.7
December 2015	0.0	0.0	–0.4
December 2016	0.3	0.3	0.3
December 2017	2.0	2.0	2.0
December 2018	2.8	2.0	2.8
December 2019	1.6	1.6	1.6
December 2020	1.3	1.3	1.3

44. *See* 5 U.S.C. §§ 8340, 8462; *see also* Cong. Research Serv., Cost-of-Living Adjustments for Federal Civil Service Annuities (Oct. 2017).

45. Cong. Research Serv., Cost-of-Living Adjustments for Federal Civil Service Annuities, 94-834 (Oct. 14, 2020).

The employee's FERS annuity will be increased for COLAs, if

1. the employee is over age 62; or
2. the employee retired under the special provision for air traffic controllers, law enforcement personnel, or firefighters; or
3. the employee retired on disability, except when the employee is receiving a disability annuity based on 60 percent of the employee's high-3 average salary (this is generally during the first year of receiving disability benefits); or
4. the employee's retirement includes a portion computed under CSRS rules.

Retirees under age 62 who do not fall into one of the categories in items 2, 3, or 4 above are not eligible for COLAs until they reach age 62.

For FERS, COLA amounts are determined by the percentage increase in the Consumer Price Index (CPI), according to the following table:

Change in CPI	COLA
0 to 2 percent	Change in CPI
2 to 3 percent	2 percent
Over 3 percent	Change in CPI, less 1 percent

For CSRS, COLA amounts are equal to the percentage change in the CPI, regardless of the amount of the change.

Supplementary annuities paid to certain survivors of deceased retirees are also increased by any COLAs payable.

Survivors of deceased employees who are receiving the Basic Employee Death Benefit in installments do not receive cost-of-living increases on the installment payments.

1.7 FERS and CSRS—The Alternative Form of Annuity

Certain FERS and CSRS participants can elect an alternative form of annuity (AFA), consisting of a lump sum payment equal to their retirement contributions and a reduced monthly annuity. Only nondisability annuitants who have a life-threatening affliction or other critical medical condition can elect this option. This option is not available if they have a former spouse entitled to a portion of the employee annuity or a survivor annuity pursuant to a court order granting rights to a spouse or former spouse (a COAP) that is already on file with OPM. A married participant must get spousal consent to elect an AFA; however, the AFA will not affect the survivor annuity election for the current spouse.

Part of the AFA lump sum is taxable in the year paid unless it is rolled over into an Individual Retirement Arrangement.[46]

1.8 CSRS and FERS Disability Pension

A federal employee is entitled to a disability pension in the event they are unable to work and the disability is expected to last at least one year. In such event, the employee will receive his or her FERS pension as a disability annuity if he or she is under age 62 and

46. *See* IRS Publ'n 721 (Dec. 2, 2019), *available at* https://www.irs.gov/pub/irs-pdf/p721.pdf.

not eligible for voluntary immediate retirement. A CSRS participant must be under age 60 to qualify for a disability pension. FERS and CSRS Offset employees must also apply for Social Security disability benefits.

To be eligible, the employee must have completed at least five years of federal civilian service for CSRS participants and 18 months for FERS participants. In addition, while employed in a participating position, the employee must have become disabled for "useful and efficient service" in both his or her current position and any other vacant position at the same grade or pay level for which he or she is qualified, as described below.

Useful and efficient service means[47]

(1) either acceptable performance of the critical or essential elements of the position or the ability to perform at that level; and
(2) satisfactory conduct and attendance. Service that is not "useful and efficient" is a level of performance or attendance that, if it were to continue, would warrant denial of a within-grade increase, demotion, separation, or other remedial action.

Application for disability must be made within one year of separation from federal service and is subject to periodic medical reexamination.

CSRS and FERS calculate the disability benefit differently, as set forth below. For both CSRS and FERS, if the employee is married, the benefit will be reduced for a survivor annuity, unless the spouse consents to the election of less than a full survivor annuity. The entitlement will also be reduced if the employee has a former spouse who is entitled to survivor benefits under a COAP.

FERS disability benefits are reduced by all or a portion of the employee's Social Security disability benefit. If an employee who is receiving a FERS disability benefit receives a Social Security disability award, the employee must notify the OPM of the amount of the Social Security benefit and the effective date of the payment immediately upon becoming eligible.[48] CSRS participants do not pay into Social Security; therefore, a disabled CSRS participant will not receive Social Security disability benefits.

1.8.1 FERS Disability Benefit—Calculated

The amount of the FERS disability benefit depends on the annuitant's age and duration of service at disability retirement. The initial FERS disability retirement benefit is recomputed after the first 12 months and again at age 62, if the annuitant is under age 62 at the time of disability retirement.

The chart below shows FERS disability computation if the employee

- is age 62 or older at retirement, or
- meets the age and service requirements for immediate voluntary retirement.

In that event, the employee must receive his or her retirement benefit based on the general FERS annuity formula:[49]

47. OPM Publ'n: Retirement Facts 4, Disability Retirement under the Civil Service Retirement System, RI 83-4 (rev. Nov. 1997).

48. OPM Publ'n: Information for FERS Annuitants, RI 90-8 (rev. May 2012).

49. *Disability*, Off. of Personnel Mgmt., https://www.opm.gov/retirement-services/fers-information/types-of-retirement/#url=Disability (last visited Nov. 12, 2020).

Age	Formula
If age 62 or older at retirement with less than 20 years of service, or	1 percent of high-3* average salary for each year of service
Under age 62 qualified for an immediate voluntary retirement	
If age 62 or older with 20 or more years of service	1.1 percent of high-3 average salary for each year of service

*"High-3" average pay is the highest average basic pay the employee earned during any three consecutive years of service. See glossary for full definition.

The following chart shows the FERS disability computation if the employee is

- under age 62 at disability retirement, and
- not eligible for immediate voluntary retirement.

Under Age 62	Formula
For the first 12 months	60 percent of high-3 average salary minus 100 percent of Social Security benefit for any month in which he or she is entitled to Social Security benefits However, employee is entitled to retirement annuity, if it is larger than this amount.
After the first 12 months	40 percent of high-3 average salary minus 60 percent of Social Security benefit for any month in which he or she is entitled to Social Security disability benefits However, employee is entitled to retirement annuity, if it is larger than this amount.
When employee reaches age 62, annuity will be recomputed using an amount that essentially represents the annuity he or she would have received if he or she had continued working until the day before his or her 62nd birthday and then retired under FERS.	If actual service plus the credit for time as a disability annuitant equals less than 20 years: 1 percent of high-3 average salary for each year of service If actual service plus the credit for time as a disability annuitant equals 20 or more years: 1.1 percent of high-3 average salary for each year of service Total service used in the computation: will be increased by the amount of time employee has received a disability annuity Average salary used in the computation: will be increased by all FERS cost-of-living increases paid during the time he or she received a disability annuity

*Disability annuities for individuals who performed service in an enhanced position such as law enforcement officer, firefighter, nuclear materials courier, air traffic controller, Capitol police, or Supreme Court police will be credited at the higher 1.7 percent for that service.

For a FERS participant under age 62, if the annuity is computed using 60 percent of the high-3 average salary, COLAs are not payable for the first 12 months.[50] After this 12-month period, COLAs are payable. For employees over age 62 at retirement, or who meet the age and service requirements for an immediate FERS annuity, all COLAs occurring after the commencing date of annuity are payable.

1.8.2 CSRS Disability Benefit—Calculated

A CSRS participant who is entitled to a disability pension is entitled to a retirement annuity computed under the CSRS general formula (see Section 1.1.1), with a guaranteed minimum, discussed further below.

The guaranteed minimum disability annuity is the lesser of the following amounts:[51]

(a) 40 percent of the employee's high-3 average salary (which provides the employee with an annuity as if the employee had worked 21 years and 11 months), or
(b) generally, the amount computed under the general formula after increasing the employee's actual years of service by the time remaining between the date of the employee's separation and the date the employee turns 60.

For example, if the employee was employed for 14 years before becoming disabled at age 48, OPM would add 12 years to the employee's 14 years of service (age 60 – 48 = 12 additional years) to arrive at 26 years of service under (b). In this example, OPM would pay 40 percent of the employee's average salary because it is the lesser of the two.

Because of the percentage and age limitations, the guaranteed minimum annuity offers no advantage to a retiring employee who has completed at least 21 years and 11 months of service or is age 60 or older.

Annuitants who are receiving military retired pay or have waived military retired pay to receive compensation from the Department of Veterans Affairs are generally not eligible for the guaranteed minimum disability annuity (unless the military retired pay is based on a disability incurred in combat under chapter 1223, title 10, U.S. Code).

The participant can work and earn some money while receiving disability retirement benefits. However, if the participant is under age 60, his or her disability annuity will stop if OPM determines that he or she is restored to earning capacity. The participant's earning capacity is restored if, in any calendar year, his or her income from wages and self-employment totals at least 80 percent of the current rate of base pay for the position from which he or she retired on disability.

CSRS participants receiving a disability pension receive COLAs.

A National Guard technician who is medically disqualified for military duty and who has five years of creditable civilian service may receive disability benefits without meeting the usual CSRS disability criteria.

50. A COLA is an increase in pay or in an annuity amount based on inflation as measured by the CPI. *See* Section 2.4.

51. 5 C.F.R. § 844.302.

1.9 Central Intelligence Agency Retirement and Disability System (CIARDS)

1.9.1 CIARDS Pension

Central Intelligence Agency (CIA) employees without prior federal service[52] are automatically covered by FERS. After completing five years of "qualifying" service, a CIA employee may be eligible to participate in the CIA Retirement and Disability System (CIARDS), a special category of FERS.[53] Qualifying service is that which is performed by a CIA employee in carrying out duties "in support of intelligence activities abroad hazardous to life or health" or "so specialized because of security requirements as to be clearly distinguishable from normal government employment."[54] Such designation is made at the discretion of the director of the CIA.

The CIARDS single-life annuity is computed by taking the product of

- the participant's high-3 average pay and
- the number of years, not exceeding 35, of service credit multiplied by 2 percentage points.[55]

CIARDS employees contribute 7 percent of their basic pay toward their pensions.[56] Revised annuity participants contribute 9.3 percent of their pay.

Contributions after 35 years of service accrue interest at the rate computed under 5 U.S.C. § 8334(e), compounded annually from the date on which the amount is deducted and withheld until the date of the participant's retirement or death.

CIARDS allows an employee to retire at age 50 with 20 or more years of service. In addition, the CIA maintains a list of "unhealthful posts," and each year of duty at such a post is counted as one and a half years in computing the length of service of a participant for the purpose of retirement.[57]

CIARDS was created in part to entice the best and brightest to serve in the CIA, to allow employees to retire early, and to enable the CIA to bring on new, younger employees. This policy is driven by the need to maintain a youthful workforce for clandestine operations overseas who can withstand the physical and mental demands of such work. An interesting, previously confidential CIA memo from 1962, recently made public, expresses as follows:

---

52. Employees who commenced employment prior to January 1, 1984, would have been covered by CSRS.

53. The terms of CIARDS are set forth in 50 U.S.C. § 38, established pursuant to the Central Intelligence Agency Retirement Act of 1964 for Certain Employees.

54. 50 U.S.C. § 2013 defines participants in the CIARDS system as follows:

> (a) Designation of participants—The Director may from time to time designate employees of the Agency who shall be entitled to participate in the system. Employees so designated who elect to participate in the system are referred to in this chapter as "participants".
> (b) Qualifying service—Designation of employees under this section may be made only from among employees of the Agency who have completed at least 5 years of qualifying service. For purposes of this chapter, qualifying service is service performed by an Agency employee in carrying out duties that are determined by the Director –
>
> (1) to be in support of intelligence activities abroad hazardous to life or health; or
>
> (2) to be so specialized because of security requirements as to be clearly distinguishable from normal government employment.

55. 50 U.S.C. § 2031.

56. 50 U.S.C. § 2021.

57. 50 U.S.C. § 2081.

> The effectiveness of our clandestine operations overseas depends in large measure upon personnel having the highest degree of vigor, resilience, adaptability, energy, aggressiveness, vitality, fearlessness, and endurance. These traits are normally found in youthful individuals and tend to deteriorate with age. The work of clandestine operations personnel is characterized by uneven and uncertain hours of work, duty in unhealthy locations with often less than adequate medical facilities, and arduous, demanding, and occasionally hazardous assignments in which employees become a direct target for activities of the opposition, susceptible to immediate attack or seizure in the event of war or civil disturbance. These conditions combine frequently to lead to physical and mental exhaustion at an age much lower than is normally the case for those engaged in more sedentary activity.[58]

CIA is the only agency that imposes mandatory retirement across the board on every employee (unless exempted by the director). A participant in the system will be automatically retired from the agency[59]

(A) upon reaching age 65, in the case of a participant in the system who is at the Senior Intelligence Service rank of level 4 or above; or
(B) upon reaching age 60, in the case of any other participant in the system.

Agency Contact Information
Contact information for the CIA Retirement and Disability System is:
Central Intelligence Agency, P.O. Box 1925, Washington, D.C. 20505

1.9.2 CIARDS Survivor Annuity for Spouse

When a married CIA employee covered by CIARDS retires, his or her spouse is entitled to a survivor annuity unless the employee waives the survivor benefit with the spouse's consent. Like CSRS, the maximum survivor annuity is 55 percent of the employee's pension. The cost of the survivor benefit is the same as CSRS, 2½ percent of the first $3,600 of retired pay plus 10 percent of any amount of retired pay over $3,600.

1.9.3 Default CIARDS Pension Rights of Former Spouse

A divorced spouse of a CIA employee who is a participant in CIARDS is entitled by default to a share of the pension and to a survivor annuity, meaning no court order is needed to secure it. 50 U.S.C. § 2032 provides an automatic pro rata share of the employee annuity for a former spouse unless expressly waived or divested by spousal agreement or court order

(A) if married to the participant, former participant, or retired participant throughout the creditable service of the participant, equal to 50 percent of the annuity of the participant; or
(B) if not married to the participant throughout such creditable service, equal to that proportion of 50 percent of such annuity that is the proportion that the number of days of the marriage of the former spouse to the participant during periods of creditable service of such participant under this subchapter bears to the total number of days of such creditable service.

---

58. Central Intelligence Agency, Agenda for Task Force on Early Retirement (Apr. 27, 1962), https://www.cia.gov/library/readingroom/docs/CIA-RDP75B00380R000800110018-7.pdf.
59. 50 U.S.C. § 2055.

The former spouse of a CIARDS participant will not be entitled to a survivor annuity if he or she remarries before age 55; however, the survivor annuity is restored if the remarriage is dissolved by death, annulment, or divorce.[60]

Note that if the former spouse is younger than age 50 at the time the participant dies, the right to the survivor annuity is postponed; the annuity will start to be paid after the former spouse reaches age 50.

Parties are free to negotiate for the spouse to receive more or less than the default rights, and the court can award more or less. The participant and former spouse may make a joint election to waive, reduce, or increase a survivor annuity within two years of divorce or at the time of retirement, whichever is later.

1.9.4 CIARDS Lump-Sum Credit

Upon separation from service, a CIARDS employee may apply for the lump-sum credit, which is a refund of employee contributions to the pension. The lump-sum credit will be paid to a married employee only with the express written concurrence of his or her spouse, which must be received by the Director of Central Intelligence. This requirement may be waived under certain circumstances described in 50 U.S.C. § 2031(b)(1)(D):

(A) only upon written notification to
  (i) the current spouse, if any,
  (ii) any former spouse, and
  (iii) any former wife or husband who has a court order covered by paragraph (3); and
(B) only if the express written concurrence of the current spouse has been received by the Director.

Unless expressly waived in a divorce settlement, the former spouse will receive a pro rata share of such lump-sum credit. The receipt of a refund of employee contributions at separation from service voids any right to a pension or survivor benefit. The employee is barred from receiving the lump-sum credit if it would defeat a survivor annuity that has been previously awarded to a former spouse by court order.

1.9.5 Voluntary Investment Plan Accounts for CIA Employees

In addition to the TSP, CIA employees are entitled to contribute to a Voluntary Investment Plan. This is an IRS-qualified 401(a) defined contribution retirement plan, with no matching employer contribution. Participant contributions are made as payroll deductions and are pooled in a tax-deferred program consisting of four investment options. Any 401(a) contributions an employee makes and any earnings on those contributions are immediately fully vested.

PRACTICE TIP

CIA employees may also contribute to a 401(a) plan in addition to a TSP. Be sure to check the employee's paystub.

60. 38 U.S.C. § 2034.

The Internal Revenue Code subjects 401(a) withdrawals to income tax withholding and a 10 percent early withdrawal penalty unless the employee is 59½, dies, is disabled, or rolls over the funds into a qualified IRA or retirement plan through a direct trustee-to-trustee transfer.

Employees who contribute to a 401(a) plan qualify for a tax credit for their pretax contributions.[61]

1.10 Congressional Pension System (CPS)

There are separate pension rules for members of Congress and congressional employees. Their pension is referred to as the Congressional Pension System (CPS). Although it has a different name, each such employee is really covered by FERS or CSRS but has the benefit of a more generous accrual rate and more generous rules regarding when a congressperson or congressional staff member may retire with a pension, as described below. The CPS is administered by OPM.

Members of Congress elected in 1984 or later are automatically covered by FERS.[62] Therefore, most congressional employees are covered by this plan. However, some long-time members or staff members may be covered by CSRS or the CSRS Offset plan.[63]

PRACTICE TIP

Members of Congress and congressional staff members are the only federal employees who are not eligible to participate in the Federal Employees Health Benefits Program (FEHB). The only health plans available to members of Congress and certain congressional staff are those plans created under the Affordable Care Act or offered through an exchange established under the act, such as DC Health Link.

According to the Congressional Research Service: "There were 611 retired Members of Congress receiving federal pensions based fully or in part on their congressional service as of October 1, 2016. Of this number, 335 had retired under CSRS and were receiving an average annual pension of $74,028. A total of 276 Members had retired with service under FERS and were receiving an average annual pension of $41,076 in 2016."[64] These figures do not include congressional employees.

Members of Congress and congressional employees contribute an additional 0.5 percent of pay to FERS as compared to participants in standard FERS.

The pension of a FERS participant covered by CPS who retires with at least five years of service as a member of Congress or as a congressional employee (or any combination of the two) is calculated as follows:

61. *See* 26 U.S.C. § 401.
62. 5 U.S.C. § 8401.
63. *See* 5 U.S.C.A. § 8331.
64. Katelin P. Isaacs, Cong. Research Serv. Rep. 7-5700 (RL30631): Retirement Benefits for Members of Congress (2017).

The employee's annuity is 1.7 percent of the high-3 average salary

multiplied by

the employee's years of service as a member of Congress or a congressional employee up to 20 years of service

plus

1 percent of the employee's high-3 average salary

multiplied by

the employee's years of service over 20

Participants receive an unreduced annuity at age 50 with 20 years of service or at any age with 25 years of service.

Members of Congress first elected after December 31, 2012, are eligible for retirement annuities at earlier ages and with fewer years of service than most other federal employees.

- They are eligible to retire at age 62 with at least five years of service.
- They are eligible to retire at age 50 if they have completed 20 years of service.
- They are eligible to retire at any age after completing 25 years of service.

The retirement annuity may not exceed 80 percent of their high-3 average salary.

Like with regular FERS, an annuity supplement is payable from the MRA to age 62 (see Section 2.7 for more information). Also, like FERS, if the employee has earnings from wages or self-employment that exceed the Social Security annual exempt amount, the employee's supplement will be reduced or stopped. COLAs are payable to congressional retirees before age 62 only if they retire for disability.[65]

1.11 Survivor Annuities under CSRS and FERS

An employee annuity under CSRS or FERS is paid monthly for the life of the plan participant. When he or she dies, the annuity stops, unless he or she elected a survivor annuity. A survivor annuity provides for an annuity to be paid to the survivor after the death of the plan participant for the survivor's life. The survivor could be a current spouse, a former spouse, or both, up to the plan-specific cap. A survivor annuity may be payable upon the death of (1) a current employee of over ten years, (2) a former employee of over ten years, or (3) a retiree, based on election or court order.

The cost of the survivor annuity for a spouse or former spouse is a fixed percentage of the self-only annuity, no matter the relative ages of the parties. The specific cost and the maximum benefit available depend on the pension system.

A surviving spouse is entitled to a survivor benefit in accordance with the following:

- *Current Employees*: If a current married employee dies, his or her spouse is eligible to receive a survivor annuity if the deceased employee had at least ten years of creditable service (18 months of which must be civilian service) and the surviving spouse was married to the deceased employee for at least nine months or is the

65. A COLA is an increase in pay or in an annuity amount based on inflation as measured by the CPI. *See* Section 2.4.

parent to a child of the deceased employee.[66] The amount of the annuity is one-half of the employee's accrued basic retirement benefit. The annuity will begin on the date the deceased employee would have been eligible for an unreduced annuity. The surviving spouse may elect to have the annuity start earlier, though it will be reduced. The surviving spouse may also elect to receive a Lump Sum Death Benefit instead.[67]

- *Former Employees:*

  FERS: The surviving spouse of a former employee is eligible for the survivor annuity if the deceased former employee had at least ten years of creditable service, five years of which must be creditable civilian service, and the surviving spouse was married to the deceased former employee for at least nine months or is the parent to a child of the deceased employee.[68] The amount of the annuity is one-half of the employee's accrued basic retirement benefit. The same start dates apply as to current employees. Additionally, the Lump Sum Death Benefit may be taken instead.

  CSRS: If a CSRS-covered employee separates from employment but is not in pay status (meaning he or she goes into "deferred status"), no survivor benefit will be paid to a spouse or former spouse, notwithstanding any election or court order that purports to award a survivor annuity.[69]
- *Retirees*: When an employee is married and making application for retirement, he or she must indicate whether or not he or she elects a survivor annuity for his or her spouse. If so, the level of the survivor benefit must be elected. The spouse must consent to an election of less than a full survivor annuity.

After retirement, if the parties are married and they elected not to provide a survivor annuity (or elected less than a full annuity), they may elect one (or increase the existing survivor annuity) within 18 months after retirement. If they do so, the employee must pay a deposit that includes

- the difference between the reduction in annuity for the new survivor election and the original survivor election; plus
- a charge of 24.5 percent of the amount of the increase from the original survivor base to the new survivor base (computed as of the time of retirement); plus
- any applicable interest.

If no survivor annuity is payable, then a Lump Sum Death Benefit is payable to the deceased employee's beneficiary. For more information on the Lump Sum Death Benefit, see Section 1.12.3.2.

A former spouse who is entitled to a survivor annuity, and who remarries prior to age 55, will lose his or her entitlement to the survivor annuity, unless the employee was married to the former spouse for 30 years or more, in which case the former spouse's remarriage before age 55 does not terminate such entitlement.[70]

66. *Survivors*, Off. of Personnel Mgmt., www.opm.gov/retirement-services/fers-information/survivors (last visited Nov. 12, 2020).

67. *Id.*

68. *Id.*

69. Note that any CSRS employee leaving government in 2020 would have at least 36 years of federal service and would more than likely be over age 55, meaning he or she would have reached MRA and be eligible to go into pay status. Therefore, there are likely to be few, or no, remaining federal employees to whom this provision applies.

70. 5 U.S.C. §§ 8341, 8445(h)(1).

1.11.1 CSRS Survivor Annuity

1.11.1.1 Postretirement Survivor Annuity Amount and Cost

Upon retirement, a CSRS participant must elect for his or her spouse a survivor annuity equal to 55 percent of the amount of the employee's annuity payable as of his or her death. With the consent of the spouse, the participant can elect a lesser amount or no survivor annuity. The employee's self-only annuity will be reduced in order to provide for the survivor annuity. The reduction in the employee's self-only annuity is referred to as the cost of the survivor annuity. For the maximum survivor benefit, the cost is 2.5 percent of the first $3,600 of the employee's self-only annual annuity, plus 10 percent of the self-only annual annuity amount over $3,600. The following example shows the cost of a maximum survivor benefit for a CSRS pension:

Self-only annual annuity without survivor benefit	$30,900
Less 2½ percent of the first $3,600	–$90
And less 10 percent of amount over $3,600	–$2,730
($30,900 – $3,600 = $27,300)	
Total annuity reduction to provide survivor benefit	**$2,820**
(cost of survivor annuity)	
Self-only annuity	$30,900
Less cost of survivor annuity	$2,820
Annual employee annuity adjusted for survivor benefit	**$28,080**

1.11.1.2 Preretirement Survivor Benefits

If a CSRS participant dies as an active employee, his or her spouse will receive a survivor annuity equal to the smaller of the following: (1) 55 percent of 40 percent of the employee's high-3 annual salary or (2) 55 percent of what the employee's annuity would have been if they had worked until age 60.

If a current employee dies and no survivor annuity is payable as a result of his or her death, the retirement contributions remaining to the deceased person's credit in the Civil Service Retirement and Disability Fund, plus applicable interest, are payable to the employee's named beneficiary, if he or she has a valid designation on file. If the employee did not have a valid Designation of Beneficiary on file, OPM will pay the first person(s) listed below who is alive on the date the payment becomes due:[71]

1. A widow or widower
2. A child or children (descendants of a deceased child may qualify)
3. Parents in equal shares or all to the surviving parent
4. The administrator or executor of the estate
5. If none of the above, next of kin as determined under state law

Unless the employee changes or cancels a designation, the person named, including a former spouse, will receive the lump-sum benefit. Divorce does not affect a preexisting beneficiary designation. Therefore, an employee who does not want a former spouse to benefit from his or her death should file a new beneficiary designation promptly.

71. *Id.*

PRACTICE TIP

Form SF 2808, Designation of Beneficiary (CSRS), is the proper form to update a beneficiary designation.

1.12 FERS Survivor Benefits

The following sections address survivor benefits that may be payable upon the FERS participant's death. These benefits may be payable upon the death of a current employee, after an employee leaves federal government service but before the employee starts receiving a retirement annuity, or after he or she retires and goes into pay status on his or her FERS pension.[72] These benefits are the Basic Employee Death Benefit, the Survivor Annuity, and the Lump Sum Death Benefit. The amount and type of benefit payable depends on whether the deceased participant was an employee, a former employee, or a retiree at the time of death.

The table below summarizes the information contained in the following sections:

Duration of Employment	Current Employee	Former Employee—Not in Pay Status	Retiree
Worked 18 months to ten years	1. Basic Employee Death Benefit 2. Lump Sum Death Benefit	Lump Sum Death Benefit	1. Survivor Annuity if one elected OR, if none, 2. Lump Sum Death Benefit if money remains to their credit in CSRD Fund
Over ten years	1. Basic Employee Death Benefit and 2. Survivor Annuity OR, if none, 3. Lump Sum Death Benefit	1. Survivor Annuity OR, if none, 2. Lump Sum Death Benefit	1. Survivor Annuity if one elected OR, if none, 2. Lump Sum Death Benefit if money remains to their credit in CSRD Fund

1.12.1 FERS Postretirement Survivor Annuity Amount and Cost

Upon the death of a FERS annuitant, the surviving spouse will be entitled to a survivor annuity of 50 percent of the amount of the employee's self-only annuity (plus a Special Retirement Supplement if the employee's spouse is younger than age 60 and not yet eligible for Social Security benefits), unless the employee elected less than 50 percent. If the annuitant is divorced at his or her death, the former spouse will be entitled to an annuity in whatever amount was agreed to or court ordered prior to retirement, so long as it does not exceed 50 percent of the employee's self-only annuity.

72. Further information regarding death benefits for retirees is covered in Section 1.11 (Survivor Annuities under CSRS and FERS).

The FERS participant's self-only annuity is reduced in order to provide for this survivor annuity. For the maximum survivor annuity (50 percent of the self-only annuity), the cost is 10 percent of the employee's self-only annuity. If a smaller survivor annuity is elected, the cost will be less. For example, if the employee elects a partial survivor annuity of 25 percent of the self-only annuity, the cost is 5 percent of the self-only annuity.[73]

1.12.2 Preretirement Survivor Annuity under FERS

Upon the death of a current or former employee with over ten years of federal government service, a Survivor Annuity is payable to the surviving spouse or to a former spouse pursuant to a court order incident to divorce (a COAP). The monthly annuity payable to the surviving spouse of an employee whose death occurs during active employment is 50 percent of the annuity computed as if the employee had retired as of the date of his or her death.

In addition to the Survivor Annuity, the beneficiary of a current employee may be entitled to the Basic Employee Death Benefit, described below.

1.12.2.1 FERS Basic Employee Death Benefit upon Death of a Current Employee

The Basic Employee Death Benefit[74] is payable to the beneficiaries of a current employee who had at least 18 months of creditable service upon death. The amount is equal to 50 percent of the employee's final annual pay (or average pay if higher), plus $15,000, adjusted for COLAs.[75] The current amount with COLAs is $33,998.05.[76]

This benefit is paid either in a lump sum or in 36 monthly installments, based on the election of the survivor receiving the benefit. When the benefit is received in installments, the installment payments are not subject to COLA increases. Remarriage does not affect eligibility for this benefit if received by a surviving spouse and the surviving spouse elects to receive the sum in monthly installments.

The Basic Employee Death Benefit is payable[77]

1. to a surviving spouse who
   - was married to the deceased for an aggregate of at least nine months (the nine-month requirement does not apply if the death was accidental); or
   - was the parent of a child born of the marriage.
2. to a surviving former spouse if an accepted court order is on file at the OPM and the former spouse was married to the deceased for a total period of at least nine months and did not remarry before reaching age 55.

1.12.2.2 FERS Lump Sum Death Benefit

The Lump Sum Death Benefit is payable to the beneficiary of a current, former, or retired employee if no survivor annuity is payable to a spouse or former spouse.[78] This benefit cannot be affected by agreement or court order.

---

73. OPM PUBL'N: INFORMATION FOR FERS ANNUITANTS, RI 90-8 (rev. May 2012).

74. Defined in 5 C.F.R. § 843.103.

75. A COLA is an increase in pay or in an annuity amount based on inflation as measured by the CPI. *See* Section 1.6.

76. U.S. OFF. OF PERSONNEL MGMT., APPLYING FOR DEATH BENEFITS UNDER THE FEDERAL EMPLOYEES RETIREMENT SYSTEM, SF 3114 (rev. May 2013).

77. *Id.*

78. *Id.*

Current or Former Employee: The amount of the Lump Sum Death Benefit for a beneficiary of a current or former employee is equal to the deceased employee's contributions to the FERS pension, plus applicable interest.[79]

Retirees: The amount of the Lump Sum Death Benefit for the beneficiary of a retiree is equal to the unexpended balance of the retiree's retirement contributions, plus interest.[80]

If the participant did not have a valid Designation of Beneficiary on file and no survivor annuity payable to anyone, OPM will pay the Lump Sum Death Benefit to the first person(s) listed below who is alive on the date the payment becomes due:[81]

1. A widow or widower
2. A child or children (descendants of a deceased child may qualify)
3. Parents in equal shares or all to the surviving parent
4. The administrator or executor of the estate
5. If none of the above, next of kin as determined under state law

Unless the employee changes or cancels a designation, the person named, including a former spouse, will receive the Lump Sum Death Benefit. Form SF 3102, Designation of Beneficiary, may be used to update a designation and can be found in the downloadable resources provided with this book, available at https://ambar.org/RepFed.

1.13 Child Survivor Benefit

A Child Survivor Benefit under CSRS or FERS is in addition to any survivor benefit that is payable to a spouse or former spouse. It may be paid to or on behalf of a child of an employee, a former employee, or a retiree as further described below.

Federal law does not permit a state court to allocate or otherwise affect, by COAP or otherwise, the statutory provisions for survivor benefits for children. Nevertheless, parties negotiating a settlement who have minor children will want to take the availability of this benefit into account in formulating terms to provide for them.

This benefit is payable to children regardless of whether a parent is still working or retired at time of death as discussed below. All of the federal pensions addressed in this book provide for survivor benefits for children. The material below summarizes only the survivor benefits under FERS and CSRS.

The amount of the Child Survivor Benefit changes from year to year. As of 2020, if there was one living parent who was married to the deceased employee, the surviving spouse would receive $545 per month per child for up to three children. If there are more than three children, the three-child payment of $1,637 is pooled and divided among the children. If there are no living parents or the deceased parent was never married to the surviving parent, the child benefit is $655 per month for up to three children or $1,965 per month pooled and divided among the children. The amount of the child benefit has no correlation to the employee annuity.

Any money payable is offset dollar by dollar by any benefits received from Social Security. As such, most children never receive this survivor benefit due to the Social Security offset. However, the main advantage of the Child Survivor Benefit is that it allows

---

79. *Id.*

80. If the retiree elected an alternative form of annuity at retirement, there will be no Lump Sum Death Benefit, as he or she will have received upon retirement a refund of the employee contributions to FERS, plus interest. *See* Section 1.7.

81. OPM Publ'n: Information for Annuitants: Civil Service Retirement System (CSRS) (rev. June 2013).

children to still have access to FEHB such that they are entitled to continue FEHB enrollment even if they don't receive the monthly payment. However, the premium for FEHB must be paid.

For a minor child ("child" includes an adopted child, stepchild, or recognized child born out of wedlock) to receive monthly survivor benefits,

- the child must be the unmarried survivor of a federal employee who had 18 months of creditable civilian service or a civil service retiree, and
- the child must have been dependent upon the deceased employee or retiree.

A child is considered dependent if he or she

- was born within wedlock to the deceased employee or retiree;
- is an adopted child of the deceased employee or retiree or a child who meets all of the following conditions:
  - the child lived with the deceased, and
  - the deceased filed a petition to adopt the child, and
  - the child was adopted by the surviving spouse after the employee or retiree died;
- is a stepchild or recognized child born out of wedlock who lived with the employee or retiree in a regular parent-child relationship at the time of the employee's or retiree's death; or
- is a recognized child born out of wedlock for whom a judicial determination of support has been obtained. A recognized child born out of wedlock is also considered dependent if there is proof that the deceased employee or retiree made regular and substantial contributions to the child's support.

The child survivor annuity is not usually paid directly to the child. A child's annuity is paid to his or her parent or legal guardian if one has been appointed. If there is no legal guardian, payments will be made at OPM's discretion to the person who is responsible for the child. When a student beneficiary reaches age 18, OPM will send the payments directly to the student if he or she requests it.

Annuity benefits generally terminate when a child reaches age 18, marries,[82] or dies. Annuity benefits can continue after age 18 if the person is incapable of self-support because of a disability incurred before age 18 or is a full-time student at a recognized institution. Annuity benefits stopped because the child attained age 18 can be resumed if the person is unmarried and becomes a full-time student at a recognized institution before reaching age 22.

When a federal employee or retiree dies, the surviving parent or other person responsible for the eligible child(ren) must complete an Application for Death Benefits, Standard Form 2800, and send it to OPM along with a death certificate.

The Foreign Services Survivor Benefit is a comparable program for children of Foreign Service employees who die in service while covered under FSRDS or FSPS and who had at least 18 months of federal service. This benefit is reduced by any child Social Security benefit, as described above.

---

82. Annuity benefits terminated because the child married can be resumed if the marriage later ends and the child still meets the requirements.

Chapter Two

How to Divide FERS and CSRS Benefits in Divorce

Chapter 1 provided a brief summary of the rights of participants and their spouses in the major federal pension programs. Chapter 2 discusses what pension benefits are divisible at divorce and how to divide them. The Office of Personnel Management (OPM) issued regulations governing the terminology and other materials of significance to lawyers preparing court orders affecting CSRS and FERS.[1] The following discussion summarizes the key points of the regulations.

2.1 Introduction

A divorce, and the accompanying division of a CSRS or FERS pension, can come at any point in the employee lifecycle: after the participant separates from federal employment but before retirement (change of job), while the participant is still employed with the federal government (active employee), or when the participant is retired (in pay status). There are no provisions that would permit a former spouse to receive a share of a CSRS or FERS pension prior to the employee's retirement, regardless of the age of the employee. A division of a CSRS or FERS pension cannot be negotiated or awarded after the participant's

1. C.F.R. §§ 838.101–.103, 838.111, 838.121–.124, 838.131–.135.

death. After the participant's death, OPM is permitted to allocate to a former spouse a share of a pension that was in pay status only if a court order incident to divorce (a COAP) had already been entered that provided for a survivor annuity.

The various features of the CSRS and FERS pensions can be divided between spouses only pursuant to a court order that complies with the requirements of the U.S. Code and applicable regulations. The court order is often called a Court Order Acceptable for Processing (COAP),[2] discussed in detail in Chapter 5. A COAP is submitted to the court at or following the entry of a judgment of absolute divorce. The COAP must state the former spouse's share as a fixed amount, a percentage, or a fraction or provide a formula with ascertainable variables, such as years of service. Division of benefits by COAP means that each spouse will receive a certain share of the annuity on a monthly basis, beginning when the employee retires.

Payments to a spouse pursuant to a COAP come directly from OPM, as opposed to coming from the employee. Each party will be taxed on the amount that he or she actually receives from OPM, and OPM will send a separate end-of-year tax statement to each party for preparation of tax returns.

Parties to a premarital agreement, a postmarital agreement, or a marital settlement agreement can waive all rights to their spouse's pension.

The following sections address each feature of the pensions and the options for dividing them that OPM will accept.

2.2 How to Divide the Monthly Employee Annuity

The employee annuity is the monthly sum that the employee will receive when he or she goes into pay status on his or her pension. Payment will continue for the rest of his or her life. When an employee retires, he or she submits an application to retire and may obtain an estimate of his or her employee annuity, also referred to as the projected basic annuity benefit. The employee annuity is computed based on the employee's length of service and his or her high-3[3] average salary, as described in Chapter 1.

Parties negotiating a settlement, or a party seeking a court award, must determine the pension benefit to be divided: the self-only annuity, the gross annuity, or the net annuity.

Then parties or the court must state the former spouse's share as a fixed amount, a percentage, or a fraction or through a formula to apply to the annuity to be divided.

When representing a party in divorce and drafting an order to divide a pension or a settlement agreement involving a FERS or CSRS pension, it is critical to use the correct terminology set forth in the Code of Federal Regulations.[4]

"Self-only annuity" means the recurring unreduced payments to a retiree whose annuity is not being reduced to provide a survivor annuity to anyone. This is also known as a single-life annuity, meaning it is paid until the employee dies.

"Gross annuity" means the amount of self-only annuity less any applicable survivor reduction but before any other deductions.

"Net annuity" under CSRS means the amount of annuity payable after deducting from the gross annuity any amounts that are owed by the retiree to the United States;

2. A court order that allocates federal retirement benefits pursuant to 5 C.F.R. § 838.103 and can affect an employee annuity, a refund of employee contributions, and a former spouse survivor annuity. *See* Section 5.1.

3. High-3 average pay is the highest average basic pay the employee earned during any three consecutive years of service. See glossary for full definition.

4. C.F.R. § 838.103.

deducted for health, Medicare, or life insurance premiums; already payable to another person based on a COAP or a child abuse judgment enforcement order; or properly withheld for federal, state, or local income tax.

"Net annuity" under FERS means the amount of annuity payable after deducting from the gross annuity any amounts owed by the retiree to the United States (like a tax lien), deducted for health benefits premiums, deducted for life insurance premiums, deducted for Medicare premiums, withheld for federal income tax purposes, withheld for state income tax purposes, or are already payable to a different payee pursuant to another COAP. There is rarely a reason to use this definition in a marital settlement agreement or a court order dividing a pension.

"Pro rata share" means one-half of the fraction whose numerator is the number of months of federal service that the employee performed during the marriage and whose denominator is the total number of months of federal service performed by the employee through the day before the effective date of phased retirement or separation for retirement, as applicable to the annuity calculation. This proportion can be and is applied to both the employee annuity and the survivor benefit. Many attorneys prefer to state the marital share fraction expressly in their agreements and COAPs; however, because this is a statutory term, it is also possible to simply state the former spouse's share as pro rata, if that is what the parties intend. The calculation of federal service will include military service, if the employee combined military and civilian service as described in Section 7.3.

Additional definitions are found in the glossary at the end of this book.

PRACTICE TIP

Dividing the employee annuity is a two-part process. First, you must define the annuity being divided; second, you must determine the spouse's share.

2.2.1 Treatment of Postdivorce Salary Adjustments

Beyond setting forth a formula, a fixed amount, a percentage, or a fraction, the regulations also allow the parties to agree, or the court to order, a variety of other terms. For example, parties could agree that OPM will not apply salary adjustments after a specified date in computing the former spouse's share of the employee's annuity.[5] If the COAP limits application of salary increases and the employee receives postdivorce pay increases, the former spouse will receive less than he or she would have otherwise received. Silence in the COAP means that postdivorce pay increases will be included.

Whether a court adjudicating property division at divorce has the authority to limit a former spouse's pension share in this manner is a state-law question. Many jurisdictions that have tackled the appropriateness of this concept have rejected it, reasoning that even after divorce, increases in pay from additional work years are closely related to efforts of the employee spouse during the marriage that made postdivorce pay increases and benefits possible. However, some states have held that capping benefits at salary as of the date

5. 5 C.F.R. § 838.622(c)(1)(ii).

of divorce is appropriate under their equitable distribution statutes.[6] Regardless of state law, parties are free to negotiate for terms acceptable to them; federal law does not stand in the way.

PRACTICE TIP

The parties can agree to limit or the court can limit the spouse's rights to a federal pension by excluding postdivorce salary increases from the pension calculation or can cut off accumulation of the marital share at date of separation or earlier. Federal law does not limit the parties or the court in formulating the spouse's share.

2.3 Survivor Benefits in Divorce

2.3.1 Survivor Annuity

A survivor annuity award in divorce can occur at various stages along the employee lifecycle:[7]

1. *The employee is currently working, or separated from federal employment, and not retired.* In such case, any survivor annuity level can be designated, up to the plan-specific cap.
2. *The employee is a retiree in pay status and designated the maximum survivor benefit.* In such case, upon entry of a COAP or a submission of an election postdivorce, the monthly reduction will continue at the same rate.
3. *The employee is a retiree in pay status and made a survivor annuity designation of less than the maximum permissible amount.* In such case, the employee has two years to increase the survivor benefit for a former spouse above what was elected at retirement if the election is for the same spouse to whom the employee was married at the time of retirement.
4. *The employee is a retiree in pay status and the spouse waived a survivor annuity.* In such case, the employee has two years to elect a survivor annuity for the spouse if the election is for the same spouse to whom the employee was married at the time of retirement. In such case, two reductions are made to the self-only annuity. One is the regular monthly reduction that will begin upon the election of the survivor

---

6. *See* 23 PA. CONS. STAT. § 3501(a) (property acquired after separation excluded from marital property); Gordon v. Gordon, 545 Pa. 391 (1996) (salary to be used to determine marital portion of pension is as of divorce, not retirement, but spouse may be entitled to higher benefit resulting from change in plan after divorce); Armstrong v. Armstrong, 34 S.W.3d 83 (Ky. 2000) (postdivorce increased earnings and resulting pension benefits are separate property of employee spouse); Rivera-Santos v. Rivera-Santos, 862 So. 2d 480 (La. 2003) (former spouse share of pension based on amount of pension payable at retirement, but employee may seek exception if meets three-part test, including proof that increase is resulting from his or her postdivorce individual efforts); Hicks v. Hicks, 348 S.W.3d 281, 287 (Tex. App. 2011) (high–36-month average should be calculated as of the date of divorce, rather than the date of retirement).

7. 5 C.F.R. § 838.911.

annuity. The second is to compensate for the missed survivor annuity reductions that had not been made from the date the retiree went into pay status through the date of his or her postretirement election. As to the second, OPM explains:[8]

> The second reduction is *permanent* even if your former spouse loses entitlement. This reduction is based on the accumulated survivor reduction owed, plus 6 percent interest compounded annually. The total amount owed and your age are used to determine an actuarial reduction for the survivor benefit. We refer to this as an actuarial reduction because it is designed to pay back the total amount owed over the average life expectancy of a person your age.[9] (The actuarial reduction does not apply if your annuity is reduced to provide a court-ordered, former-spouse survivor annuity.)

Whether the soon-to-be former spouse must specifically ask for an award of the survivor annuity or whether the survivor annuity is treated as an integral part of the pension is a matter of state law and practice.[10]

PRACTICE TIP

If the client wants the survivor annuity, make an affirmative request for it in settlement negotiations or at trial. Failure to request the survivor annuity expressly may result in a dispute about whether it is to be included in the order dividing the pension with no guarantee the dispute will be resolved in the client's favor.

A COAP is preferable to an election to maintain a survivor benefit entitlement because a COAP cannot be changed without spousal agreement or further court order. The participant can unilaterally revoke an election for a former spouse. A COAP awarding a former spouse the survivor benefit cannot be revoked unilaterally.

---

8. OPM Publ'n: Information on Electing a Survivor Annuity for Your Former Spouse, RI 20-64B (rev. Sept. 2013).

9. 5 C.F.R. § 838.806(c)(3).

10. Harvey v. Harvey, 905 S.W.2d 760, 764 (Tex. 1995) (survivor benefits subject to division as part of retirement benefits division at divorce absent evidence the pension plan survivor benefit is an asset separate from retirement benefits); 23 Pa. Cons. Stat. § 350(a); Palladino v. Palladino, 713 A.2d 676, 679 (Pa. Super. Ct. 1998) (survivor benefits are marital property); Cal. Fam. Code § 2610(a) (court has authority to order spouse to elect survivor benefit as part of division of community property upon the dissolution of marriage); *In re* Marriage of Smith, 148 Cal. App. 4th 1115, 1126 (2007) (husband ordered to participate in optional Survivor Benefit Plan (SBP) for U.S. Army members; SBP election is neither separate property nor community property but rather equitable tool that allows court to preserve wife's right to her share of property in her lifetime; costs ordered split between the parties); *In re* Marriage of Cooper, 160 Cal. App. 4th 574 (2008) (survivor benefit is community property, subject to equal division as mandated by the community property distribution rules); Va. Code Ann. § 20-107.3(G)(2) (court can order spouse to maintain survivor benefits for former spouse and has discretion to decide who pays the cost); Potts v. Potts, 142 Md. App. 448 (2002) (spouse seeking share of survivor benefits as part of pension division must make express request); Pleasant v. Pleasant, 97 Md. App. 711, 725 (1993) (survivor annuity is marital property, and court can award former spouse survivor annuity and can decide who pays the cost).

Any survivor benefit level can be agreed to or court ordered, up to the plan-specific cap if the former spouse meets the following conditions:[11]

1. The election is timely.
2. The marriage lasted at least nine months.
3. The former spouse has not remarried before age 55 (if the marriage lasted 30 years or longer, this provision doesn't apply).
4. The employee had at least 18 months of service subject to civil service retirement deductions.
5. If the employee is remarried, the new spouse must consent in writing to provide a survivor annuity for the former spouse.

As to #1 above, "timely" means the employee must complete an election form that must be received by the OPM (a) within two years after the date the marriage ended or (b) within two years after the date another former spouse lost entitlement to a survivor annuity for which the employee annuity was reduced.[12]

A common misconception is that if the employee is in pay status and has already designated the spouse to receive the survivor benefit, no COAP or election is necessary to continue it after divorce. This is wrong.[13] Any predivorce survivor annuity election automatically terminates upon divorce.[14]

Note that the law does not allow the surviving spouse or former spouse to choose a lump-sum payment instead of the monthly survivor benefit; however, the survivor can choose a refund of remaining contributions (if any) and waive the survivor annuity.

Parties to a premarital agreement, a postmarital agreement, or a marital settlement agreement can waive all rights to a survivor annuity. Parties who intend to waive these benefits should say so expressly in their agreement. A general waiver of marital rights, a general waiver of property rights, or a general waiver of rights to share in a pension, without express reference to survivor rights, may not be sufficient.

PRACTICE TIP

Discuss with your client whether or not the survivor annuity is important to him or her. The survivor annuity is more meaningful in the case of an older employee and spouse with a long marriage. It is less valuable to a 30-year-old spouse who is likely to remarry. A young employee may wish to preserve his or her full survivor benefit for a future spouse. It's worth talking to your client about what is worth negotiating for and what is not.

---

11. OPM Publ'n: Information on Electing a Survivor Annuity for Your Former Spouse, RI 20-64B (rev. Sept. 2013).
12. OPM Publ'n: Information for FERS Annuitants, RI 90-8 (rev. May 2012).
13. 5 C.F.R. § 838.912; 5 U.S.C. §§ 8339(j)(5), 8341(h)(1).
14. OPM Publ'n: Information for FERS Annuitants, RI 90-8 (rev. May 2012).

2.3.2 Allocating the Cost of the Survivor Annuity in Divorce

Once the election of a former spouse survivor annuity is given effect (by COAP[15] or election), the monthly annuity will be reduced if the employee is already retired and in pay status or when he or she retires in the future. The employee annuity will be adjusted based on the amount of the survivor benefit he or she elects or that the court orders.

A common scenario involves the employee who retired and had previously designated his or her spouse as the survivor; as a result, the reduction in the self-only annuity is already in effect when the parties decide to divorce. In such event, a COAP or election must be made to maintain the survivor benefit postdivorce. With regard to the monthly reduction, if the employee annuity has been reduced for survivor benefits and the COAP provides the same amount of survivor annuity, no change to the employee annuity will occur. If the COAP provides that the employee maintains a smaller amount of survivor annuity, the monthly employee annuity would be increased by the difference between the current and the new (lower) reduction amount.

How the cost of providing the survivor annuity should be allocated can be determined by party negotiations or by the court. Federal law merely creates default rules to allocate the cost when the court order dividing the pension is silent on this subject.

PRACTICE TIP

Check your jurisdiction for guidance on how your court typically allocates the cost of the survivor annuity. But keep in mind that, by agreement, either party can pay the cost, or the cost can be paid off the top (proportionally) or equally. This is a point that can be negotiated.

2.3.3 Payment of the Former Spouse Survivor Annuity

If the employee is retired and in pay status at the time of his or her death, the former spouse survivor annuity awarded at divorce begins on the first day of the first month following the death of the employee.

If a FERS participant was still employed with the federal government at his or her death, or was separated from federal employment but not yet in pay status (deferred status), the former spouse survivor annuity begins on the date the deceased participant would have been eligible for an unreduced annuity, unless the survivor chooses to have it begin at a lower rate on an earlier date.

Under CSRS, if the employee was separated from federal employment but not yet retired (on deferred status) at the time of death, there will be no survivor annuity payable notwithstanding an election for a spouse to whom the employee was married at separation from service or a COAP on file that purports to award a survivor annuity to a former spouse.

15. A court order that allocates federal retirement benefits pursuant to 5 C.F.R. § 838.103 and can affect an employee annuity, a refund of employee contributions, and a former spouse survivor annuity. *See* Section 5.1.

2.3.4 Basic Employee Death Benefit

The Basic Employee Death Benefit is payable to a former spouse (in whole or in part) if an accepted court order is on file at the OPM and the former spouse was married to the deceased for a total period of at least nine months and did not remarry before reaching age 55.

2.4 How to Divide Cost-of-Living Adjustments (COLAs)

Parties to a settlement can agree, or the court can order, that OPM will either apply or not apply cost-of-living adjustments (COLAs) to the former spouse's share of the employee's annuity.[16] If the COAP is silent as to the COLA, and if the former spouse's share of the pension is expressed as a percentage, a fraction, or a formula, OPM will apply the COLA to the former spouse's share. However, if the COAP is silent about the COLA and it provides only that the former spouse will receive a specific dollar amount, then the former spouse will not receive a COLA. Parties entering into a settlement providing for a specified dollar amount of the pension, and who intend that the former spouse receive the COLA, need to say so expressly in the settlement agreement. Similarly, counsel for the former spouse who has been awarded a specified dollar amount of an employee's annuity must ask the court to expressly provide for the COLA in the COAP.

PRACTICE TIP

Be explicit about addressing the COLA in the settlement agreement. If your settlement agreement is silent as to the award of the COLA, opposing counsel may object to including it as a term in the COAP, and the court may agree and refuse to include it.

2.5 Treatment of Refund of Employee Contributions

A refund of employee contributions voids the CSRS or FERS annuity. A COAP should tell OPM what to do if an employee who is not retired applies for a refund of employee contributions. The COAP can either prohibit the employee from taking a refund of employee contributions or award a portion of the refund to the former spouse. The refund of contributions may be shared between them pro rata, equally, or by some other allocation.[17]

The lawyer for the spouse should consider what is in his or her best interests; it may be in his or her best interests to have the COAP prohibit the refund and preserve the right to pension benefits. The lawyer should address this in the settlement agreement or request it of the court in a contested matter.

16. 5 C.F.R. § 838.622(c)(2). *See* Peterson v. Off. of Personnel Mgmt., 180 Fed. App'x 153 (2006) (affirming decision of Merit Systems Protection Board that COLA applied to the former spouse's fraction of pension even though no express provision for COLA in divorce order).

17. 5 U.S.C. § 8342(j)(1)(B) permits state courts to block payment of a refund of employee contributions from a CSRS pension, but only if a former spouse has been awarded a portion of the employee annuity or a survivor annuity. 5 U.S.C. § 8424(b)(1)(B) is the FERS corollary provision.

PRACTICE TIP

Best practice, if you represent the spouse, is to include in the marital settlement agreement a prohibition on the refund of employee contributions and in a contested case to ask the court to prohibit a refund. Otherwise, if the employee elects a refund, there will be no pension that the spouse can receive a share of, nor will there be a survivor benefit.

2.6 Treatment of the CSRS Voluntary Contribution Account and Excess Deductions

Two types of deductions from a CSRS participant's pay (in addition to the employee contribution to the pension and contributions to the Thrift Savings Plan (TSP)) may create a fund that could constitute divisible property at divorce under state law but that federal law does not permit to be divided by COAP: voluntary contributions and excess deductions (discussed in Section 1.1.3).

A state court order may affect pension payments under CSRS "which would otherwise be made to an employee or Member based upon his service."[18] Voluntary contributions and excess deductions are not based upon the employee's service; they fall outside the statutory authorization for court orders to affect CSRS benefits. Therefore, a COAP cannot require OPM to pay a former spouse a portion of a lump-sum withdrawal comprised of voluntary contributions or excess deductions, nor can it require a division between the employee and former spouse of the portion of the annuity attributable to them. Whether a court can fashion an equitable property award to account for the value of the voluntary contribution account or excess deductions is a matter of state, not federal, law. There is nothing in federal law that suggests it preempts state law as to how a family court may treat voluntary contributions.

PRACTICE TIP

Just because federal law does not allow for division of a voluntary contribution account or excess deductions through a COAP does not mean they cannot be divided another way. The parties are free to negotiate a property division that takes their value into account and provides for the spouse to receive other property, and a party is free to ask the court to take their value into account in the equitable division of property.

18. *See* 5 U.S.C. § 8325(j).

2.7 FERS Annuity Supplement (FAS)—How to Divide It

Parties negotiating a settlement to divide a FERS pension should address expressly the FERS annuity supplement (FAS) (see Section 1.4). The agreement should either provide how the FAS will be allocated between the parties or state expressly that the spouse waives his or her claim to it. A spouse in a contested case should specifically ask the court to include the FAS in allocating a share of a FERS pension.

The treatment of the FAS when the court order is silent is an open issue. Prior to 2016, OPM interpreted a FERS COAP that was silent as to the FAS to mean the FAS was not allocated between the parties and the employee would retain the benefit for him- or herself; only if the COAP explicitly divided the FAS between the parties did OPM divide it. There is no specific mention in the regulations as to how OPM should treat this benefit when a COAP is silent.

In July 2016, OPM changed its longtime policy and started allocating the FAS between the parties even in those cases where the state court order was silent.

Under its revised policy, OPM determined to

(1) provide a lump-sum payment to the former spouse for all months of underpayment of the monthly annuity; and
(2) deduct from the retiree's monthly annuity the requisite amount of overpayment of an annuity supplement.

Moreover, and to the chagrin of many retirees, OPM also retroactively applied its reinterpretation of the regulations and reopened old cases in which the parties had divorced years before 2016 and after OPM had already processed the COAP without allocating the FAS. The inspector general of OPM disagreed.[19]

PRACTICE TIP

Be clear in the COAP and marital settlement agreement providing for division of a FERS pension as to whether or not the FAS is to be divided between the parties. Find out if the employee has the potential for early retirement and include the FAS in your negotiations or request that the court allocate it.

---

19. OPM Off. of the Inspector Gen. Off. of Legal & Legislative Affairs, Review of the U.S. Office of Personnel Management's Non-Public Decision to Prospectively and Retroactively Re-Apportion Annuity Supplements, Rep. No. L-2018-1, at 14 (2018) sets forth in detail the history of the change in OPM's decision. The culmination of the investigation by the Office of the Inspector General (OIG) was the following: "The OIG disagrees with OPM's position. OPM's response is contradicted by its nearly three decades of acknowledged practice of interpreting the Basic Annuity to *not* include the Annuity Supplement."

On April 16, 2018, a single judge of the Merit Systems Protection Board (MSPB) ruled in favor of a retired employee who had been required to repay FAS benefits to his former spouse.[20] The judge took issue with OPM's argument that 5 U.S.C. § 8421(c) "unambiguously requires" that the FAS be deemed part of any court-ordered division of a FERS annuity, noting that the FAS "is treated as a separate and distinct entitlement from a basic annuity."[21] OPM appealed to the full MSPB. The MSPB had not resolved the issue as of July 2020. For more information regarding the MSPB, see Section 7.14.

2.8 Sample Language for Settlement Agreements

Language for a settlement agreement to be incorporated into a COAP should be crafted to lead to a COAP that OPM deems acceptable. It is important to address the employee annuity, the survivor annuity (including who pays the cost), a refund of employee contributions, COLAs, and, in the case of FERS, the annuity supplement. The following are some examples of acceptable language. The lawyer must tailor the agreement to the needs of each specific client.

Former spouse pays cost of survivor annuity

> *Brian is entitled to a FERS pension. Bonita will receive a pro rata share of Brian's self-only annuity and the maximum survivor annuity. The cost of the survivor annuity shall be deducted from Bonita's share.*

Parties equally pay cost of survivor annuity

> *Caroline is a participant in FERS. Maddy will receive a pro rata share of Caroline's self-only annuity and a 25 percent survivor annuity. The cost of the survivor annuity shall be paid by the parties equally.*

Dividing pension pro rata with no survivor annuity

> *Kate was previously employed by the federal government and is vested in a FERS pension, which is partially marital property. Alfonso shall receive 50 percent of the marital share of Kate's self-only annuity. Alfonso waives any right to a survivor annuity with respect thereto.*

Dividing pension by other dollar amount or percentage

> *Sarah shall receive 35 percent of the marital share of Nauman's CSRS pension on an "if, as, and when" basis.*
>
> *Or*
>
> *Sarah shall receive $500 per month of Nauman's CSRS pension.*

Death of former spouse—paid to former spouse's estate

> *Brenda is a participant in FERS. Jose will receive a pro rata share of Brenda's self-only annuity and a pro rata share of the survivor annuity. The cost of the survivor annuity shall be paid by the parties equally. In the event that Jose predeceases Brenda, his share shall be paid to his estate.*

---

20. *See* Moulton v. OPM, MSPB Docket No. DE-0841-18-0053-I-1 (Apr. 16, 2018).
21. *Id.*, 2018 MSPB LEXIS 4903, at *14.

A spouse may waive an interest in the federal employee's FERS or CSRS pension. In such an event, it is important to be clear if the spouse is waiving an interest in the annuity, the survivor benefit, or both. Here is sample language for the spouse to waive his or her interest:

> *Tushar is a participant in FERS. Lily hereby waives any and all interest she may have in his FERS annuity and any survivor benefit to which she may be entitled as his former spouse.*

A plan participant retiring on disability may be eligible to receive workers' compensation in lieu of a disability annuity.[22] If the participant elects to receive workers' compensation, the funds will not be divisible by a court order, whereas a disability pension can be divided by court order. The lawyer for the spouse can protect his or her client's interests by negotiating to include in a settlement agreement that the employee will not opt for workers' compensation over a disability annuity.

> *The parties acknowledge that Joy is applying for disability retirement. The parties agree that Joy shall not opt to receive workers' compensation in lieu of a disability annuity.*

22. For more information regarding disability and its relationship to workers' compensation, see Section 1.8.

Chapter Three

Foreign Service Pensions

Chapter 3 discusses a distinct category of federal employee, the Foreign Service employee. There are three retirement systems for members of the Foreign Service: the Foreign Service Retirement & Disability System (FSRDS), the older retirement system, comparable to CSRS; the Foreign Service Pension System (FSPS), the newer retirement system; and the hybrid system, the FSRDS Offset. There are unique aspects of these pension systems and extra steps the lawyer may need to take to protect the interests of the Foreign Service client or spouse at divorce.

3.1 Foreign Service Retirement & Disability System (FSRDS), Foreign Service Pension System (FSPS), and FSRDS Offset

There are two main retirement pension plans for employees and retirees of the Foreign Service—Foreign Service Retirement & Disability System (FSRDS) and the Foreign Service Pension System (FSPS)—plus a third, hybrid, pension, FSRDS Offset.

Where to Find the Law

The statutes pertaining to the FSRDS are codified in 22 U.S.C. § 4041 *et seq*. The FSPS was created by 22 U.S.C. § 4071. The regulations related to both pensions are found in 22 C.F.R. part 19.

FSRDS is the old system and is most comparable to the Civil Service Retirement System (CSRS). Participation in FSRDS is limited to career Foreign Service employees who entered federal service prior to January 1, 1984, and (1) have been continuously employed by the United States government since December 31, 1983, or before or (2) have had a break in federal service of one year or less since 1984. Employees who are enrolled in FSRDS contribute 7.25 percent of their basic pay to the accrual of their pensions and, like CSRS participants, do not contribute to Social Security.[1] FSRDS participants can voluntarily contribute to the Thrift Savings Plan (TSP) without a government contribution.

The FSPS is the new system and is comparable in many ways to the Federal Employees' Retirement System (FERS). FSPS participants have a defined benefit pension, contribute to Social Security, and participate in the TSP with government contribution.

Participation in FSRDS and FSPS is open only to Foreign Service personnel of the following agencies:

- U.S. Department of State
- U.S. Agency for International Development (USAID)
- U.S. Foreign Agricultural Service and the Animal, Plant, and Health Inspection Service of the Department of Agriculture
- U.S. Foreign Service of the Department of Commerce
- U.S. Peace Corps

FSRDS Offset is a third Foreign Service pension, comparable to CSRS Offset. This pension was developed between 1984 and 1986 when Congress implemented a policy to have new Foreign Service employees contribute to and participate in Social Security coverage. Participants in this pension are covered by both FSRDS and Social Security. In general,

1. *Comprehensive Retirement Information*, The Retirement Network of the U.S. Dep't of State, https://rnet.state.gov/cri1.htm (last visited Nov. 13, 2020).

PRACTICE TIP

Many employees of the State Department are not Foreign Service officers and are covered by CSRS or FERS In addition, some Foreign Service officers are actually employees of the CIA and may be covered by the CIA Retirement and Disability System (CIARDS). Be sure to correctly identify the pension system by examining the paystub and asking the right questions.

participation in this pension is limited to career Foreign Service employees who had at least five years of creditable civilian federal service prior to January 1, 1987, and those who rejoined the federal service after January 1, 1984, after a break of CSRS or FSRDS coverage of more than one year.[2]

The Foreign Service pension participant accrues percentage points for each year of service, in accordance with the chart below. The pension is calculated on the basis of the total number of percentage points multiplied by the average of the employee's high-3[3] salary as follows:

FSRDS	2 percent for each year of service up to 20 years, plus 1.7 percent for each year of service over 20 years, multiplied by high-3 average salary
FSPS	1.7 percent for each year of service multiplied by high-3 average salary
FSPS special category	2.3 percent for each year of service multiplied by high-3 average salary
FSRDS special category	2.5 percent for each year of service multiplied by high-3 average salary

The basic FSRDS annuity cannot exceed 70 percent of the high-3 average salary; however, the employee is entitled to credit for unused sick leave in calculating the amount of the pension, which can result in an annuity that exceeds 70 percent. A Foreign Service employee who continues to work after reaching the 70 percent ceiling will receive a refund of retirement deductions withheld from pay, plus interest.

The annuity for an employee covered by FSRDS Offset is computed in the same manner as if he or she was covered under FSRDS only. The annuity is reduced when the employee becomes eligible for Social Security. The offset is applied in the same manner as CSRS Offset.[4]

2. *Id.*

3. "High-3" average pay is the highest average basic pay the employee earned during any three consecutive years of service. See glossary for full definition.

4. See Section 1.2 herein for details of the CSRS Offset plan.

3.2 Eligibility for Retirement

Eligibility for Foreign Service retirement is set forth in the following chart:[5]

Type of Retirement		
Voluntary	FSRDS	Age 50/20 years service*
	FSPS	Age 50/20 years service*
	FSPS (only)	Ages 55–57/10 years service****
Deferred	FSRDS	Age 60/five years service**
	FSPS	Age 62/five years service***
	FSPS (only)	Ages 55–57/ten years service****
Involuntary	(sections 607, 608, 611, and 813 of FS Act)	FO-1 and above: FSRDS and FSPS are eligible for immediate annuity regardless of age and service. FO-2 and below: FSRDS and FSPS are eligible for immediate annuity provided the age and service requirements for voluntary retirement are met at the time of the involuntary retirement.
	FSPS (only)	Any age/25 years service*
Mandatory	FSRDS and FSPS (section 812, FS Act)	Age 65/five years service
	FSRDS and FSPS (section 812, FS Act)	Age 57/20 years law enforcement service, if covered by PL 105-382/AID LE retirement
Disability	FSRDS	Any age/five years civilian service
	FSPS	Any age/18 months civilian service

*Requires at least five years of service in the Foreign Service.

**An employee covered by FSRDS with five years of service is entitled to an annuity upon separation from service if then 60 or older.

***An employee covered by FSPS with five years of service is entitled to an annuity upon separation from service if then 62 or older.

****Minimum Retirement Age (MRA) eligibility provisions: The FSPS annuity payable at ages 55–57 (MRA) with a minimum of ten years of service is subject to an age-based reduction. The reduction is calculated as 5 percent for each year the annuitant is under age 62.

The Minimum Retirement Age (MRA) provisions for FSPS are the same as for FERS.[6] FSPS participants are also eligible for an annuity supplement like that which FERS participants can receive.[7]

3.3 Enhanced Pension Benefits

As with FERS and CSRS, there are enhanced pension benefits under FSRDS and FSPS for law enforcement and other special categories of workers, such as special agents and security personnel of the Department of State.[8]

---

5. *Comprehensive Retirement Information*, *supra* note 1.
6. See Section 1.3.3 for further information about the MRA and related annuity reductions.
7. 3 Foreign Affairs Manual § 6186.
8. 50 U.S.C. § 4071(d).

The annuity of an employee in a special category is computed in the same way as the annuity of a federal law enforcement officer covered by CSRS or FERS.[9] In such cases, the maximum annuity is 80 percent of the high-3 average salary. However, sick leave credit is added to the calculation of time in computing years of service, which could result in an annuity that exceeds 80 percent. The principal may also be eligible to receive extra service credit due to service at an unhealthful post.

A Foreign Service employee may also work on the basis of recall service. In the event an employee who was previously in retirement pay status is recalled to service, while serving in the recall service, he or she will be entitled to the full salary of the class in which he or she is serving in lieu of his or her annuity. During such service, the recalled annuitant will make contributions to the retirement fund and accrue additional service credit.[10] An annuitant may qualify for a supplemental (additional) annuity as a result of such recall service. In such a case, if the annuity of the participant is discontinued or reduced so that the amount payable to the Former Spouse is less than the amount of the pension to which the Former Spouse was entitled, the employee's salary will be reduced by the amount necessary to make the Former Spouse whole, and the spouse's payments will continue at the amount to which he or she is otherwise entitled.

An annuitant who is reemployed by a federal government agency may not receive a combination of salary and annuity that exceeds his or her Foreign Service salary at the time of retirement.

Foreign Service pensions receive cost-of-living adjustments (COLAs).[11] Annuitants receiving benefits under the FSRDS received a 2.8 percent COLA in 2019. Annuitants receiving benefits under the FSPS received a 2.0 percent COLA in 2019.

3.4 Terminology

As with CSRS and FERS, the Foreign Service pensions (both FSRDS and FSPS) have their own terminology.

Principal[12]—A participant or former participant whose service in the Foreign Service forms the basis for a benefit for a spouse, Former Spouse, Previous Spouse, or child of a participant.[13]

Former Spouse[14]

1. Must have become divorced from the principal after February 15, 1981; and
2. must have been married to the principal for at least ten years during service of the principal, which is creditable for retirement, with at least five years of such service occurring while the principal was a member of the Foreign Service.

Previous Spouse[15]—Any previous spouse of a principal, whether or not he or she meets the definition of Former Spouse.

9. *See* Sections 1.1.4 and 1.3.5.1.
10. 22 C.F.R. § 19.10-6.
11. A COLA is an increase in pay or in an annuity amount based on inflation as measured by the Consumer Price Index. *See* Section 1.6.
12. 22 C.F.R. § 19.2(q).
13. The term "principal" in this context is synonymous with the term "participant."
14. 22 C.F.R. § 19.2(k).
15. 22 C.F.R. § 19.2(p).

Full Annuity[16]—If a principal retires and does not provide a survivor annuity to a spouse, Former Spouse, or designated beneficiary, the principal receives a full annuity. A full annuity means an annuity computed without any reduction in the amount of the annuity to provide for the survivor.

Reduced Annuity with Regular Survivor Annuity[17]—A survivor annuity provides for an annuity to be paid to the survivor after the death of the former employee. The survivor could be a current spouse, a Former Spouse, or both, up to the cap. The maximum regular survivor annuity or combination of regular survivor annuities that may be provided is limited to 55 percent under FSRDS and 50 percent under FSPS of the principal's full annuity. The maximum regular survivor annuity or combination of regular survivor annuities that a principal who was married at retirement may elect or provide is *limited* to the amount provided at the time of initial retirement or reversion to retired status following recall service.

Additional Survivor Annuity[18]—This option is comparable to the FERS/CSRS insurable interest annuity. This option is available when the retired principal has already elected the maximum regular survivor annuity or a court has awarded it. The principal must be in normal health for his or her age and must pass a physical exam. The additional survivor annuity is generally more expensive than the regular survivor annuity.

Pro Rata Share[19]—A percentage of the principal's service, which is calculated by the following formula: the number of years and months during which the Former Spouse was married to the principal while the principal was earning creditable service divided by the total number of years and months of the principal's creditable service. For purposes of the calculation, a month equals 30 days; a fraction of a month is not included in the calculation.

3.5 Spouse and Former Spouse Entitlement

When a married principal retires, the principal must elect a Reduced Annuity with Regular Survivor Annuity unless the spouse waives it. The Regular Survivor Annuity is the maximum amount available after providing for any Former Spouse entitled to it.

A spouse or divorced spouse may receive an entitlement to a share of the principal's pension, a survivor annuity, or extra credit for service at an unhealthful post, by virtue of one of the following mechanisms:

(1) Statutory default rights
(2) A written spousal agreement
(3) By retirement benefits court order

The other pensions in this book require a court order expressly allocating a share of a pension and a survivor annuity to a spouse in the event of divorce. As explained ahead, a Former Spouse of a Foreign Service officer may have certain default rights regarding the pension and the survivor benefits upon divorce that do not require a spousal agreement or court order expressly allocating these benefits. The Former Spouse has an automatic entitlement unless his or her rights are divested by spousal agreement or court order.

There is no default rule entitling a spouse or Previous Spouse to a share of the Foreign Service employee's TSP account.

16. 22 C.F.R. § 19.10-1.
17. 22 C.F.R. § 19.10-2.
18. 22 C.F.R. § 19.10-5.
19. 22 C.F.R. § 19.2(s).

In the event a principal is divorced after retirement (commencement of annuity), the maximum survivor annuity that may be provided for the spouse to whom he or she was married at retirement is the amount provided for him or her at the time of retirement.

PRACTICE TIP

The level of the survivor annuity elected at Foreign Service retirement cannot later be increased.

3.5.1 Statutory Default Rights for Certain Former Spouses

A divorcing spouse who qualifies as a Former Spouse (defined in Section 3.4) has certain default pension rights. Specifically, the Former Spouse is entitled to a pro rata share of 50 percent of the participant's retirement annuity and a pro rata share of the maximum survivor annuity.[20] The Former Spouse is entitled to both pension and survivor benefits unless those benefits are waived expressly by a spousal agreement or a court order divests him or her of these rights.[21]

In the event of divorce, the principal must notify Department of State, Office of Retirement (HR/RET) of the divorce on or prior to its effective date. The spouse may also do so. The notice must include the effective date of the divorce; the full name, mailing address, and the date of birth of the Former Spouse; and the date of the principal's marriage to that person, and it must enclose a certified copy of the divorce decree. If there is a court order or a spousal agreement concerning payment or waiver of Foreign Service benefits, the original or a certified copy of the order or agreement must also be forwarded to HR/RET. In the absence of a court order or spousal agreement providing otherwise, the department will pay a pro rata share of the principal's benefits to the Former Spouse.

A Former Spouse also has a default right to a pro rata share of any lump-sum credit payable to a principal. See Section 3.10.

The principal may be eligible to receive extra service credit due to service at an unhealthful post. The spouse or Former Spouse will be entitled upon divorce to a pro rata share of the pension based on such extra service credit if the Former Spouse resided with the principal in the unhealthful post. If he or she declined to travel with the principal to the unhealthful post, the Former Spouse will not be entitled to a default pro rata share of the extra service credit in the event of a divorce.[22]

3.5.2 Creation and Waiver of Spousal Rights in Written Spousal Agreement

A spousal agreement is any written agreement between a participant and the participant's spouse or Former Spouse.[23] Spouses can file an agreement addressing the division or allocation of any portion of the pension with HR/RET at any time, whether or not a divorce is

20. *See* 22 U.S.C. §§ 4054-4055, 4071j.

21. The Foreign Service Act of 1980 provides a procedure in the event a spouse or Former Spouse is missing. 22 C.F.R. § 19.11-4.

22. 22 C.F.R. § 19.5-3.

23. 22 C.F.R. § 19.2(t).

thereafter obtained. This makes the division of Foreign Service pensions unique in that a spouse or Former Spouse[24] can receive a portion of the employee's pension by direct pay on an "if, as, and when" basis, while parties are still married and without a court order.

Parties to a spousal agreement may vary the rights of the Former Spouse; they are not bound by the default rights. The agreement may waive, reduce, or increase the allocation of the principal's pension, survivor annuity, supplemental survivor annuity for recall service, or lump-sum credit and need not adhere to the statutory entitlement. An agreement can also provide an additional survivor annuity. Either party may file a spousal agreement with HR/RET at any time prior to a divorce and must file upon divorce or retirement, whichever occurs first. If the divorce occurs after retirement, it must be filed within 12 months after the divorce becomes final.[25] To be valid, a spousal agreement must be either authenticated by a court or notarized.

PRACTICE TIP

Any spousal agreement filed with HR/RET remains valid and binding in the event of divorce, but only if the spouse qualifies as a Former Spouse (see Section 3.4). If the definition of Former Spouse is not met, the spousal agreement will not be binding on HR/RET, and a court order will be required to effectuate the terms of the agreement.

If an agreement is filed with HR/RET, it will guarantee the spouse that the agreed-upon level of survivor annuity will be paid, irrespective of a future divorce, provided the survivor meets the definition of Former Spouse[26] as opposed to merely being a Previous Spouse.[27] If the parties are divorced without filing an agreement with HR/RET, if the spouse meets the definition of Former Spouse, that person will be entitled only to a *pro rata* share of the survivor annuity even if a spousal agreement provided for him or her to receive more than a pro rata share.

If the Former Spouse intends to waive interest in any of the principal's pension, survivor annuity, supplemental survivor annuity for recall service, or lump-sum credit, it must be done expressly in a spousal agreement. An express waiver must refer to pension or retirement benefits; a general waiver of marital rights is insufficient to waive rights to a Foreign Service pension. However, a waiver that generally identifies retirement benefits, or specifically identifies the Foreign Service pension, may be sufficient, even if it does not identify all of the elements thereof.[28] It will be in the best interests of the Foreign Service

---

24. *See* Section 3.4.
25. 22 C.F.R. §§ 19.7-3, 19.11-2.
26. 22 C.F.R. § 19.2(k) defines a Former Spouse as "a former wife or husband of a participant or former participant who was married to such participant for not less than ten years during periods of service by that participant which are creditable . . ."
27. 22 C.F.R. § 19.2(p) defines a Previous Spouse as "any person formerly married to a principal, whether or not such person qualifies as a former spouse" pursuant to 22 C.F.R. § 19.2(k).
28. Oshinaike v. Oshinaike, 140 A.3d 1206, 1209 (D.C. 2016) held that "an unambiguous waiver of all pension, annuity, and survivor benefits" sufficed to effect a Former Spouse's waiver of all interest in the Foreign Service officer's pension, survivor annuity, supplemental survivor annuity for recall service, and lump-sum credit.

employee to promptly file the spousal agreement waiving pension and survivor rights with HR/RET; a failure to do so means the spouse may receive the default pro rata share. Likewise, a waiver of a supplemental annuity based on recall service must be filed prior to payment going into effect.

PRACTICE TIP

A spousal agreement filed with HR/RET may be sufficient to secure Foreign Service pension benefits for a client who lives overseas and is not immediately able to obtain a divorce. Advise the client that the spousal agreement alone is not sufficient to divide a TSP account. For a TSP division, the spouse must obtain a divorce and a Court Order Acceptable for Processing (COAP).

3.5.3 Court Adjudication of Spousal Rights

Some divorcing or divorced spouses are not eligible for the default rights to a share of a Foreign Service pension or a survivor benefit. A divorcing spouse who was married to a Foreign Service member between nine months and ten years *may* receive a survivor benefit if elected by the employee or ordered by the court; it is not an automatic entitlement at divorce. If parties are unable to agree on terms for settlement, any entitlement must be provided for expressly in a judgment of divorce. Parties may argue for a different allocation in accordance with the laws of the jurisdiction.

Similarly, a court may decide to make an award that differs from what the divorcing spouse would get if he or she were eligible for and received the statutory share of the pension. For example, a court could award a Former Spouse less than 50 percent of the pro rata share or could deny him or her a survivor annuity.

3.6 Foreign Jurisdiction Divorce

By the nature of Foreign Service employment, parties are stationed worldwide, usually together, but not always. A Foreign Service officer or the spouse may obtain a divorce in another country or in a state of the United States that does not have personal jurisdiction over the other party. How will this affect his or her retirement rights? The answer is, it depends.

In one scenario, a Foreign Service officer may obtain a divorce via an ex parte proceeding in a court at his or her overseas station. This may be out of convenience or in an attempt to divest the spouse of rights. If a participant receives an ex parte divorce where the court did not have personal jurisdiction over the spouse, the participant cannot unilaterally divest the other spouse's interest in his or her pension or TSP. The Supreme Court has long recognized that a court cannot adjudicate a personal claim or obligation unless it has personal jurisdiction over the defendant.[29] In other words, a participant may obtain an ex parte divorce, but such order cannot effect an elimination of the other spouse's eco-

29. Estin v. Estin, 334 U.S. 541 (1948).

nomic rights.[30] Accordingly, an ex parte divorce without personal jurisdiction may not serve to defeat the statutory entitlement of a Former Spouse.

The court that has authority to enter a COAP to grant a spouse rights to a Foreign Service pension is defined as a court of any state or the District of Columbia; the Commonwealth of Puerto Rico, Guam, the Northern Mariana Islands, or the Virgin Islands; and any Native American court.[31] Therefore, a court of a foreign nation will not be able to issue an order dividing a Foreign Service pension, or denying a spouse a share thereof, that the Department of State will implement.

In another scenario, a spouse living in the United States may seek to obtain a divorce in a court of his or her home state. If the spouse meets the definition of Former Spouse, he or she will automatically receive a pro rata share of the participant's pension and survivor benefits even if the court did not have personal jurisdiction over the participant. Unless the spouse's home state court has personal jurisdiction over the Foreign Service spouse, it will not have jurisdiction to award a share of the participant's TSP unless the participant submits to the court's jurisdiction, nor will it have jurisdiction to make an award of Foreign Service pension benefits to a spouse who does not meet the definition of Former Spouse.

PRACTICE TIP

If your client becomes aware of a Foreign Service spouse's possible or attempted ex parte divorce proceeding, discuss the considerations in allowing such a divorce to go forward or contesting. Advise him or her of his or her statutory rights and right to ask for more, and consider that such a proceeding may result in the loss of a claim to other marital property, including the TSP.

Initiating an ex parte divorce could have unintended consequences. Consider that a client who obtains an ex parte divorce in a foreign jurisdiction, in an attempt to defeat the statutory rights of the Former Spouse, may actually cut off the participant's own claim to share in the Former Spouse's other property.

3.7 Remarriage of Former Spouse with Default Rights

The Former Spouse loses his or her entitlement to the regular pension annuity benefit permanently if he or she remarries before age 60, whether such entitlement was pursuant to default rights or spousal agreement or secured by COAP.[32]

30. Mattwell v. Mattwell, 565 N.Y.S.2d 961, 963 (Sup. Ct. 1990).
31. 22 C.F.R. § 19.2.
32. 22 C.F.R. § 19.9-2.

PRACTICE TIP

This draconian remarriage restriction bears a warning, in writing, by the divorce attorney to the client. It is worthwhile to underline and bold this advice.

If a Former Spouse remarries before age 60 but after a survivor annuity has commenced, the survivor annuity is also terminated. However, the survivor annuity may be restored if the remarriage is dissolved by death or divorce.[33] In the case of an FSPS annuity, restoration of the survivor annuity is contingent upon the Former Spouse's election to receive the survivor annuity in lieu of other federal survivor benefits and upon return of any lump sum paid upon termination of the annuity.[34]

In the case of an FSPS annuity, there will be no termination if the Former Spouse was married to the annuitant for more than 30 years.[35]

3.8 Surviving Spouse Annuity

The statutory survivor benefit in the event of a divorce is a pro rata share of the regular survivor annuity. The maximum survivor annuity is 55 percent of the annuity under the FSRDS and 50 percent for FSPS.

Moreover, in the case of multiple spouses (current or former), the maximum possible combined total of all current and Former Spouse survivor annuities is 55 percent of an FSRDS annuity and 50 percent of an FSPS annuity. This is relevant for second marriages. In the case of the death of a spouse or Former Spouse who is entitled to a survivor annuity, if there is no surviving spouse, the department will restore the retiree's annuity to its full amount.

Note that for FSRDS, as with CSRS, if an employee leaves service and dies before entering pay status, no survivor annuity will be paid. With FSPS, however, if an employee leaves service and dies prior to entering pay status, the survivor annuity payable pursuant to a court order or pursuant to a spousal agreement filed with HR/RET will be paid as agreed or ordered, beginning on the date the deceased employee would have been eligible or required to go into pay status.[36]

33. 22 C.F.R. § 19.11-5.

34. *Id.*

35. Foreign Service Divorce Handbook, Retirement Network of the U.S. Dep't of State (Sept. 2014), Subsection I-3, https://rnet.state.gov/pdf/FS%20Divorce%20Handbook%20Revised%20September%202014.pdf.

36. 22 U.S.C. § 4071(j)(e).

3.9 Child's Survivor Benefit

If a principal who has at least 18 months of civilian service credit under FSRS or FSRDS dies in service, or if an annuitant dies, an annuity is payable to a surviving child as statutorily defined. If a surviving wife or husband dies, or the annuity of a child is terminated, the annuities of any remaining children will be recomputed and paid as though such spouse or child had not survived the participant. If the annuity to a surviving child who has not been receiving an annuity is initiated or resumed, the annuities of any other children will be recomputed and paid from that date as though the annuities to all currently eligible children in the family were then being initiated.[37]

A court order cannot award or otherwise affect entitlement, or nonentitlement, to an annuity for a surviving child. However, parties negotiating a settlement who have minor children will often find it useful to have this information.

3.10 Lump-Sum Credit

The lump-sum credit is comprised of the mandatory and special contributions by the principal to his or her Foreign Service pension fund during the principal's first 35 years of service with the Foreign Service, plus the interest thereon.[38] If a participant dies and no survivor annuity is payable, the lump-sum credit is paid to surviving individuals in the following statutory order of preference:

1. To the beneficiary(ies) designated in a signed/witnessed writing received before his or her death
2. Second, if there is no designated beneficiary, to the widow(er)
3. Third, if none, to child(ren)
4. Fourth, if none, to a surviving parent
5. Fifth, if none, to the duly appointed executor/administrator of the estate
6. Sixth, if none, to such other next of kin

A Former Spouse of a participant or annuitant is entitled to a pro rata share of 50 percent of any lump-sum credit authorized to be paid to a former participant who separated from the service on or after February 15, 1981, unless otherwise directed in a court order or a spousal agreement.[39]

3.11 FSRDS, FSRDS Offset, and FSPS Disability—Employee and Former Spouse Rights

As with the other pensions discussed in this book, participants in FSRDS, FSRDS Offset, and FSPS have entitlement to receive disability retirement under certain circumstances.[40] A participant who meets the eligibility requirements for disability retirement may elect to retire voluntarily in lieu of disability retirement if the participant meets the eligibility requirements for an immediate voluntary retirement.

37. 3 Dep't of State, Foreign Affairs Manual § 3652.2.
38. 22 C.F.R. § 19.13-1.
39. 22 C.F.R. § 19.13-2.
40. 3 Dep't of State, Foreign Affairs Manual § 6161 *et seq.*

Requirements for disability retirement for the three systems are as follows:

System	The participant must
FSRDS	(a) become totally disabled or incapacitated for useful and efficient service by reason of disease, illness, or injury (not due to vicious habits, intemperance, or willful conduct of the participant); and (b) have at least five years of creditable service toward retirement under the system (excluding credit for military and naval service).
FSRDS Offset	Same as above plus: (a) Must provide evidence that he or she has filed (and not withdrawn) an application for Social Security disability insurance benefits under section 223 of the act or an official statement from the Social Security Administration that the individual is not insured (eligible) for disability insurance benefits for insufficient work history* (b) A participant under the age of 62 and eligible for Social Security disability benefits must give notice of increases to the Social Security disability payment.
FSPS	Same as FSRDS Offset

*42 U.S.C. 423.

Generally speaking, for FSRDS and FSRDS Offset, if a participant has fewer than 20 years of service, his or her annuity will be computed as if he or she had 20 years of service credit. For most FSPS participants, the annuity will be equal to 60 percent of their high-3 salary, with reduction for the Social Security disability benefit received. The Department of State Foreign Affairs Manual succinctly sets forth the manner in which disability retirement annuity is computed for each system:

> In the case of a former spouse of a disability annuitant, the pension of such former spouse will commence on the latter of:
>
> (1) The date the principal would qualify for an annuity (other than a disability annuity) on the basis of his or her creditable service;
> (2) The date the disability annuity begins; or
> (3) The first of the month in which the divorce becomes final.
> (4) A pension to a former spouse of a disability annuitant will be calculated on the basis of an annuity for which the participant would qualify if not disabled.[41]

3.12 Obtaining Information from the Foreign Service

The Department of State will provide to the employee an annuity estimate if the employee is at or near retirement, calculated with and without survivor benefits included. However, it will not provide an estimate that requires speculation about future promotions, program changes, or any other nonfactual information and does not give annuity estimates for employees who are not close to retirement.

41. 3 Dep't of State, Foreign Affairs Manual § 6166.3.

PRACTICE TIP

The Department of State is the source of information regarding FSRDS and FSPS retirees and former participants. It will supply information *regarding active employees, calculation of an annuity and survivor benefits,* and *determination of Former Spouse benefits.* An employee may obtain the information on his or her own behalf. In addition, the attorney for the spouse may send a subpoena, or the employee may sign a release and send it to

Office of Retirement
Department of State, SA-1, H-620
2401 E Street, NW
Washington, D.C. 20522-0108
Tel: (202) 261-8960
Fax: (202) 261-8988
Website: RNet.state.gov
E-mail: HRSC@state.gov

A current employee's agency (State Department, USAID, etc.) can supply employment and pay information.

Chapter Four

Retirement Benefits for Employees of the Federal Reserve System (FRS)

Chapter 4 focuses on the retirement plans for employees of the Federal Reserve System (FRS) and the Consumer Financial Protection Bureau (CFPB). Such employees participate in the Federal Reserve Board Retirement Plan (Board Plan for employees hired before January 1, 1984, who do not pay into Social Security) or the Retirement Plan for the Employees of the Federal Reserve (Bank Plan for employees hired after December 31, 1983), collectively known as the Federal Reserve Employee Benefits System. Both plans include within them a unique feature, the Portable Cash Option (PCO). FRS employees also participate in a defined contribution plan, the Federal Reserve Thrift Plan.

4.1 Board Plan

The Board Plan is a defined benefit pension plan. It covers employees of the FRS and the CFPB who entered government service before January 1, 1984. The Board Plan remains open to some employees with previous participation and some employees who transferred from a different agency of the federal government and were not covered by Social Security during that service.[1]

The employee and the government both contribute to the pension. The employee contributes 7 percent of his or her basic pay to his or her future pension benefit. As with the Civil Service Retirement System (CSRS), employees do not pay into Social Security

1. 12 U.S.C. §§ 226, 241.

and receive no Social Security benefits on account of this employment. The employee is fully vested after five years of creditable service or attaining age 65 while employed by the Board or the CFPB. If an employee leaves after fewer than five years, he or she automatically receives a refund of his or her contributions, plus interest.

The benefit can be paid in the form of a monthly annuity, as a self-only annuity or as a reduced annuity for the participant with a surviving spouse annuity, similar to CSRS, but with some differences explained further below. If the employee takes a refund of his or her contributions, the right to the pension is voided entirely; there will be no pension payable.

Generally, an employee must retire no later than age 70½ and may retire at the following ages:[2]

- Age 62 or older with at least five years of creditable service
- Age 60 with at least 20 years of creditable service
- Age 55 with at least 30 years of creditable service

As with most of the other governmental pensions discussed in this book, cost-of-living adjustments (COLAs) are paid on the monthly annuity payments.[3]

Similar to CSRS, the employee may also make additional voluntary contributions to the plan to increase the amount of the monthly retirement benefit. Voluntary contributions are capped at 10 percent of the employee's annual basic pay on an after-tax basis, subject to certain limits imposed by the Internal Revenue Code (IRC). The employee can make voluntary contributions through a payroll deduction or one or more lump-sum payments. The contributions receive interest compounded annually at a rate determined by the Secretary of the Treasury. The employee may receive a refund of voluntary contributions at any time without negatively affecting the amount of the normal employee pension entitlement.

As with other governmental plans, the Board Plan also offers payment of an alternative form of annuity, if the employee has a life-threatening illness. See Section 1.7 for further information.

4.1.1 How the Board Plan Pension Benefit Is Calculated

The pension benefit is based in part on the final average salary, which is the employee's highest average annual compensation during any 36 consecutive months (three years) before retirement. It includes base pay, any regularly paid shift differential, variable pay, lump-sum merit increases, and any salary deferred under the Thrift Plan, contributed to a cafeteria plan, and/or reduced for qualified transportation expenses.[4] Final average salary does not include other forms of deferred compensation, periods of unpaid leaves of absence, contributions by the employer, bonuses, overtime pay, or special holiday pay.

The employee accrues 1.5 percentage points per year for the first five years, 1.75 percentage points for the next five years, and 2 percentage points for all years over ten; the total percentage points are then multiplied by the final average salary. The pension benefit is calculated as expressed in the following chart:

---

2. Your Federal Reserve Retirement Plan Handbook, Information for Board of Governors and Consumer Financial Protection Bureau Participants (Federal Reserve Employee Benefits System 2019).

3. A COLA is an increase in pay or in an annuity amount based on inflation as measured by the Consumer Price Index. See Section 1.6 for further information.

4. I.R.C. § 132.

1.5 percent of final average salary ***multiplied by*** the first five years

plus

1.75 percent of final average salary ***multiplied by*** the second five years

plus

2 percent of final average salary multiplied by the remaining years beyond ten

The pension benefit as calculated above is reduced if any portion of the pension is taken as a PCO payment (discussed in Section 4.3).

The basic annuity cannot exceed 80 percent of the final average salary, a percentage typically reached at 41 years and 11 months of service.

The IRC establishes limits on pension payments affecting employees with very high pension benefits that may affect this pension plan.[5] The IRC also limits the compensation the Board Plan can use to calculate benefits. The limits change from year to year and are indexed for the Consumer Price Index.[6] To get around these caps, the Federal Reserve has established a nonqualified Retirement Benefit Equalization Plan (BEP). Together, the Board Plan and BEP pay retirees the amount that they would have received from the Board Plan if not for the IRC compensation and pension limits.

The Board Plan may pay the employee a pension benefit in the form of an annuity, a lump sum, or a combination of the two. The Board Plan uses two different formulas to calculate the benefit: a traditional annuity formula based on final average salary and years of creditable service, and the PCO, which provides for a lump-sum payment. In determining the employee's benefit, the Board Plan will use the formula that produces the larger benefit. The employee could receive a lump-sum distribution from the Board Plan, up to the value of the PCO, a monthly annuity, or both.

If the traditional formula produces the larger benefit, and if the employee withdraws the value of the PCO as a lump sum, the difference between the value of the traditional formula pension benefit and the PCO is payable as a residual annuity, beginning as early as age 62. The PCO may be rolled over into the Thrift Plan, an Individual Retirement Account (IRA), or another employer's qualified plan. If the employee takes the PCO as a cash distribution and does not roll it over, the distribution will be treated as a taxable event.

PRACTICE TIP

A Board Plan participant's form of benefit payment won't be known until retirement. In drafting an agreement or arguing for equitable distribution of FRS or CFPB retirement benefits at trial, be sure to address the possibility of an annuity, the lump-sum option, or a combination of the two.

---

5. 26 C.F.R. § 1.401(a)(17)-1.

6. The limit in 2019 was $280,000 for employees hired on or after January 1, 1996, and $415,000 for employees hired before January 1, 1996.

4.1.2 Death and Survivor Benefits

The maximum survivor annuity under the Board Plan is equal to 55 percent of the basic monthly annuity. Married employees must receive spousal consent to elect a payment option at retirement that provides less than full survivor benefits.

If the employee elects a survivor annuity at retirement, the reduction in the employee's basic monthly annuity will be calculated in the same manner as CSRS:

- 2.5 percent of the designated base, up to $3,600 per year, plus
- 10 percent of the designated base in excess of $3,600.

In the event that an employee retires without a survivor annuity and wishes to add a survivor beneficiary after retirement, he or she must make the election within 18 months of retirement and must pay a lump sum to the plan to account for the missed payments.

In the event an employee is unmarried at retirement and marries thereafter, he or she has 24 months to designate the new spouse as the survivor beneficiary.

An employee's survivor may also be entitled to a lump-sum death benefit, consisting of unexpended contributions to the plan. This benefit is similar to that which is paid by CSRS and the Federal Employees' Retirement System (FERS).

As with FERS and CSRS, there may also be a survivor annuity payable to, or for the benefit of, an unmarried surviving child under age 18; a child between the ages of 18 and 21 who is a full-time student at an accredited educational institution; or a child of any age if he or she is incapable of supporting him- or herself due to a mental or physical disability that began before age 18. The amount of the annuity, which is periodically changed for COLAs, depends on the number of eligible children and whether there is a surviving parent. See Section 1.13 for further information.

As with CSRS, there is an option for a survivor annuity to someone other than a spouse (someone with an insurable interest) (see Chapter 6). However, in the Board Plan, it is referred to as "survivor benefit to your designated person." Payments to the beneficiary are equal to 55 percent of the reduced annuity of the employee.

4.2 The Bank Plan

Federal Reserve Bank employees hired after December 31, 1983, participate in the Retirement Plan for the Employees of the Federal Reserve (the Bank Plan). Participants in the Bank Plan pay into Social Security (like FERS participants); however, Bank Plan participants do not make any contribution to the plan.

Like the Board Plan, Bank Plan participants have a PCO (see Section 4.3) and receive their retirement benefit in the form of a lump sum (PCO), an annuity, or both.

4.2.1 How the Bank Plan Pension Benefit Is Calculated

The Bank Plan employee annuity is based on

(a) final average salary (highest average annual compensation during any 60 consecutive months);
(b) creditable service; and
(c) Social Security Integration Level.

The Social Security Integration Level is the average of the Social Security wage base (the maximum amount on which the employee pays Social Security taxes) for each of the 35 years before the date of retirement. The Social Security wage base was $137,700 in 2020.

The traditional benefit formula payable at age 65 is calculated as follows:

1.3 percent ***times*** the final average salary up to the Social Security Integration Level

plus

1.8 percent ***times*** the final average salary in excess of the Social Security Integration Level

times

years of creditable service

If the final average salary is more than the Social Security Integration Level, the calculation of the benefit is illustrated in the example below:

Assume the final average salary was $90,000 and the employee had 30 years of creditable service when he or she separated from service at age 65 in 2019. The applicable Social Security Integration Level was $80,532.

Step 1. Determine if the final average salary ($90,000) is more than the Social Security Integration Level ($80,532). The answer is yes.

Step 2. Multiply 0.013 (1.3 percent) by $80,532 (final average salary up to the Social Security Integration Level). The answer equals $1,046.92.

Step 3. Multiply 0.018 (1.8 percent) by $9,468 (final average salary in excess of the Social Security Integration Level). The answer equals $170.42.

Step 4. Add $1,046.92 and $170.42 (the answers from Steps 2 and 3). The answer equals $1,217.34.

Step 5. Multiply $1,217.34 (the answer from Step 4) by 30 (years of creditable service). The answer equals $36,520.20. This is the annual benefit payable at age 65.[7]

7. Your Federal Reserve Retirement Plan Handbook Information for Federal Reserve Bank, Board and Bureau Participants 13 (Federal Reserve Employee Benefits System 2019).

If the final average salary is less than the Social Security Integration Level, the calculation of the benefit is illustrated by the example below:

> Assume the final average salary was $40,000 and the employee had 20 years of creditable service when he or she separated from service at age 65 in 2018. The applicable Social Security Integration Level was $80,532.
>
> **Step 1**. Determine if the final average salary ($40,000) was more than the Social Security Integration Level ($80,532). The answer is no.
>
> **Step 2**. Multiply 0.013 (1.3 percent) by $40,000 (final average salary). The result is $520.
>
> **Step 3**. Multiply $520 (the answer from Step 2) by 20 (years of creditable service). The result is $10,400. This is the annual benefit payable at age 65.[8]

The maximum pension amount is 80 percent of the employee's final average salary.

If the total present value of the pension is $5,000 or less, the employee will receive a lump-sum payment in lieu of an annuity.

Eligibility to retire is summarized as follows:[9]

Retirement eligibility—unreduced benefit	Age 65 with five years of service Age 60 and meets rule of 90 (age + service = 90)
Retirement eligibility—reduced benefit	Minimum: Age 50 with five years of service (37.5 percent of full benefit) Reductions based on actuarial tables
Retirement computation formula	1.3 percent x high-5 average salary up to Social Security Integration Level, plus 1.8 percent x high-5 average salary over Social Security integration level, times total years of service Reduction for retirement before eligibility date (based on actuarial table) Maximum annuity—80 percent of high-5 average salary
COLAs	Upon approval of Board of Governors—on average, 40–60 percent of CPI-W change after CPI-W increases at least 8 percent
Employee contributions	None

Full vesting occurs at age 65 or five years of service. The employee may retire at or after he or she reaches age 65 (normal retirement age) to receive a normal retirement pension (based on the traditional formula, discussed above).

8. *Id.* at 14.

9. *Service Credit under the Federal Employees Retirement System, Hearing before the H. Subcommittee on Civil Service*, 106th Congress (1999) (testimony of Gov. Edward W. Kelley, Jr.), Attachment A, *available at* https://www.federalreserve.gov/boarddocs/testimony/1999/19990225.htm#AttachmentA.

An employee hired prior to January 1, 2009, may elect to retire and receive an annuity at a reduced rate after reaching age 50, after five years of service. The reduction rate can be located on the following chart:[10]

Age When Payments Begin	Total of Age at Retirement Plus Years (at Least Five) of Vesting Service											With 5 Years of Service
	90	88	86	84	82	80	76	72	68	64	60	
65	100%	100%	100%	100%	100%	100%	100%	100%	100%	100%	100%	100%
64	100%	99.6%	99.2%	98.8%	98.4%	98%	96%	94%	—	—	—	92.5%
62	100%	98.8%	97.6%	96.4%	95.2%	94%	89.5%	85%	80.5%	—	—	79.4%
60	100%	98%	96%	94%	92%	90%	84%	78%	72%	—	—	67.5%
58	92%	90%	88%	86%	84%	82%	77%	72%	67%	62%	—	60.8%
56	84%	82%	80%	78%	76%	74%	69.7%	65.4%	61.1%	56.9%	—	53.6%
54	76%	74%	72%	70%	68%	66%	62.5%	59%	55.5%	52%	48.5%	47.6%
52	—	—	64%	62%	60%	58%	55.3%	52.7%	50%	47.3%	44.7%	42.7%
50	—	—	—	—	52%	50%	48%	46%	44%	42%	40%	37.5%

An employee hired after January 1, 2009, may elect to retire and receive an annuity at a reduced rate after reaching age 55, after five years of service. The reduction rate can be located on the following chart:[11]

Age When Payments Begin	Total of Age at Separation from Service Plus Years (at Least Five) of Vesting Service						Early Retirement Factors with Less Than 80 Points (at Least Five Years of Vesting Service)
	90	88	86	84	82	80	
65	100%	100%	100%	100%	100%	100%	100%
64	100%	99.6%	99.2%	98.8%	98.4%	98%	95%
62	100%	98.8%	97.6%	96.4%	95.2%	94%	85%
60	100%	98%	96%	94%	92%	90%	75%
58	92%	90%	88%	86%	84%	82%	67%
56	84%	82%	80%	78%	76%	74%	59%
55	80%	78%	76%	74%	72%	70%	55%

4.2.2 Death and Survivor Benefits

Like all other government pensions, the Bank Plan provides for a single-life annuity, and the employee has options to provide for a survivor. However, the Bank Plan offers more payment options than just the single-life annuity and the joint and survivor annuity. Those options may be modified by one or more of the following features:

(a) Guaranteed payment (with spousal consent)
(b) Lump-sum payment (with spousal consent)
(c) Level income payment
(d) 100 percent COLA

10. Your Federal Reserve Retirement Plan Handbook Information for Federal Reserve Bank, Board and Bureau Participants 20 (Federal Reserve Employee Benefits System 2019).
11. *Id.* at 21.

An employee in the Bank Plan electing a pension with survivor annuity at retirement may elect a 50 percent, 75 percent, or 100 percent survivor annuity. The cost is not a fixed percentage of the pension, as it is with FERS and CSRS. Rather, the cost is based on the age of the employee, the beneficiary's age, the date the employee begins receiving payments, and the level of survivor benefit elected. The cost of the survivor annuity can best be compared to the FERS and CSRS insurable interest option. The Bank Plan includes an option for a subsidized survivor benefit that does not exist with the other pension plans discussed in this book.

A married employee may elect a 50 percent survivor annuity without spousal consent but must receive spousal consent to elect a 75 percent or 100 percent survivor annuity. An employee who wishes to elect a guaranteed payment or a lump-sum payment must also get spousal consent.

An employee may receive a subsidized survivorship option if

- he or she chooses to provide the surviving spouse or a parent, brother, sister, son, or daughter with a survivor benefit of at least 50 percent of the converted pension payable to the employee over his or her lifetime; *and*
- the employee is at least 60 years old at retirement; *or*
- his or her age plus years of vesting service equal at least 90 at retirement.

Under the subsidized survivorship option, the amount of the reduction is less than the reduction under the regular survivorship option. In such case, the single-life pension is actuarially reduced by half the regular rate for the first 50 percent of the survivor benefit. The true rate is used to reduce the portion of the survivor benefit over 50 percent, if any.

The guaranteed payment option allows the employee to receive pension payments that are guaranteed for a certain period of time. The available guaranteed payment options include

(a) five or ten years for a single-life pension benefit; or
(b) five years for a survivorship pension benefit.

An employee who elects the single-life pension benefit may designate a beneficiary to receive any payments remaining if the employee dies before receiving the guaranteed number of payments. With a survivorship pension benefit, if the employee dies before receiving five years of payments, the designated beneficiary will continue to receive the same payments for the remainder of the period. After that, the designated beneficiary's benefit will be paid in accordance with the survivorship benefit.

The lump-sum payment option provides a lump-sum payment from the pension benefit of $1,000 or more, in $100 increments, from the pension benefit to the annuitant's designated beneficiary, payable after the annuitant dies.

The level income payment option provides that if the employee retires early and starts receiving benefits before he or she reaches age 62, larger payments are made before age 62. When the annuitant reaches age 62 and is eligible to receive Social Security, benefit payments are reduced.

The 100 percent COLA option provides full inflation protection when inflation is at 2 percent or below and partial inflation protection when CPI-W exceeds 2 percent. The COLA also is paid to the survivor, if any.

As with other government pensions, statutory lump death benefits may be paid as well. The amount of the benefits and the manner in which they are paid (lump sum or annuity) are dependent on whether death occurred during active service or in deferred retirement status, as well as whether there is an eligible spouse or dependent child. The lump-sum death benefit cannot be affected by court order.

The Bank Plan allows for a domestic partner to be a beneficiary of a survivor annuity or the lump-sum death benefits. In order to qualify as such, the employee and domestic partner must provide a valid certificate of domestic partnership issued by a state or local government and a signed affidavit.

4.3 Portable Cash Option (PCO)

On January 1, 2002, the Federal Reserve established the Portable Cash Option (PCO), an option for eligible employees of the Federal Reserve to receive their pension benefit as a cash balance rather than a monthly annuity. Existing employees had to be grandfathered in, so old and new employees received different treatment, as discussed below.

For each employee who started employment after 2001, the PCO account was or is credited as follows:

- for the first 60 months of employment (generally years 1–5), the Federal Reserve contributes 5 percent of the employee's pay to the account; and
- for the next 120 months of employment (generally years 6–15), the Federal Reserve contributes 10 percent of the employee's pay to the account.

For existing employees of the Federal Reserve Bank who were working prior to 2002, the PCO account was funded retroactively. For service between January 1, 1992, and December 31, 2001, the PCO account was credited with an initial account balance that was calculated as follows: 5 percent of pay for each year of Federal Reserve employment up to five years; for years 6–10, 10 percent of pay.

PCO accounts are credited with employer contributions on a monthly basis and earn interest. After 15 years of service, new contributions to the PCO account end; however, the account continues to earn interest. The employee is fully vested after five years of service. PCO accounts do not receive COLAs. If the employee separates from service or retires and takes the PCO as a lump sum, it will be taxable to the employee unless he or she rolls it over into an appropriate account, such as the Thrift Plan, an IRA, or another employer-sponsored retirement account.

The following provisions of the PCO are applicable only to the Bank Plan:

- If the employee terminates employment before age 50, he or she may receive the total value of the PCO account in a lump sum.
- If the PCO account produces a larger benefit than the pension, then the lump-sum PCO distribution will be the only benefit payable from the plan; in such case, no annuity will be paid.
- If the traditional formula produces the larger benefit, then the employee may receive the value of the PCO account as a lump sum. The difference between the value of the traditional formula benefit and the PCO lump-sum payment is payable as a residual annuity, beginning as early as age 50. However, if the present value of the residual annuity is $25,000 or less, then it is also paid immediately as a lump sum.
- If the employee terminates employment at age 50 or later, he or she may also elect to receive the value of the PCO account as a lump sum. The rules are similar to those that apply to employees under age 50, except that the employee may elect to receive a portion of the PCO, instead of the total value of the PCO, as a lump sum.

4.4 Dividing Federal Reserve Employee Benefits System Plans in Divorce

The Federal Reserve Employee Benefits System pension and retirement plans may only be divided by court order incident to divorce. If the participant has already retired when the parties divorce, the options for division are limited to dividing whatever benefits the employee already elected.

When parties divorce before the participant retires, the former spouse may elect any form of benefit available to the employee under the terms of the plan (other than a joint and survivor annuity with a new spouse as the survivor).[12] The Federal Reserve Plan pensions may be paid as a shared interest or as a separate interest annuity.

The Federal Reserve Plan pensions are the only pensions covered in this book that offer a separate interest annuity option. This option is only available when parties divorce and a pension order is submitted and qualified prior to retirement. Under the separate interest approach, the actuarial value of the participant's retirement benefit is divided into two as of a certain date (date of separation; date of divorce; another date chosen by the parties or the court), permitting the participant and the former spouse to each separately elect from the benefit options available under the plan. This obviates the need for a survivor annuity, as the former spouse's rights are not affected by the death of the participant. It also means that the former spouse will not benefit from any subsequent salary increases received by the employee.

The former spouse with a separate interest can elect to receive benefits at a time and in a form different than that chosen by the participant. For example, the former spouse can elect an annuity for his or her life. The amount of the former spouse's pension benefit is actuarially determined based on his or her life expectancy. The former spouse may begin receiving payments before the employee spouse begins to receive benefits (but only on or after the employee's earliest retirement age); in such case, the benefit may be reduced. The former spouse must start receiving his or her share of the retirement benefits no later than the date the employee begins to receive his or her retirement benefits. Under a separate interest approach, the benefit of the former spouse does not revert to the participant in the event the former spouse dies first.[13]

In the case of division at divorce prior to retirement, the parties must agree on a separate interest or a joint interest division, or the court can determine the form of division. In either case, the court order must say expressly whether the pension benefit will be paid as a shared interest or as a separate interest.

In cases where the participant has already retired and has started receiving a pension, the spouse can only receive a shared interest division. Thus, the former spouse will receive his or her share of the participant's pension if, as, and when paid to the participant (as is the case with the division of a CSRS or FERS pension). The benefit payable to the former spouse may be a dollar amount or percentage of the employee's vested accrued benefit as of a valuation date chosen by the parties or determined by the court. The vested accrued benefit is the dollar amount that the participant has a nonforfeitable right to receive and is the greater of the annuity formula's actuarial equivalent lump-sum value or the

---

12. However, in the event a former spouse with a separate interest dies, any unexpended contributions to the plan that had been assigned to him or her may be paid to his or her designated beneficiary.

13. Patricia Shewmaker & James R. Lewis, The Complete QDRO Handbook (4th ed. 2019).

participant's PCO account balance. Additionally, unless the court order states otherwise, any voluntary contributions will also be divided between the parties.

Pension payments to the former spouse under the shared interest approach will cease upon the earlier of the former spouse's death or the participant's death (unless there is a survivor annuity). If a participant is already in pay status, any survivor benefits will be paid pursuant to the election that the participant made before benefits commenced. If the former spouse predeceases the employee, the former spouse's benefit will revert to the employee unless the retirement benefits court order states otherwise. If the participant is not retired when the order dividing the benefit is entered, the former spouse can receive a share of the participant's preretirement annuity and the postretirement survivor annuity; however, these rights must be provided for with specificity in the retirement benefits court order.

Upon receipt of a proposed order, the pension will be frozen. A party or counsel may submit a proposed order with the last four digits of each party's Social Security number. Review can take up to 30 days.

The Office of Employee Benefits of the FRS, acting as agent for the Committee on Plan Administration, is the plan administrator for the Bank Plan. The Office of Employee Benefits of the FRS has contracted with Alight Solutions LLC to establish procedures and administer qualified domestic relations orders (QDROs) for the Bank Plan. Alight Solutions, LLC, preapproves orders that are submitted by facsimile to the following number: 1-847-554-1963. The final order must be sent for processing to

Federal Reserve Employee Benefit System Qualified Order Team
Post Office Box 7144
Rantoul, IL 61866-7144

The Office of Employee Benefits of the FRS, acting as agent for the Committee on Plan Administration, is the plan administrator for the Board Plan. The Qualified Order Team preapproves orders that are submitted by facsimile to the following number: 1-847-554-1963. The final order must be sent for processing to

Federal Reserve Benefits Express Center Attention: Qualified Order Team
Post Office Box 1433
Lincolnshire, IL 60069-1433

4.5 Federal Reserve Thrift Plan

Employees of the Federal Reserve and the CFPB may participate in the Federal Reserve Thrift Plan.[14] This is an entirely different plan than the Thrift Savings Plan discussed in Chapter 9. Employees entitled to participate in the Thrift Plan do not participate in the Thrift Savings Plan. The Thrift Plan is qualified under sections 401(a) and 501(a) of the IRC, and the contributions meet the requirements of sections 401(k) and 401(m) of the IRC.

The Thrift Plan allows employees to save on a pretax and/or after-tax basis. There are some commonalities between the Federal Reserve Thrift Plan and the Thrift Savings Plan.[15] There are some important differences.

14. 12 U.S.C. § 5584.
15. 5 U.S.C. § 8401 *et seq.*

The Federal Reserve Board makes a matching contribution up to the first 7 percent of the employee's salary contributed to the Thrift Plan. However, if the employee chooses not to contribute, the board contributes 1 percent. The plan includes the option for Roth contributions (the savings account) and pretax investing (the Deferred Compensation account).

Employees are immediately vested in their own contributions and any investment earnings on those contributions. The remainder of the account vests on a five-year schedule: the employee vests at 20 percent of their employer matching contribution for each year of service, becoming 100 percent vested after completing five years of service.

The employee may contribute up to $40,000 per year, or the equivalent of 100 percent of his or her salary (whichever is less), on either a pretax or an after-tax basis or a combination of both. This overall contribution limit includes employer matching contributions.

As is the case with the Thrift Savings Plan, the employee may take a loan from his or her Thrift Plan. There are two types of loans available through the plan: a General Purpose Loan (repayable between six and 60 months) and a Primary Residence Loan (repayable between 61 and 180 months). The term of a loan may not extend beyond December 31 of the year in which the employee reaches age 70½. Loan funds are taken pro rata from each investment. The minimum is $1,000 and maximum is 50 percent of the vested balance, up to $50,000 (minus any outstanding loan balance) for up to two loans outstanding at a time.

As is the case with a Thrift Savings Plan account, if an employee leaves the Federal Reserve before repaying a loan, the entire loan is due immediately. If not repaid in full, the loan will be considered a taxable distribution.

Between August 1, 1982, and December 31, 1986, Thrift Plan participants were eligible to establish a deductible employee contribution account. Those accounts, known as DEC/IRA accounts, are held in a separate subaccount under the plan, to which contributions can no longer be made.

If an employee separates from the Federal Reserve before reaching age 55, he or she has the option of receiving installment payments prior to age 59½ without incurring the 10 percent early withdrawal penalty. This option, called restricted installment payments, requires the employee to elect to receive installment payments over his or her own life expectancy or joint life expectancy with a spouse.

If an employee is married, his or her spouse is automatically the sole primary beneficiary of the Thrift Plan. The spouse must consent in writing (with notarization) to have the employee designate someone other than the spouse as beneficiary.

The plan administrator is

Office of Employee Benefits
Federal Reserve Employee Retirement Benefits System
744 Broad Street
Newark, NJ 07102

The Federal Reserve Thrift Plan is divided by a QDRO, like private-sector retirement accounts.[16]

16. *See* The Complete QDRO Handbook, *supra* note 13.

4.6 Pension Purchase Option (PPO)

The Pension Purchase Option (PPO) allows a retired employee or a survivor currently receiving a survivor annuity to roll funds from the Thrift Plan to his or her Federal Reserve pension plan, or survivor benefits, as the case may be, and purchase an additional annuity that can be paid as a single-life annuity or an annuity with survivorship options and with or without COLAs. At least $25,000 of eligible Thrift Plan funds must be available. Multiple PPO rollovers may be made, but no more than once per year. The amount of the resulting annuity depends on market conditions at the time and the age of the person making the rollover. This option is also available to a former spouse, but only if he or she received a portion of the employee's Thrift Plan and only if the former spouse transferred his or her share to his or her own Thrift Plan account and did not roll it over to an IRA or another retirement account.

Chapter Five

Court Orders Acceptable for Processing (COAPs)

Chapter 5 explains the mechanics of implementing the division of pension benefits pursuant to a Court Order Acceptable for Processing (COAP). A complete court order should provide detailed instructions on each type of benefit that the court order can affect. The regulations treat the employee annuity, refund of employee contributions, survivor annuity (including pre- and postretirement survivor annuities), cost-of-living adjustments (COLAs), and annuity supplements independently.[1] The Office of Personnel Management (OPM) considers each type of benefit award as separate and distinct from the others; therefore, the lawyer should exercise care in describing each type of benefit that the order is intended to affect. The benefits are also interrelated. For example, as discussed in the preceding chapters, a former spouse survivor annuity results in a reduction of the employee annuity.

5.1 Requirements for a FERS or CSRS COAP

A COAP may be created as a court order separate from the judgment of divorce, or the terms for division of a pension may be incorporated in the text of the judgment of divorce. OPM does not require a separate court order to be considered a COAP. If all the language

1. OPM Publ'n: A Handbook for Attorneys on Court-Ordered Retirement, Health Benefits and Life Insurance under the Civil Service Retirement Benefits, Federal Employees Retirement Benefits, Federal Employees Group Life Insurance Program, RI 38-116 (rev. July 1997).

necessary to divide the pension is contained in the judgment of divorce, the judgment itself will be the COAP. However, often a separate COAP is preferable. Among other reasons, it will not have extraneous material, such as provisions regarding custody and support of minor children.

Where to Find the Law

5 U.S.C. § 8345(j) permits state courts to award a former spouse certain CSRS pension benefits payable while the participant is alive and to award a former spouse entitlement to a survivor annuity in the event that the employee or retired employee predeceases the former spouse.

Similarly, 5 U.S.C. § 8467 permits state courts to award a former spouse certain FERS benefits payable while the participant is alive. 5 U.S.C. § 8445 permits state courts to award a former spouse entitlement to a survivor annuity in the event that the employee or retired employee predeceases the former spouse.

On July 29, 1992, OPM issued regulations published in the Federal Register (Vol. 57, No. 146) to improve the processing of court orders affecting retirement benefits under the CSRS and FERS.

When reviewing a COAP or preparing one, the lawyer should be sure that it includes the following to meet the minimum requirements set forth in the regulations to be approved and processed.

Mandatory Terms:

- **Title.** Commonly used titles are Court Order Acceptable for Processing, Qualifying Court Order, Court Order Allocating CSRS (or FERS) Benefits, or some such variant.[2] OPM will reject an order labeled QDRO (Qualified Domestic Relations Order) unless it expressly states it is governed by 5 C.F.R. part 838.[3]
- **Identification of Retirement System.**[4] The COAP must identify the retirement system to which it applies, FERS or CSRS.[5] It is not necessary to make the additional category distinctions such as CSRS Offset, FERS-RAE, or FERS Special.
- **Express Statement of Division.** The COAP must expressly state that the former spouse is entitled to a portion of the participant's annuity.[6]
- **Direct Payment to Former Spouse.** If the parties intend that OPM pay the former spouse directly, this must be stated explicitly. In such case, the COAP should instruct OPM to pay the former spouse his or her share of the retirement annuity directly, so that OPM will send out two monthly checks, one to each party.

2. Federal Reserve Plans accept court orders labeled QDRO (Qualified Domestic Relations Order).
3. 5 C.F.R. § 838.302.
4. 5 C.F.R. §§ 838.303; 838.611; 838.911.
5. Requirements for submission of FSRDS or FSPS retirement court orders are discussed in Section 5.5.2.
6. 5 C.F.R. § 838.303(b)(2).

- **State the Spouse's Share or Amount.** The COAP must state the former spouse's share of the retirement annuity as a fixed amount, as a percentage or a fraction of the annuity, or by a formula with variables, such as length of the participant's employment, that can be determined by OPM from its files.[7]
- **Identify the Type of Annuity.**[8] The COAP must correctly identify the type of employee annuity (i.e., phased retirement,[9] composite retirement, net, gross, or self-only annuity) to which it applies so that OPM can determine to what to apply the percentage, fraction, or formula. Although the code requires specificity as to the type of annuity to which the COAP applies, the regulations state that OPM will interpret a COAP providing for a generic division of an employee's annuity to mean any annuity (including the phased retirement annuity and the composite retirement annuity). OPM will accept a COAP that divides a phased retirement annuity or composite retirement annuity, but such an order must state whether it is directed at the self-only, gross, or net annuity.[10] If the COAP is ambiguous, OPM will interpret it to apply to the gross phased retirement annuity or gross composite retirement annuity. However, if an order provides for division of the phased retirement annuity or composite retirement annuity, without expressly providing for the possibility that an employee will retire in the usual manner, then it will not effectively award an annuity for the latter event. OPM will not divide disability retirement benefits when such a division would be contrary to state law unless the order expressly directs division of disability benefits.[11]

The following are Optional Terms:

- **An Award of the Former Spouse Survivor Annuity.** The COAP may award a former spouse a portion of the surviving spouse annuity.[12] If the COAP awards a survivor annuity but is silent as to the amount of the survivor annuity, OPM will interpret it as awarding the maximum survivor annuity. If the employee wishes to retain some survivor benefits for a subsequent spouse, the COAP must provide a formula for the former spouse's share of the survivor annuity,[13] e.g., only the marital share of the survivor annuity; otherwise, there is nothing left for a subsequent spouse. The COAP must expressly provide for the survivor annuity using terms such as "former spouse annuity" or "survivor annuity."[14] OPM will reject as not acceptable for processing an order that states that the former spouse will continue to receive pension benefits after the death of the employee.
- **Allocation of the Cost of the Survivor Annuity.** OPM will honor a COAP allocating the cost of the survivor annuity to either party or providing that the cost be shared; however, the COAP must correctly express the parties' or the court's intent. If the COAP provides for the gross annuity to be divided, OPM

---

7. 5 C.F.R. § 838.305.
8. 5 C.F.R. § 838.306.
9. See Chapter 7 for an explanation of phased and composite retirement.
10. See Section 2.2.
11. 5 C.F.R. Part 838, Subpart J, Appendix A—Guidelines for Interpreting State Court Orders Dividing Civil Service Retirement Benefits.
12. A survivor annuity provides for an annuity to be paid to the survivor after the death of the former employee. The survivor could be a current spouse, a former spouse, or both, up to the plan-specific cap. The amount of the cost and the maximum benefit available depend on the pension system. *See* Section 2.3.1.
13. 5 C.F.R. § 838.305.
14. 5 C.F.R. § 838.304.

will deduct the cost of the survivor annuity first and then divide the remaining pension benefit; the result is the parties will share the cost pro rata. However, if the COAP provides for division of the self-only annuity, the COAP should state the allocation of the cost of the survivor annuity explicitly; for example, the COAP can provide that the entire cost of the survivor benefit be deducted from the spouse's share or that it be deducted equally from each party's share. When the COAP divides the self-only annuity, absent an express provision allocating the cost, the cost will be allocated to the participant's share of the monthly pension benefit so that the participant will bear the entire cost of providing the survivor annuity for his or her former spouse.[15]

- **Refund of Employee Contributions.** A COAP should direct OPM what to do if an employee who is not retired applies for a refund of employee contributions upon separation from federal service prior to retirement or upon applying for retirement. A COAP can award a portion of an employee refund to a former spouse or prohibit the employee from receiving a refund.[16] If a refund is allowed, there will be no annuity payable. If the COAP is silent, the employee may receive a refund of contributions, which would defeat the other terms of the COAP providing for the former spouse to receive a share of the pension and survivor benefits. A COAP can bar OPM from making a refund of employee contributions. OPM will not accept a COAP that bars a refund unless the COAP also awards the former spouse a portion of the employee annuity or a survivor benefit.[17]
- **COLAs.** Unless the COAP expressly states otherwise, an allocation of a share of a pension to a former spouse expressed as a percentage or in a formula will entitle the former spouse to receive his or her pro rata share of any postretirement COLAs.[18] A former spouse whose share is a fixed dollar amount will not receive COLAs unless the order expressly so provides.[19]
- **Former Spouse Dies First.** The COAP can provide for the former spouse's share of the annuity to revert to the former spouse's estate if he or she predeceases the employee.[20] In the absence of such a provision, if the former spouse predeceases the employee, the former spouse's share will revert to the employee.
- **FERS Annuity Supplement.** If the COAP is silent as to division of the FERS annuity supplement, it will be divided proportionally between the spouses.[21] It is best practice to specify whether the annuity supplement, if any, will be shared with the former spouse.

---

15. 5 C.F.R. § 838.807(c).
16. 5 C.F.R. § 838.802.
17. 5 C.F.R. § 838.805.
18. A COLA is an increase in pay or in an annuity amount based on inflation as measured by the Consumer Price Index. *See* Section 1.6. *See also* 5 C.F.R. § 838.622(b)(1).
19. 5 C.F.R. § 838.622(b)(2).
20. The regulations state that OPM will not pay heirs directly but rather will pay in accordance with a court order to pay to a bank account or trust account, or the registry of the court from which the distribution to heirs will be made. There is one exception; a court order may provide that the deceased former spouse's share of the employee's annuity be paid directly to the children of the former spouse and employee. OPM, Court Orders Affecting Retirement Benefits, 57 Fed. Reg. 146 (July 29, 1992).
21. *See* Section 2.7.

PRACTICE TIP

Part 838 of title 5, Code of Federal Regulations, contains extensive model language that OPM encourages attorneys to use in preparing court orders.

The regulations contain instructive guidance on most, but not all, features of the pensions.

5.2 What Cannot Be Achieved by COAP

The following benefits cannot be awarded by COAP:

- **Continuing the Employee Annuity after the Annuitant's Death.** A former spouse's entitlement to a portion of an employee annuity terminates upon the death of the employee.[22] Therefore, OPM will reject a court order that purports to extend the former spouse's entitlement to a portion of an employee annuity past the death of the employee.
- **Division of CSRS Voluntary Contributions.** The employee may receive an additional annuity or a lump-sum refund of his or her contributions, plus interest, as a result of his or her voluntary contributions.[23] Voluntary contributions are not based on service. As such, voluntary contributions fall outside the statutory authorization for court orders to affect CSRS benefits that are based on service.[24] Therefore, the court has no authority to award a share of that portion of the annuity or refund to the spouse.
- **Division of CSRS Excess Deductions.** Excess deductions are not subject to division by COAP. Excess deductions are retirement deductions taken from the salary of a CSRS participant whose service exceeds the amount necessary to qualify for the maximum annuity (80 percent of high-3 average salary).[25] When OPM pays excess deductions to the employee, it is paying back voluntary contributions.[26]
- **Assign the CSRS or FERS Lump-Sum Death Benefit.** OPM must pay any accrued annuity that is not paid before a retiree's death and any unexpended balance of an employee's retirement contributions as a death benefit in accordance with the order of precedence established by federal law. Such repayments cannot be divided or assigned pursuant to a COAP.[27]

---

22. 5 C.F.R. § 838.302(b).

23. See 5 U.S.C. § 8325(j), which provides that state courts may affect payments under CSRS "which would otherwise be made to an employee or Member [of Congress] based upon his service" (discussed in Section 2.6).

24. There is no such benefit in FERS.

25. 5 U.S.C. § 8342(h) provides that, at the retirement or death of the employee, the balance of excess deductions not applied toward the service credit deposits is deemed a voluntary contribution (discussed in Section 2.6).

26. There is no such benefit in FERS.

27. See Lump Sum Death Benefit discussed in Section 1.14.

- **Assign the Children's Survivor Benefit.** Eligibility for children's survivor benefits is governed entirely by federal law and cannot be affected by state court orders.[28]
- **Create a Separate Interest.** A COAP cannot create a separate interest in a federal pension or entitle the former spouse to receive annuity payments before the employee has retired and entered pay status. The former spouse may receive a share of a federal government pension only if, as, and when paid to the employee. The only federal pension that allows a separate interest to be created is the Federal Reserve Board Plan.
- **Order the Employee to Maintain Health Insurance for the Former Spouse on the Employee's Plan.** A court order cannot directly order a federal government employee to maintain health insurance for a former spouse.[29] However, the spouse can get access to Federal Employees Health Benefits (FEHB) coverage after divorce by securing a portion of the employee annuity and survivor benefit through a COAP.
- **Life Insurance.** A COAP cannot require an employee to maintain life insurance.[30]
- **Order Retroactive Payments.** The COAP cannot require OPM to make payments retroactive to a date prior to the first day of the second month after OPM received the court order,[31] with limited exceptions.[32]
- **Order Payment Based on a Contingency.** A COAP cannot make payment to a former spouse contingent upon events other than those provided by law on which the right to pension payments are based, such as retirement of the employee; a provision that the former spouse will receive a share of the employee annuity only if he or she remains unmarried, for example, will cause OPM to reject the COAP.
- **Call the Order a QDRO.** Labeling the order a QDRO will be cause for rejection unless the text of the order cites the applicable federal regulations.[33]

5.3 COAP Submission and How to Avoid Rejection

Once the court enters a COAP that meets the requirements described in Section 5.1, the lawyer must then submit it to the Court Ordered Benefits Branch (COBB) of OPM. Make note of the following to avoid the COAP being rejected:

- Provide the signature of the appropriate judicial official. COBB does not review draft court orders; it will treat any order submitted without the appropriate judicial signature as a draft and will reject it.
- Include the spouse's current address, Social Security number (SSN), and date of birth in the body of the order or in a separate letter forwarding the certified copy of the order. If such information is not provided within the court order, it may be submitted only by the employee, the spouse, or either party's attorney of record.
- Include the employee's current address, as well as the SSN and date of birth, the latter two items either in the body of the order or in a separate letter forwarding the certified copy of the order.

28. *See* Sections 1.13 and 3.9 herein.
29. *See* Section 7.4 and Chapter 14 generally.
30. Other provisions permit an order to maintain Federal Employees Group Life Insurance (FEGLI) coverage. *See* Chapter 12.
31. 5 C.F.R. § 838.231(a).
32. *See* Sections 5.5.3 and 8.9.
33. 5 C.F.R. § 838.302.

- If the judgment of divorce makes mention of a settlement agreement, consent order, or marital settlement agreement, it must also be produced.

When a COAP is rejected, it is often for a simple reason such as failing to include one of the foregoing items. According to Tanisha Elliott, attorney in the COBB of OPM, the most frequent cause of rejection is that the COAP or judgment of divorce is not certified.

Eventually, after receipt of a COAP, COBB will send a determination letter to both parties and to the attorney who submitted the order. This could take many months. If the employee is not in pay status, the determination letter will accept or reject the COAP, and summarize its major terms, but will not include an estimate of the pension amount payable to the former spouse. If COBB rejects the order, the parties must submit an amended COAP, again signed by the appropriate judicial officer. Follow the same process described above.

PRACTICE TIP

Submit the COAP for division of a CSRS, FERS, Congressional Pension System, or the Central Intelligence Agency Retirement and Disability System (CIARDS) pension to OPM at

COBB (Court Ordered Benefits Branch)
PO Box 17
Washington, DC 20044-0017

Send the COAP via certified mail, with tracking, so you can ensure it's received. Do not close the file and assume your work is done until you have a copy of the determination letter that the COAP is accepted.

When the employee retires, he or she will receive another letter setting forth in detail how the previously accepted COAP will affect the pension payments, using actual dollar figures. An employee who is already retired will similarly receive a letter setting forth how OPM interprets the COAP. This is the first time that OPM tells the parties how much each party is set to receive. It is at this stage that disagreements sometimes occur as to the interpretation of the COAP. What are the steps to resolve a disagreement about COBB's interpretation of the COAP?

1. The employee, former spouse, or counsel, if any, may contact COBB in writing stating an objection to the determination letter. COBB will attempt to work out the dispute by telephone, if possible. If the employee or former spouse still does not agree with the determination made by COBB, he or she will receive a revised letter from COBB advising on his or her reconsideration rights and delineating the process. An employee must avail him- or herself of reconsideration rights within 30 days of receiving such decision letter. COBB advises that only approximately 10 percent or so choose this process, and this percentage is comprised of cases where a former employee is in pay status. If the employee is not in pay status, an amended COAP is the most efficient route. In some cases, parties may believe that the COAP is worded correctly and that the math applied by COBB is wrong. It is only those cases that are appropriate for the reconsideration process. This

reconsideration process concludes with a written determination of how the COAP will be implemented.

2. If either party is still unsatisfied with the results of the reconsideration process, he or she may file an appeal with COBB. Appeals are handled by COBB as well but are passed to a different department. That process is likewise comprised of phone calls and the submission of documentation. It concludes with another written determination.
3. If a party is still unsatisfied with the results of the COBB appeal process, he or she may appeal to the Merit Systems Protection Board as set forth in Section 7.14.

5.4 The First Order Rule and the Survivor Annuity

When the employee is already in pay status, the First Order Rule requires that the survivor annuity be addressed in the first order dividing the CSRS or FERS pension. This means that if the COAP omits an award to the former spouse of a survivor annuity with respect to a retiree, or awards a share of the survivor annuity that a party considers erroneous, and the COAP is submitted to OPM and accepted, OPM will reject an amended COAP that purports to make or revise the award of the survivor annuity. The rule provides in part:[34]

> **(1)** In this section, the "first order dividing the marital property of the retiree and the former spouse" means
>
> > **(i)** The original written order that first ends (or first documents an oral order ending) the marriage if the court divides any marital property (or approves a property settlement agreement that divides any marital property) in that order, or in any order issued before that order); or
> >
> > **(ii)** The original written order issued after the marriage has been terminated in which the court first divides any marital property (or first approves a property settlement agreement that divides any marital property) if no marital property has been divided prior to the issuance of that order.
>
> **(2)** The first order dividing marital property does not include—
>
> > **(i)** Any court order that amends, explains, clarifies, or interprets the original written order regardless of the effective date of the court order making the amendment, explanation, clarification, or interpretation; or
> >
> > **(ii)** Any court order issued under reserved jurisdiction or any other court order issued subsequent to the original written order that divide any marital property regardless of the effective date of the court order.

34. 5 C.F.R. § 838.806.

The First Order Rule does not apply prior to the employee's retirement; the COAP can be amended as many times as necessary prior to retirement, including to fix the omission of a survivor annuity. It also does not apply after retirement to an amended COAP that merely shifts the cost of the survivor annuity.

5.5 Foreign Service COAPs

As is the case with FERS and CSRS, the spouse with rights to share a Foreign Service pension cannot receive his or her portion of the pension until the employee actually enters pay status. Unlike a spouse of a FERS or CSRS participant, a Foreign Service spouse may not need a COAP to secure pension rights at divorce. A Foreign Service COAP is necessary when the parties intend to depart from default rights, or the court orders a division that departs from the default rights, or the spouse will not meet the definition of Former Spouse and the parties agree that he or she should receive a share of the pension.[35] Note there are no default rights to the Thrift Savings Plan, so an order will be needed to divide it.

A Foreign Service COAP may[36]

1. fix the amount of a principal's[37] pension to be paid to the former spouse or deny an award of default rights;
2. fix the amount of any regular survivor annuity or deny an award of default rights;
3. order an additional survivor annuity;
4. fix the amount of any benefit based on recall service payable to a former spouse to whom the principal was married during any portion of the recall service or order that no amount be paid;
5. fix the amount of any lump-sum credit refund of contribution payable to a former spouse or order that no amount be paid; and
6. order that any payment that would otherwise be made by the Foreign Service Retirement and Disability Fund to a principal based on his or her service will be paid (in whole or in part) to a previous spouse or child.

A Foreign Service COAP may not do the following:[38]

1. direct payment of an amount in excess of funds available to be paid;
2. direct that the principal, rather than the Secretary of State or the government, make the payments, unless the principal does not object during the 30-day notice period provided under 22 C.F.R. § 19.6-6;
3. make payment contingent upon events other than those on which other payments from the fund are based, such as age, marital status, and school attendance; and
4. be in conflict with any previously issued court order that remains valid.

---

35. 22 C.F.R. § 19 *et seq*. See Section 3.5.1 for an explanation of default spousal statutory rights.

36. 22 C.F.R. § 19.6-1.

37. In the Foreign Service Pension System, the term "principal" is defined as a participant or former participant in the Foreign Service Pension System whose service forms the basis for a benefit for a spouse, former spouse, previous spouse, or child of the participant or former participant. 22 C.F.R. § 19.2(q).

38. 22 C.F.R. § 19.6-1. See Section 5.2 for additional provisions that are prohibited in all federal pension orders.

The court that has authority to enter a COAP is defined as a court of any state or the District of Columbia; the Commonwealth of Puerto Rico, Guam, the Northern Mariana Islands, or the Virgin Islands; and any Native American court.[39] This is particularly important for foreign service families stationed abroad. An employee of the Foreign Service or spouse who procures a divorce in a court of a foreign nation will not be able to get an order dividing a Foreign Service pension, or denying a share thereof, that the Department of State will implement. However, a divorce from a court of a foreign nation may be a basis for pro rata share payments and a survivor annuity to a former spouse under the default rules.[40]

As is the case with any other retirement benefit court order, the former spouse's share of the principal's annuity must be stated explicitly. It may be stated

- as a fixed amount;
- as a percentage or a fraction of the principal's annuity; or
- by another formula, provided that it does not contain any variables whose values are not readily ascertainable from the face of the court order or normal Department of State files.

When the court order or spousal agreement contains a formula for dividing the principal's annuity, how the principal's service is expressed can affect the parties' rights. A formula that requires a computation of service that uses "years of service," "total service," "service performed," or similar terms will exclude time credited to the principal that is attributable to unused sick leave. However, when the order or spousal agreement contains a formula that requires a computation of "creditable service" (or some other phrase using "credit" or its equivalent), unused sick leave will be included.

PRACTICE TIP

In a spousal agreement or court order, always expressly address the division of each of the pension's elements—principal's pension, survivor annuity, supplemental survivor annuity for recall service, and lump-sum credit—and either allocate or waive each element.

It is important to use the correct terminology when preparing a Foreign Service COAP. The terminology for Foreign Service COAPs differs from that of FERS and CSRS COAPs.

The term "full annuity" is defined as follows: "If a participant [principal] retires and does not provide a survivor annuity to a spouse, former spouse or designated beneficiary, the participant receives a full annuity."[41] A full annuity means an annuity computed without any survivorship cost reduction.[42]

39. 22 C.F.R. § 19.2.
40. *Id.*
41. 22 C.F.R. § 19.10-1.
42. This is most comparable to the self-only annuity in FERS/CSRS parlance. Language that is also acceptable to effect the same outcome would be "gross annuity," "life rate annuity," "unreduced annuity," or "annuity without survivor benefit."

The term "net annuity" refers to the "disposable annuity" or the "retirement check." Unless one of these terms is used, the Department of State will presume that the court order refers to a full annuity. There is rarely a reason to use a term other than "full annuity."

PRACTICE TIP

When dividing a Foreign Service annuity, it is usually best to use the term "full annuity," since it constitutes the entire annuity before deductions.

As with FERS/CSRS, the former spouse's share of the principal's annuity will terminate upon the death of the principal, and the former spouse will receive no pension payments thereafter unless the COAP provides for a survivor annuity. In the event that the former spouse dies first, his or her share of the annuity can revert to the principal, or it can be paid to

(1) the court;
(2) an officer of the court acting as a fiduciary;
(3) the estate of the former spouse; or
(4) one or more of the principal's children.

PRACTICE TIP

If you represent the principal, he or she will want the spouse's share to revert back if the spouse dies first. This is the default if the COAP is silent. Spouses may want their share to be paid to their estate if they predecease the principal. The COAP can provide for this if the parties agree or the court orders it.

5.5.1 Lump Sum in Lieu of Annuity—Foreign Service Pensions

The former spouse of a Foreign Service retiree may be paid a lump sum in lieu of an annuity.[43] The amount awarded would be a portion of the present value of the principal's annuity, determined as of the date of the award. In such case, the court order should specifically state the present value of the principal's annuity and award the former spouse either a percentage or a specific dollar amount to be paid as a lump sum. The U.S. Department of State, Office of Retirement (HR/RET) will not calculate a present value, nor will it check the accuracy of the value stated in the order. It will simply make payment in the

43. Foreign Service Divorce Handbook, Retirement Network of the U.S. Dep't of State (Sept. 2014), https://rnet.state.gov/pdf/FS%20Divorce%20Handbook%20Revised%20September%202014.pdf.

amount or percentage directed in the order. Specifically, the former spouse will receive payment of his or her lump sum in equal monthly installments at 50 percent of the principal's full annuity beginning at the time of retirement or the date of the order, whichever comes later, until the lump-sum amount is paid.

There are few reasons for parties to negotiate such an arrangement. One situation where it may be useful is where the parties want to set off the present value of the pension against other assets, such as a house.

Note that there is no authority for how such a lump-sum division will be affected by remarriage of the spouse before age 55. When using this method of division, it would be safest to assume that such payments will continue despite remarriage.

5.5.2 Submission of Foreign Service COAP; Timing

The First Order Rule, discussed in Section 5.4, also applies to Foreign Service pensions. Therefore, if the Foreign Service principal is already retired and in pay status, and the former spouse wants survivor benefits, the first COAP submitted to the Department of State must make those provisions.

A Foreign Service COAP may be sent to Department of State (HR/RET), Room H-620, SA-1, Washington, DC 20522-0108. The application must be typed or printed, be signed by the beneficiary, and include[44]

(1) the full name, date of birth, current address, and current marital status of the beneficiary;
(2) full name and date of birth of the principal or other identifying information;
(3) relationship to the principal and, if a spouse or former spouse, date of marriage to and/or divorce from the principal; and
(4) a statement that the court order has not been amended, superseded, or set aside. The original or a recently certified copy of the court order must be enclosed with the application or a statement appended that such a copy has been sent to the Department of State by other means.

The lawyer should be aware of the following time limitations when representing a Foreign Service employee or spouse and preparing a COAP:

- A spousal agreement affecting pension benefits may be filed at any time and will govern payments made after its acceptance by HR/RET. Note: the parties need not be divorced.
- A court order directing or barring payment of a pension to a former spouse may not be given effect if it is issued more than two years after the divorce becomes final.
- A spousal agreement affecting supplemental survivor benefits or lump-sum payments must be filed before the supplemental annuity of the principal begins or lump-sum payment is made.
- A spousal agreement between a principal and a former spouse may be filed with HR/RET at any time to provide an additional survivor annuity for the former spouse.
- A court order adjusting the amount of a regular or additional survivor annuity to a former spouse may not be given effect by the Department of State if it is issued after the death of the principal.

44. 22 C.F.R. § 19.6-3.

- A spousal agreement may be revised or voided by agreement of the parties (by filing a new agreement) subject to the above limitations, except a spousal agreement for an additional survivor annuity; such agreements are irrevocable.
- A valid spousal agreement entered into subsequent to the issuance of a court order will override the court order.

After the Department of State accepts a COAP, if the principal objects to the implementation, he or she has 30 days to initiate legal action. In such case, the amount of the proposed payment will be withheld from the former spouse, and no payment will be made to him or her until the dispute is resolved.

5.5.3 Retroactive Payments—Foreign Service Pensions

A COAP dividing a Foreign Service pension can require the Department of State to make payments retroactively. The Foreign Service Handbook for Attorneys on Court Orders and Spousal Agreements states it succinctly:[45]

> A court order issued within 12 months after a divorce becomes final, directing payment of a pension to a former spouse, may be made retroactively effective to the first of the month in which the divorce becomes final if so specified by the court. In such event, the Department will adjust any future payments that may become due to an annuitant and a former spouse by increasing one and correspondingly reducing the other in order to give effect to the order of the court. However, if future payments to one party are not due, as for example if a court orders that no payments be made to a former spouse, or that 100 percent of an annuity be paid as pension to a former spouse, the Department will not give retroactive effect to a court order by collecting overpayments from one party in order to pay them to the other party and will not make overpayments from the Fund.

If the COAP is not submitted during the final divorce hearing, *and* the Foreign Service employee is in pay status at the time of the divorce, in order for the former spouse to receive payments beginning as of the date of divorce, the COAP must specify that payments shall be retroactive to the date of divorce *and* the COAP must be received by the Department of State within 12 months of the date of divorce.

45. Am. Foreign Serv. Ass'n, Foreign Service Handbook for Attorneys on Court Orders and Spousal Agreements 11–12 (2014), *available at* https://www.afsa.org/sites/default/files/FSdivorcehandbook.pdf.

Chapter Six

The Insurable Interest Annuity

Chapter 6 introduces the insurable interest annuity feature of CSRS and FERS pensions. If a CSRS or FERS employee is in good health at retirement, he or she may elect a reduced annuity naming a beneficiary with an insurable interest, such as a domestic partner or other nonspouse family member, to receive a survivor annuity after his or her death.

6.1 Overview

An insurable interest annuity is an alternative to the regular survivor annuity for a spouse or former spouse.[1] If an employee is in good health at retirement and retires for reasons other than disability, he or she may elect a reduced retirement annuity and name a beneficiary to receive an annuity after the employee's death. The beneficiary must be a person who has an insurable interest in the employee, such as a domestic partner, other nonspouse dependent family member, or other person who could reasonably expect to derive financial benefit from the employee's continued life. If the employee is married, he or she must obtain spousal consent to elect an insurable interest annuity for the spouse in lieu of the regular survivor annuity. However, the employee does not need spousal consent to elect an insurable interest annuity for a third person. A retired employee could have both a regular survivor annuity for a spouse and an insurable interest annuity for someone else, such as a domestic partner.

The insurable interest annuity can provide a survivor annuity to a person who would not otherwise be eligible to receive one, such as a domestic partner, an adult disabled child, or a second spouse when a prior spouse is entitled to the entire regular survivor annuity.

1. 5 C.F.R. § 831.613.

6.2 Eligibility for an Insurable Interest Annuity

An insurable interest is presumed to exist in a spouse, a blood or adopted relative closer than first cousin, a former spouse, a fiancé(e), and a current same-sex domestic partner or person with whom the employee is living in a relationship that would constitute a common-law marriage if the parties lived in a jurisdiction that recognizes common-law marriages.

The term "same-sex domestic partner"[2] means a person in a domestic partnership with an employee or annuitant of the same sex, and the term "domestic partnership" is defined as a committed relationship between two adults, of the same sex, in which the partners

(i) are each other's sole domestic partner and intend to remain so indefinitely;
(ii) maintain a common residence, and intend to continue to do so (or would maintain a common residence but for an assignment abroad or other employment-related, financial, or similar obstacle);
(iii) are at least 18 years of age and mentally competent to consent to contract;
(iv) share responsibility for a significant measure of each other's financial obligations;
(v) are not married or joined in a civil union to anyone else;
(vi) are not the domestic partner of anyone else;
(vii) are not related in a way that, if they were of opposite sex, would prohibit legal marriage in the U.S. jurisdiction in which the domestic partnership was formed; and
(viii) are willing to certify, if required by OPM, that they understand that willful falsification of any documentation required to establish that an individual is in a domestic partnership may lead to disciplinary action and the recovery of the cost of benefits received related to such falsification, as well as constitute a criminal violation under 18 U.S.C. 1001.

An employee who wants to provide an insurable interest annuity to someone who does not have a presumptive insurable interest, including an opposite-sex domestic partner, must provide an affidavit from one or more people with personal knowledge of relevant facts, including financial dependency. The Office of Personnel Management (OPM) requires the affidavit to state the relationship between the employee and the person, the extent to which the person named is dependent on the employee, and the reasons why the person might reasonably expect to derive financial benefit from the employee's continued life.

An employee may name only one natural person as the beneficiary of an insurable interest annuity. OPM will not accept the designation of a contingent beneficiary; such a beneficiary designation is void.

6.3 Cost of the Annuity and Amount of the Benefit

The employee may elect for the beneficiary to receive up to 55 percent of the amount of the employee's annuity, after reduction for the cost of the survivor benefit. The cost of the insurable interest annuity depends on the difference between the employee's age and that

2. 5 C.F.R. § 842.605(e)(2).

of the beneficiary and the amount of the employee's annuity that is used as a base. The base amount varies depending on whether there is anyone else who has an entitlement to a survivor benefit and, if so, how much. If at retirement the employee is entitled to a self-only annuity (i.e., he or she does not have a spouse or former spouse entitled to a survivor annuity), the reduction to provide an insurable interest benefit is computed as follows:[3]

- If the person named is older, the same age, or less than five years younger than the retiree, the reduction is 10 percent;
- if the person named is at least five but less than ten years younger than the retiree, the reduction is 15 percent;
- if the person named is at least ten but less than 15 years younger than the retiree, the reduction is 20 percent;
- if the person named is at least 15 but less than 20 years younger than the retiree, the reduction is 25 percent;
- if the person named is at least 20 but less than 25 years younger than the retiree, the reduction is 30 percent;
- if the person named is at least 25 but less than 30 years younger than the retiree, the reduction is 35 percent; or
- if the person named is 30 or more years younger than the retiree, the reduction is 40 percent.

If the employee wants to provide an insurable interest annuity for a child, the cost is substantial. In such a circumstance, life insurance might be a more economical option. See Chapter 12.

Note the difference between the maximum possible amount of the insurable interest annuity benefit compared to a regular spousal survivor annuity. With a regular spousal survivor annuity, the surviving spouse receives 55 percent (CSRS) or 50 percent (FERS) of the unreduced (i.e., self-only) benefit, whereas with an insurable interest annuity, the surviving annuitant will receive 55 percent under CSRS, or 50 percent under FERS, of the reduced benefit.

These examples illustrate the math:

Example 1:
Elena is a CSRS participant who will be retiring in September 2020 at age 62. Elena is a single person who is supporting her mother, age 91. Elena decides to give her mother an insurable interest survivor annuity. Elena's single-life annuity will be $40,000 per year. In order to give the insurable interest survivor annuity to her mother, Elena's annuity will be reduced by 10 percent of $40,000, or $4,000. Elena's annuity will therefore be reduced to $36,000. If Elena dies before her mother, her mother will receive a survivor annuity equal to 55 percent of $36,000, or $19,800.

Example 2:
Janelle is a FERS participant who will retire on June 1, 2020, at age 60. Janelle was approved for an insurable interest survivor annuity to her partner, Lili, age 35. Janelle's self-only annuity before the reduction for the insurable interest survivor annuity was $75,000. Janelle's annuity will be reduced by 35 percent ($26,250) in order to give Lili, who is 25 years younger, a survivor annuity benefit. Janelle's FERS annuity will then be $75,000 less $26,250, or $48,750. At her death, Lili will receive an insurable interest survivor annuity of 50 percent of $48,750, or $24,375.

The amount of the annuity payable to the retired employee who elects an insurable interest annuity will be affected by whether he or she has a spouse at retirement who will

3. 3 Dep't of State, Foreign Affairs Manual § 6187.4; 5 U.S.C. § 8420.

get a regular spousal survivor annuity or a former spouse who has a COAP[4] providing for a spousal survivor annuity. The employee's annuity will be reduced by the cost for both.

PRACTICE TIP

If your client is the plan participant, or a second spouse, advise him or her that under certain circumstances, a second spouse can obtain a spousal survivor annuity, even if a first spouse is already entitled to the maximum regular survivor annuity. Specifically, if the former spouse dies or loses entitlement to the survivor annuity, such as by remarrying before age 55, the participant has two years to opt to convert the insurable interest annuity to a current spouse survivor annuity.

6.4 Insurable Interest Election: How to Provide It and When It Ends

For the civil service employee to elect an insurable interest benefit, he or she must arrange for and pay the cost of any medical examination required to demonstrate good health. The employee must furnish to OPM a copy of the exam, signed and dated by a licensed physician, on such forms and at such time and place as OPM prescribes. A Foreign Service member must pass a physical examination that is conducted by the Department of State, Office of Medical Services.[5]

After receipt of all required evidence to support an election of an insurable interest annuity, OPM will notify the employee of initial monthly annuity rates with and without the election of an insurable interest annuity and the initial amount payable to the proposed beneficiary. No election of an insurable interest annuity is effective unless the employee confirms the election in writing, dies, or becomes incompetent within 60 days after the date of the notice.

The reduction to provide an insurable interest survivor annuity stops, and the insurable interest annuity is therefore cancelled, when (1) the person named to receive the insurable interest benefit dies, or (2) the person named is the current spouse of the annuitant and the annuitant changes the benefit from an insurable interest election to a regular current spousal survivor annuity within two years after the last reduction to provide a former spousal survivor annuity ends, or (3) the annuitant marries and elects to provide a survivor annuity for his or her new spouse and chooses to cancel the insurable interest designation, or (4) the annuitant marries the person named to receive the insurable interest annuity and elects to provide a regular spousal survivor annuity for him or her.[6]

---

4. A COAP is a Court Order Acceptable for Processing, i.e., a court order that allocates federal retirement benefits pursuant to 5 C.F.R. § 838.103 and can affect an employee annuity, a refund of employee contributions, and a former spouse survivor annuity. *See* Section 5.1.

5. 3 Dep't of State, Foreign Affairs Manual § 6187.4; 5 U.S.C. § 8420.

6. OPM Publ'n: Information for Annuitants: Civil Service Retirement System (CSRS) (rev. June 2013).

6.5 Insurable Interest Annuity and Divorce

Federal law has no provision for recognition of a court order awarding an insurable interest annuity, meaning that it cannot be secured pursuant to a COAP. There is rarely a good reason to negotiate for an insurable interest annuity in a divorce settlement. One advantage over the regular spousal survivor annuity is that the insurable interest annuity does not terminate upon remarriage before age 55. However, the insurable interest annuity can be voided by the annuitant's later election for a spousal survivor benefit on behalf of a subsequently acquired spouse. In the context of a divorce settlement, it is difficult to secure and easy to frustrate.

For parties negotiating a settlement and considering whether to provide an insurable interest annuity or life insurance, it is important to evaluate a few factors.

First, with an insurable interest, if the beneficiary dies, so does the benefit. The employee cannot name a contingent beneficiary as he or she can with life insurance.

Second, consider the benefits of a lump-sum life insurance payout versus annuity payments, assuming that a party must choose. With an insurable interest, the beneficiary will receive a monthly annuity, whereas with life insurance, the beneficiary will receive a lump sum. This might be important in a case where the parties to a settlement intend to provide for a child. If the parties intend that the child be able to use money for payment of college expenses, a lump-sum payment might be more beneficial than a monthly payment. Conversely, if the employee intends to provide for a disabled child, a monthly payment might be more advantageous.

Third, consider tax consequences. The insurable interest annuity is fully taxable as income; by contrast, life insurance proceeds are generally tax free.

Chapter Seven

Often Overlooked Issues Pertaining to Federal Government Pensions

Chapter 7 explains other nuances, features, and considerations not described in previous chapters. Understanding these will allow the lawyer to add further value to the representation of the client in his or her divorce.

7.1 Phased Retirement under CSRS and FERS

On August 8, 2014, the Office of Personnel Management (OPM) issued the final regulation to implement phased retirement pursuant to section 100121 of the Moving Ahead for Progress in the 21st Century Act, or MAP-21.[1] This law authorized changes to the Civil Service Retirement System (CSRS) and the Federal Employees' Retirement System (FERS) by amending 5 U.S.C. §§ 8336(a) and 8412(a).[2] Effective November 6, 2014, certain employees became eligible to apply for phased retirement with consent of their employing agency.

1. 23 U.S.C. § 64.

2. U.S. Off. of Personnel Mgmt. Benefits Admin. Letter No. 14-208, Phased Retirement and Federal Employees' Group Life Insurance (FEGLI) Program Guidelines (Oct. 7, 2014).

Employees in phased retirement are able to work 50 percent time and receive 50 percent of their monthly pension annuity. No other proportions of work to retirement were being offered as of 2019.

Phased retirement is intended to retain employees who would have fully retired but who are willing to continue in federal service for a period of time on a part-time schedule while engaging in mentoring. Employees participating in phased retirement will receive additional credit toward their full retirement. These employees will also begin receiving partial annuity payments, prorated based on the portion of the workweek that they are not scheduled to work.

In general, to qualify for phased retirement, the employee must have been employed on a full-time basis for not less than the three-year period ending on the effective date of entry into phased retirement status. The employee must also be a retirement-eligible employee and must be a participant in CSRS or FERS. Participants in other federal pension systems are not eligible.

For CSRS participants, participation is limited to a person who

- is eligible for an immediate retirement with at least 30 years of service, and
- is at least age 55 or has at least 20 years of service and is at least age 60.

For FERS participants, participation is limited to those persons who

- are eligible for an immediate retirement with at least 30 years of service, and
- have attained their minimum retirement age (between ages 55 and 57 depending on year of birth) or who have at least 20 years of service and who are at least age 60.

For purposes of health insurance under the Federal Employees Health Benefits Program (FEHB) and life insurance under Federal Employees' Group Life Insurance (FEGLI), the phased retiree is considered to be working full time. Phased retirement is creditable toward the five years of service needed to continue FEGLI coverage as an annuitant.

If an employee in phased retirement status dies before separating for full retirement benefits, the employee will be deemed to be a deceased employee (as opposed to a deceased retiree) for purposes of awarding survivor benefits to a spouse or former spouse. If a Court Order Acceptable for Processing (COAP) is on file, it will govern. However, while an employee is in phased employment status, there is no deduction from the annuity to maintain a survivor benefit.

The employee continues to accrue creditable service toward calculation of the pension benefits he or she will receive upon final retirement, known as composite retirement. Composite retirement annuity means the annuity computed when a phased retiree attains full retirement status.

Phased retirement status will potentially complicate settlement agreements that predate the availability of phased retirement, provide for alimony to terminate upon the retirement of the federal employee, and are premised on the former spouse starting to receive a portion of the employee's pension. Parties entering into a settlement in the future should take account of the potential for phased retirement in their settlement agreement.

An OPM benefits letter provides apt examples of how phased retirement works.[3]

---

3. U.S. Off. of Personnel Mgmt. Benefits Admin. Letter No. 14-108, Phased Retirement Frequently Asked Questions (Aug. 8, 2014).

The example below is for a FERS employee with 35 years and 9 months of service.

FERS Phased Retirement Income		
	Annual	**Monthly**
Current Salary $68,275 x 50%	$34,137	$2,844.75
Current Annual Annuity $23,868 x 50%	$11,934	$994.50
Total Employee Income in Phased Retirement	$46,071	$3,838.75

*No FERS annuity supplement is payable in phased retirement.

The example below is for a CSRS employee with 35 years and 9 months of service.

CSRS Phased Retirement Income		
	Annual	**Monthly**
Current Salary $68,275 x 50%	$34,137	$2,844.75
Current Annual Annuity $45,296.30 x 50%	$22,648	$1,887.00
Total Employee Income in Phased Retirement	$56,785	$4,731.75

For discussion of how to address phased retirement in a COAP, see Section 5.1 of this book.

7.2 Obtaining a Present Value of the Pension

The lawyer may consider obtaining a formal pension valuation in order to obtain a present value of the employee's pension. A pension valuation is a determination of the present value of a future stream of income. The question being answered is: in today's dollars, what is the value of all future payments to be received from the pension? The valuation itself is more of an art than a science, since it is based on many assumptions.

In order to obtain a sound pension valuation, the lawyer will need to engage an expert, such as an actuary or a certified public accountant. There may be others who have qualifications and training to qualify as an expert. The pension value depends on what variables/assumptions are used by the expert in the calculation. These variables include factors such as life expectancy, interest rates, and tax discounts.

Obtaining a pension valuation may make good strategic sense in some cases. For example, determining the present value of the pension could allow parties to compare its value with other assets, such as a house, so that parties could trade off.

Another example is the case of two federal employees participating in different pension systems, such as CSRS and FERS. The parties might get two pension valuations so that they could compare the value of one spouse's FERS entitlement combined with the Thrift Savings Plan with the value of the CSRS entitlement of the other spouse.

7.3 Purchase of Creditable Military Service

A military member may separate from military service and enter federal civilian employment. Generally speaking, unless a service member reaches 20 years of active duty, he or she will not be entitled to a military pension.[4] In the event that a service member with less than 20 years of service enters federal employment, he or she may be able to apply his or her creditable military service to the federal pension entitlement.[5] A military member who retired with a pension may also be able to waive the military pension and use the years of military service to count toward a civilian pension.[6] This must be done prior to retiring or separating from federal employment.

Because pension entitlement is based on both high-3[7] salary and years of service, applying years of military service to federal service credit can result in a much higher pension upon retirement from federal civilian employment. Applying military service can also result in the employee being able to retire from civilian service in the federal government sooner than he or she could have otherwise.

Applying military service to federal pension entitlement is referred to as buying back military service. Military members do not contribute a portion of their pay to their pension. A former service member who wants to buy back military service so as to apply it to accrual of a federal civilian pension must therefore make a deposit into the pension system. To receive credit for military service toward a FERS pension, generally, the employee must make a lump-sum deposit of between 3 percent and 3.4 percent of his or her military basic pay, plus interest. The precise amount depends on the years served. The CSRS deposit is generally 7 percent of military basic pay.

In terms of procedure, the employee must first petition the Defense Finance and Accounting Service (DFAS) to get a history of his or her base pay during his or her time in the military. The second step is a request to the current employing agency to determine the amount he or she would have contributed to the pension as a civilian employee and to calculate interest on the unpaid amounts. The sum of the two is the cost to buy back the service. The agency provides a letter so stating. The applicant and the agency both complete Form SF 3108 (FERS) or Form SF 2803 (CSRS).

A federal employee who is already receiving a military pension can also request a buyback and must make a deposit. The military retiree must waive his or her entitlement to a military pension and receive only the civilian pension. The procedure is the same.

Whether in a given case it makes economic sense for the former military member to buy back military service, or waive a military pension in favor of a civilian pension, depends upon the facts of each case. Parties negotiating a settlement will need to consider a variety of factors, including the cost of the deposit compared with the expected increase in pension benefits and whether the funds are available to make the deposit. This may be more enticing if the employee left the military as a midgrade service member and then went on to earn a high salary in government employment. The calculation of what he or she would owe would be based on the lower military earnings, and the amount of the deposit might not be large compared to the potential gain. In such a situation, a buyback could make financial sense.

---

4. 10 U.S.C. §§ 1176, 8323.

5. As a general rule, military service in the Armed Forces of the United States is creditable for retirement purposes if it was active service terminated under honorable conditions and performed prior to separation from civilian service for retirement. OPM Publ'n: Retirement Facts 1, RI 83-1 (rev. Nov. 1997). Service in the National Guard, except when ordered to active duty in the service of the United States, is generally not creditable.

6. 5 U.S.C. §§ 8334(j), 8422(e); 5 C.F.R. §§ 831.2104, 842.307.

7. High-3 average pay is the highest average basic pay earned by the employee during any three consecutive years of service. See glossary for full definition.

Counsel for the nonemployee spouse should also consider that the former service member who served less than 20 years could wait until after the divorce to buy back his or her military service. Whether the order dividing the pension should take account of that contingency depends on what the parties include in their settlement or ask the court in a contested case to address.

When a retired military member is divorced with a court order dividing his or her military retired pay, he or she cannot waive military retired pay to receive a civilian pension without first consenting for OPM to continue payment to the former spouse. In other words, the employee/retired military member will receive only the civilian pension, but OPM must pay the former spouse the amount he or she would be entitled to from the military pension if paid directly from the military pay center.

PRACTICE TIP

The cost to the couple for an ex-military member to buy back service years could be small relative to the yield in increased pension benefits to their mutual benefit. They might agree to use marital property before divorce to do this. It might mitigate potential spousal support or in other ways help to negotiate a settlement.

7.4 $1 Award to Secure FEHB Coverage

A former spouse can continue to receive health insurance coverage under FEHB through a COAP by receiving a portion of the employee's annuity and a portion of the survivor benefit.[8] The former spouse need only receive one dollar per month to secure this benefit.

Parties negotiating a settlement may agree each will keep his or her own retirement benefits. However, they may want to consider an award of one dollar a month to the spouse who is not a federal employee. That would allow him or her to maintain FEHB coverage at his or her own expense for life.

PRACTICE TIP

A COAP granting the former spouse a portion of the retiree's annuity qualifies him or her for continued FEHB coverage until the employee dies. A COAP providing both a portion of the retirement annuity and a survivor annuity provides continued FEHB coverage until the former spouse dies. The COAP must provide for a former spouse annuity of at least $1.00 per month. 5 U.S.C. § 8905.

8. *See* Section 11.1.

There is little downside to negotiating the $1 per month, for either side. The cost is so little, and there still remains the rest of the survivor benefit in case the employee expects to remarry. In the case of remarriage, the former spouse of the employee can still have FEHB for the employee's life. However, if remarriage occurs before age 55, he or she will lose the entitlement to the survivor annuity, along with the entitlement to FEHB after the death of the employee.

7.5 Factoring Social Security When Dividing Federal Government Pensions

Federal preemption prevents state courts from dividing or assigning Social Security benefits upon divorce.[9] Congress has made an exception to this anti-assignment rule to allow garnishment or attachment to collect child support and alimony,[10] but not for the purpose of equitable division of property at divorce. A state court has no power to enter an order directed to the Social Security Administration to pay a portion of a recipient's Social Security benefits to his or her former spouse, nor does a state court have the power to order the recipient to pay a portion of his or her Social Security benefit to his or her former spouse as part of a division of property.

This presents a problem for a state court attempting to equitably divide marital property in a divorce proceeding where one spouse may receive Social Security and the other may not—for example, where one spouse is a participant in CSRS and has no Social Security benefits and the other spouse is a participant in FERS with a smaller pension and Social Security. In such cases, state courts have struggled with how to divide marital property and reach a result that is fair to both parties. An equal division of the pensions, without considering Social Security benefits, may produce an inequitable result.[11]

A court could consider the existence of Social Security benefits in determining what division of pension benefits is equitable, or it could expressly offset the amount of a pension awarded to a spouse with Social Security benefits by the value of those benefits.

The extent to which federal law permits a state court to consider the existence of Social Security benefits in deciding how to divide pension benefits, or to expressly offset Social Security benefits against a pension award, has not been resolved. In *Hisquierdo v. Hisquierdo*,[12] the United States Supreme Court decided that the retirement benefits under the Railroad Retirement Act, which the Court likened to Social Security, could not be assigned, attached, or offset in a state court proceeding.

Several state courts have looked to *Hisquierdo* for guidance on how to treat the Social Security benefits in a divorce proceeding. Some state courts have read *Hisqueirdo* as completely prohibiting even mere consideration of Social Security benefits in a property distribution proceeding,[13] while other states have allowed for consideration of Social Security

9. 42 U.S.C.A. § 407.

10. 42 U.S.C.A. § 659(a).

11. *See* Kelly v. Kelly, 198 Ariz. 307 (2000) (wife participated in FERS, which included a Social Security component, while husband participated in CSRS, which gave an increased annuity in lieu of Social Security benefits).

12. Hisquierdo v. Hisquierdo, 439 U.S. 572 (1979).

13. *In re* Marriage of Peterson, 243 Cal. App. 4th 923 (2016) (husband's Social Security is separate property not subject to division, while wife's pension is community property and thus subject to equal division under California law).

benefits in determining a distribution of property.[14] Some state courts have not found *Hisquierdo* decisive, as it does not address the issue of Social Security directly. Courts in these states have permitted offsetting a pension against the other spouse's Social Security benefits.[15]

PRACTICE TIP

Parties negotiating a settlement are free to factor Social Security benefits into their discussions. Nothing in the law of Social Security prevents them from doing so. Think about each party's Social Security entitlement when negotiating the division of a federal pension and alimony.

7.6 Different Accrual Rates for Different Pensions

As described in other parts of this book, participants accrue percentage points toward calculation of a pension based on the type of employment and the agency by which they are employed. The Central Intelligence Agency Retirement and Disability System and Foreign Service provide for additional benefit accruals for dangerous work locations. Some examples of these varying accrual rates follow:

- CSRS—Employee accrues between 1.5 and 2 percent per year depending on length of service.
- FERS—Employee accrues 1.0–1.1 percent per year based on age and length of service.
- FERS Special—Employee accrues 1.7 percent per year for the first 20 years, then 1 percent per year.
- Congressional Pension—Employee accrues 1.7 percent per year.
- FSRDS (Foreign Service Retirement & Disability System)—Employee accrues 2 percent per year for 20 years, 1.7 percent per year thereafter.
- FSPS (Foreign Service Pension System)—1.7 percent per year
- FSPS Special—2.3 percent per year
- FSRDS Special—2.5 percent per year
- Federal Reserve Board Plan—1.5–2 percent per year depending on length of service

14. Jackson v. Sollie, 449 Md. 165 (2016) (consideration of Social Security benefits received by one spouse is the same as dividing or offsetting and is permissible; monetary award to the nonparticipating spouse in order to equalize the parties does not violate federal preemption); *In re* Marriage of Rockwell, 141 Wash. App. 235 (2007) (court reduced community portion of wife's CSRS pension by what she would have received if her retirement plan had included Social Security benefits).

15. Cornbleth v. Cornbleth, 397 Pa. Super. 421 (1990) (where husband and wife's salaries and employment histories were similar but wife received Social Security and husband CSRS pension, court allowed a portion of husband's CSRS pension to be exempted to account for his lack of Social Security).

When determining the division, keep in mind that the participant may have been accumulating pension benefits at a different rate at different times during the marriage or prior to the marriage or may do so after divorce. Therefore, a straight division by use of the pro rata share formula may disadvantage one party or the other.

7.7 Former Spouse Predeceases Plan Participant

If the former spouse dies before the employee, what happens to the annuity? It depends on the terms of the COAP.

Upon the death of the former spouse, his or her share of the annuity will

(i) revert to the employee by default if the COAP does not explicitly state otherwise, or

(ii) pass to the court, pass to an officer of the court acting as a fiduciary, pass to the estate of the former spouse, or pass to one or more of the employee's children.[16]

A "child" is defined in 5 U.S.C. §§ 8341(a)(4) and 8441(4) as an unmarried child under 18 and can include a stepchild and an adopted child; an unmarried dependent child of any age who is incapable of self-support due to a disability that occurred before the age of 18; and an unmarried child between the ages of 18 and 22 who is a full-time student.

If parties entering into a settlement intend that the pension revert to the participant if the former spouse dies first, the settlement agreement and the COAP should say so expressly. If the pension reverts to the participant, OPM will adjust the annuity by eliminating the reduction to fund the survivor benefit.

However, if an actuarial reduction was made to the annuity to provide survivor benefits, that reduction will not stop.[17]

7.8 Participant Remarriage and Second Divorce

A retired participant who was unmarried at retirement, who had no living former spouse with a COAP and thus elected a self-only[18] annuity, and who later marries can elect a survivor annuity for his or her new spouse. He or she has two years to designate the new spouse as a survivor annuitant under CSRS, FERS, or one of the Federal Reserve plans.[19] An annuitant with a Foreign Service pension has one year after marriage to make this selection.[20] In such case, two reductions are made to the self-only annuity. One is the regular monthly reduction that will begin upon the election of the survivor annuity. The second is an actuarial reduction to compensate for the missed survivor annuity reductions that had not been made from the date the retiree went into pay status through the date of his or her postretirement election, plus interest.

16. 5 C.F.R. § 838.237.

17. See Section 2.3.1 for an explanation of the two reductions that occur to provide for a survivor annuity.

18. *See* Section 2.3.1.

19. 5 U.S.C. §§ 8339(j)(5)(C)(i), (k)(2) (2012). *See also* Briggs v. Off. of Personnel Mgm't, No. 2012-3023 (Fed. Cir. 2012); Taylor v. Off. of Personnel Mgm't, No. 2016-1822 (Fed. Cir. 2016); Schoemakers v. Off. of Personnel Mgm't, 180 F.3d 1377, 1382 (Fed. Cir. 1999).

20. 22 C.F.R. § 19.10-3; 3 Dep't of State, Foreign Affairs Manual § 6187.3(c).

The new spouse will be entitled to receive benefits if

- the annuitant dies after nine months of marriage or as a result of an accident; or
- the new spouse is a parent of a child born or adopted during the marriage.

However, if at retirement the employee elected a maximum survivor annuity for a former spouse, or a COAP provides the maximum survivor annuity to the former spouse, and the participant later remarries, there is no survivor annuity benefit available for a new spouse unless the former spouse (i) dies or (ii) remarries prior to age 55 (unless the employee was married to his or her former spouse for 30 or more years, in which case the former spouse's remarriage before age 55 does not terminate entitlement to a survivor annuity).[21] If the former spouse dies, and the second spouse has been timely designated within two years of marriage, the survivor annuity coverage will then move to cover the new spouse.[22]

It is possible to divide a survivor benefit between a former spouse and a subsequent spouse. In the event that a remarriage is possible or expected, the participant may want to negotiate in the divorce to limit the first spouse's entitlement to a survivor benefit to a pro rata share, so something remains for a potential second spouse. The maximum amount of all survivor annuities payable based on the death of a retiree, employee, or former employee is subject to the usual caps (50 percent for FERS; 55 percent for CSRS).

PRACTICE TIP

Because the former spouse's entitlement could terminate, the remarried employee should consider electing the survivor annuity for the new spouse within two years of marriage. In that event, if the previous spouse loses entitlement to the survivor annuity, the new spouse will become entitled with no change in the retiree's annuity; the annuity reduction will continue for the benefit of the current spouse.

In the event that a former spouse is entitled to receive the maximum survivor benefit, leaving no survivor benefit available for the subsequent spouse, the annuitant might elect an insurable interest annuity. If the employee elects an insurable interest survivor annuity for the employee's current spouse and the employee's former spouse loses entitlement before the employee dies, the employee can have the insurable interest annuity converted to a survivor annuity within two years of the employee's former spouse losing entitlement to the regular spousal survivor annuity.

It is possible for a subsequent spouse to receive FEHB coverage in the event that he or she is the surviving spouse of the employee. In such event, the surviving spouse can request that OPM establish an account for payment of the premiums and maintain FEHB coverage. The surviving spouse will be responsible for paying the full monthly premiums for the continued FEHB coverage directly to OPM.

---

21. 5 U.S.C. § 8445(h)(1).
22. OPM Publ'n: Applying for Deferred or Postponed Retirement under the Federal Employees Retirement System (FERS), RI 92-19A (rev. May 2012).

7.9 Former Spouse Remarriage and Effect on Survivor Annuity

Remarriage of the former spouse can result in a loss of the survivor benefit. The effect of remarriage is dependent upon length of marriage, whether the first marriage ended by death or divorce, and age of the former spouse, summarized as follows:

First Marriage Ends in . . .	Marriage Lasted 30 or More Years	Marriage Lasted Fewer Than 30 Years
Divorce	• Former spouse may remarry anytime and maintain survivor annuity.	• Former spouse may remarry after age 55 and keep survivor annuity. Former spouse who remarries before age 55 loses survivor annuity. • If lost, never reinstated
Death	• Surviving spouse may remarry anytime and maintain survivor benefit.	• If surviving spouse remarries, survivor annuity will be lost, but if second marriage ends, it may be restored.

As shown above, if a federal employee dies, leaving a widow or widower, his or her survivor benefits will continue regardless of remarriage, if the marriage to the employee lasted 30 or more years. If the marriage was fewer than 30 years, and he or she remarries before age 55, the survivor benefit will cease. However, if the surviving spouse's second marriage ends, the survivor annuity can be restored. Before the benefit can be restored, the survivor must pay back any lump sum paid to anyone at the time the survivor annuity ended.[23]

By contrast, when a divorced former spouse who is receiving a survivor annuity pursuant to a COAP remarries before age 55, likewise the survivor annuity will cease. However, unlike the surviving spouse who remarries before age 55, if the second marriage of the surviving former spouse ends, the survivor annuity can never be restored, unless the marriage to the employee lasted for 30 years or more.[24]

Some former spouse remarriages result in entitlement to more than one federal government survivor annuity, which complicates matters even further. Under both FERS and CSRS, a former spouse who is entitled to a survivor annuity, and who remarries prior to age 55, will lose his or her entitlement to the survivor annuity, unless the employee and the former spouse were married for 30 years or more, in which case the former spouse's remarriage before age 55 does not terminate such entitlement.[25] If the remarriage of a divorced spouse who lost survivor rights terminates by divorce or by the death of the subsequent spouse, his or her survivor annuity is reinstated if the marriage to the employee lasted 30 years or more.[26] In the event the former spouse acquired a federal government pension plan survivor annuity as a result of the subsequent marriage, he or she cannot keep both the reinstated survivor benefit and a survivor annuity based on the remarriage. The former spouse must elect which survivor benefit they want to receive. For example:

23. Lump-sum payments are infrequent because there usually is no unexpended balance of retirement fund contributions.
24. OPM Publ'n: Information for Survivor Annuitants, RI 25-26 (rev. Sept. 2013).
25. 5 U.S.C. § 8445(h)(1).
26. 5 C.F.R. § 843.305.

Bonnie was married to Jim for 30 years, and then they divorced, at which time they entered a FERS COAP entitling Bonnie to a former spouse survivor annuity. Jim died, and Bonnie started to receive a former spouse survivor annuity. However, Bonnie got remarried to Bill when she was 54, and so her entitlement to the former spouse survivor annuity under Jim's pension ceased. Bill was also a federal employee. Bill later died. Bonnie must choose which survivor benefit to receive and is entitled to choose the higher of the two, Jim's or Bill's.

7.10 Social Security Windfall Elimination Provision

The Social Security law's windfall elimination provision may affect the amount of Social Security benefits payable to a retired federal employee.[27] This provision affects employees who spent part of their careers participating in CSRS or FSRDS, during which time they did not contribute to Social Security, and part working at a private-sector job where they paid Social Security taxes long enough to qualify for Social Security old-age payments. Under the windfall elimination provision, the Social Security Administration uses a formula to calculate a lower Social Security payment to the recipient. The modified formula applies to employees who reach age 62 after 1985 and who thereafter become eligible for a CSRS or FSRDS annuity. This rule does not affect the amount of the pension that OPM pays the annuitant, only the amount of his or her Social Security old-age benefits.[28]

7.11 Government Pension Offset

If a retiree receives a federal pension, such as a CSRS pension, and did not pay Social Security taxes, some or all of that person's Social Security spouse's, widow's, or widower's benefit may be offset due to receipt of that pension. This offset applies to the retired federal employee if[29]

- the annuitant is covered by CSRS (or transferred to FERS but serves less than five years under FERS); and
- based on the annuitant's work history, he or she is eligible for no Social Security benefit on his or her own account or only a small Social Security benefit; and
- the spouse (or former spouse) on whose work and Social Security participation the annuitant is entitled to Social Security spousal benefits is eligible for a full Social Security benefit.

The following illustrates the effect of the law:

Lauren receives a CSRS pension of $1,200 per month from her federal government employment and never contributed to Social Security. She has a former spouse and is entitled to a spousal benefit under her ex-husband's Social Security account. Lauren's former husband earned a full Social Security benefit of $3,000 per month; therefore, Lauren's spousal Social Security benefit, at her full Social Security retirement age, would be $1,500 per month without the offset. However, Lauren's spousal benefit under her former husband's Social Security account will be offset by $800, or $2 for every $3 of her CSRS pension; her Social Security spousal benefit will be $700 per month.

27. 42 U.S.C. § 415(a)(7); 20 C.F.R. § 404.213.

28. OPM Publ'n: Information for Annuitants: Civil Service Retirement System (CSRS) (rev. June 2013).

29. FERS Transfer Handbook, A Guide to Making Your Decision, RI 90-3 (rev. Dec. 2008).

The government pension offset does not apply to employees who are covered by CSRS Offset provisions, as these employees pay into Social Security.

7.12 When Both Spouses Are Federal Employees

It is common that both parties to a divorce are current or past federal employees. In such cases, the instinct of the parties and attorneys may be to equally divide the marital share of each pension pursuant to a COAP and maintain survivor benefits for each. However, this may not be the most economical option. See the following example.

Marcela and Sam are married federal employees, and both participate in FERS. They have been married 20 years. Sam has 15 years of service and a lower high-3 salary. Marcela has nine years of service and a higher high-3 salary. Should they divide both pensions and maintain survivor benefits for each?

There are various factors to consider when both spouses have a federal government pension. In the above example, to maintain one another as survivor beneficiaries, each pension will be reduced by 10 percent, if they each elect the maximum benefit. If a pension pays out approximately $50,000 per year, that's a cost of $5,000 per year for just one pension. Life insurance might be less expensive, assuming they had a reason to provide for the surviving spouse, such as if they had a minor child who would be in that spouse's care. Moreover, they would pay the cost of two survivor benefits that only one of them will live to enjoy. Note also that if they split both of their lifetime annuities, when one dies, if the deceased spouse's share reverts to the annuitant, the survivor then has his or her entire annuity as well as the survivor annuity. Parties negotiating a settlement should consider whether that is appropriate or necessary.

One option is to divide the marital share of each employee's self-only annuity but waive the survivor annuity. If they each agree to waive the survivor annuity, and Sam dies first, his pension dies with him, and his share of Marcela's pension reverts to Marcela. Marcela will therefore have her full pension after Sam's death. In this scenario, the parties save the significant expense they would otherwise incur to provide each with a survivor annuity.

Other factors to consider are whether one party expects to remarry, if one party is significantly older or in poorer health than the other, the size of the pensions, and whether the amount of the benefit is expected to be very different due to a significant salary difference or different systems (FERS versus CSRS).

7.13 Same-Sex Couples, Domestic Partners, and Treatment of Gender-Diverse People

Domestic partners are not eligible for FEHB health coverage with the exception of same-sex domestic partners of members of the Foreign Service and Federal Reserve. Same-sex domestic partners of Foreign Service employees are eligible to enroll in federal health benefits. Opposite-sex domestic partners are not.[30] In the event a domestic partnership is

30. 3 Dep't of State, Foreign Affairs Manual § 1612, *available at* https://fam.state.gov/searchapps/viewer?format=html&query=3%20FAM%201600&links=3,FAM&url=/FAM/03FAM/03FAM1610.html#M1612.

terminated, it is incumbent upon the Foreign Service employee to notify the Department of State within 30 days.

There are personnel policies and procedures in place that protect transgender federal employees from discrimination and protect their access to federal benefits. President Barack Obama signed an executive order in 2014 to "take further steps to promote economy and efficiency in Federal Government procurement by prohibiting discrimination based on gender identity."[31] For example, no carrier participating in the FEHB may have a general exclusion of services, drugs, or supplies relating to gender transition or "sex transformations." This protection is worth keeping in mind if a member of a divorcing family needs access to medical services, drugs, and/or supplies as a result of a gender transition or "sex transformation" and at the time of the divorce is covered by FEHB. A family member requiring FEHB coverage for the services, drugs, and/or supplies to be affordable could be severely harmed if access to such services, drugs, and/or supplies were suddenly terminated.

7.14 Merit Systems Protection Board Appeals

Under the Civil Service Reform Act of 1978, federal employees may appeal certain personnel actions to the U.S. Merit Systems Protection Board (MSPB). The MSPB is an independent quasi-judicial agency in the executive branch of the federal government, composed of three members with seven-year terms. The board is bipartisan, and no more than two of its three members can be from the same political party. OPM determinations in employment matters, including the rights of divorcing employees and their spouses relating to benefits, are among the issues handled by the MSPB.[32]

Where to Find the Law

C.F.R. § 1201.118 allows the MSPB to reopen any "final decisions" issued by OPM for redetermination. C.F.R. § 1201 provides a guide for the process.

The form and content of pleadings and procedural rules are set forth in 5 C.F.R. part 1201. All pleadings and motions are filed with the Clerk of the Merit Systems Protection Board, 1615 M Street NW, Washington, DC 20419. In an appeal, special counsel for MSPB represents the interest of OPM. The specifics of how to handle an appeal to MSPB are beyond the scope of this book.

---

31. Further Amendments to Exec. Order 11478, Equal Employment Opportunity in the Federal Government, and Exec. Order 11246, Equal Employment Opportunity, 79 F.R. 42971 (2014). Discrimination on the basis of sexual orientation was added to existing law in 1998 by Further Amendment to Executive Order 11478, Equal Employment Opportunity in the Federal Government, 63 F.R. 30097.

32. "Determinations affecting the rights or interests of an individual under the Federal retirement laws" pursuant to the following sections: 5 U.S.C. §§ 8347(d)(1)–(2), 8461(e)(1); 5 U.S.C. § 8331 note; 5 C.F.R. parts 831, 839, 842, 844, and 846.

The MSPB has lacked a quorum since January 8, 2017; moreover, since March 2019, the MSPB has lacked any presidentially appointed, Senate-confirmed board members. Due to the lack of membership, the MSPB is precluded from issuing decisions on petitions for review at headquarters. Administrative law judges throughout the country, however, are still working on recommendations sent to the MSPB.[33]

Further information and forms can be found at www.mspb.gov.

33. Nomination to Merit Sys. Protection Board, Julia Akins Clark, PN183 (Jan. 16, 2019), https://www.congress.gov/nomination/116th-congress/183; Nomination to Merit Sys. Protection Board, Dennis Dean Kirk, PN186 (Jan. 16, 2019), https://www.congress.gov/nomination/116th-congress/186; Nomination to Merit Sys. Protection Board, B. Chad Bungard, PN695 (Apr. 30, 2019), https://www.congress.gov/nomination/116th-congress/695.

Chapter Eight

Avoiding Pitfalls in Dividing Federal Government Pensions

Chapter 8 highlights common errors in dividing government pensions and how to avoid them.

8.1 Inquire at the Consultation about Current and Past Federal Employment and Military Service

At the first consultation, the lawyer should ask whether either party is a current federal employee, has been in the past, or has any military service that could affect the amount of a future federal pension. The lawyer should find out how many years the employee worked for the federal government and the agency, if he or she had military service, whether he or she made a deposit to buy back that service toward accrual of a federal pension, and whether he or she left federal service with the right to a future pension. The lawyer should also ask whether he or she has a Thrift Savings Plan (TSP) account that remained and was not rolled over after leaving federal employment.

Federal employment could be relevant and helpful to know about, even if a client is already divorced or never married. For example, if the client comes in with a postjudgment dispute about child support arrears, review the retirement provisions of the settlement agreement or court order. If the child support payor is in pension pay status, he or she may have income that can be used to calculate or collect child support. The lawyer should also find out if a Court Order Acceptable for Processing (COAP) called for by the settlement agreement has been entered.

8.2 Correctly Identify the Retirement System

It is quite important to correctly identify the retirement system in which the federal employee participates when negotiating a marital settlement or preparing for a divorce trial. The Office of Personnel Management (OPM) will not accept a COAP that vaguely references a federal government pension. The correct pension system must be identified; this starts with seeking information in discovery, such as the employee's pay statements, TSP statement, or monthly pension statement.

Moreover, there are differences among the pensions of which the lawyer must be aware. For example, with FERS and CSRS, the maximum survivor benefit is different (50 percent versus 55 percent). For several of the government plans, there is a remarriage restriction before age 55 or 60 that divests a former spouse of the survivor benefit. However, with respect to the Foreign Service plans, the remarriage restriction divests the former spouse of both a share of the retirement annuity and the right to a survivor annuity. It may be significant to know whether the plan participant also paid into Social Security. If the lawyer fails to identify the plan, he or she may miss important opportunities or fail to give correct advice to the client.

8.3 Use Correct Terminology

It is very important to know and use OPM's terminology in the order dividing a pension. For example, the gross monthly annuity is the annuity amount for CSRS or FERS **after** the cost of the survivor annuity has been deducted. This means that if parties agree to an equal division of the gross monthly annuity, they will absorb the cost of the survivor annuity equally because it comes out first before division. If parties intend that the former spouse bear the cost of the survivor annuity, the order should divide the self-only annuity and then allocate the cost of the survivor annuity to the former spouse's share of the self-only annuity. Failure to use the correct terms in the pension order can produce the wrong result.

Example:
Husband's self-only pension is estimated at $3,000 per month and is 100 percent marital. Husband has separated from federal employment. The parties agreed at mediation to split Husband's pension equally and that Wife would pay the cost of the survivor benefit. However, the mediator used the wrong terminology, and their settlement agreement stated as follows:

> *The parties will equally divide Husband's gross annuity from his FERS pension. Wife will be entitled to a 50 percent survivor annuity. From Wife's share of Husband's pension, the cost of the survivor benefit will be deducted.*

The gross annuity is the resulting annuity after the cost of the survivor annuity has been deducted. However, in the example, the cost is deducted again from Wife's share with the result that she will pay double the cost of the survivor annuity. The math would look as follows:

Employee pension: $3,000/mo

Less cost of survivor annuity: – $300

$2,700 remaining to divide (gross annuity)

× 50% = $1,350 to Wife

Less cost of survivor annuity: $300

$1,050 to Wife

Had the agreement been drafted correctly, it would read as follows:

The parties will equally divide Husband's self-only annuity from his FERS pension ("Wife's Share"). Wife will be entitled to a 50 percent survivor annuity. From Wife's Share, the cost of the survivor benefit will be deducted.

Employee pension: $3,000/mo

x 50% = $1,500 to Wife

Less cost of survivor annuity: $300

$1,200 to Wife

As written, Husband will retain one-half of his self-only annuity, $1,500, and Wife will receive $1,200 per month, $1,500 minus the cost of the survivor annuity.

It is also important to note that the term "Qualified Domestic Relations Order" (QDRO) is for plans governed by ERISA, the Employee Retirement Income Security Act of 1974, and should not be used in orders dividing federal government plans.

8.4 Forward the Correct Documentation to the Federal Agency

When submitting a COAP to OPM, include the certified COAP; the certified judgment of divorce; the settlement agreement or other document evidencing the division of the pension; a certification that the agreement or order terms have not been set aside; and the addresses, Social Security numbers, and dates of birth of each party.[1]

If the former spouse is also signing up for Federal Employees Health Benefits Program coverage, forward a copy of the above, with the SF 2809 form, to the proper contact at the employing agency, if the employee is still employed, or to OPM if retired.

8.5 Do Not Overlook the Survivor Annuity

In cases where it is appropriate for the former spouse to receive the survivor annuity as part of the division of a pension, the attorney must make sure to include provisions in the settlement agreement and COAP expressly providing for it. OPM will treat a COAP that awards a share of a pension, but does not expressly award the survivor annuity, as awarding only a share of the pension. In that event, if the annuitant predeceases the former spouse, the annuity will terminate. See Section 2.3.1 for further information about survivor annuity options.

8.6 Allocate the Cost of the Survivor Annuity Correctly

Be intentional about who pays the cost of the survivor annuity. The cost can be paid by either party, by the parties pro rata (off the top), or equally. If the COAP identifies the pension to be divided as the gross annuity, the cost will be deducted off the top of the annuity before division. The result is that each party bears a proportionate share of the cost of the annuity, and it is not necessary to make an explicit statement in the COAP to that effect. Proportionate sharing means the party who will receive the larger share of the pension will pay more of the cost of the survivor benefit; for example, if the pension is divided

1. 5 U.S.C. § 838.221.

such that the employee receives two-thirds of the pension, he or she will pay two-thirds of the cost of the survivor annuity.

If the COAP identifies the pension to be divided as the self-only annuity, then the cost of the survivor annuity can be allocated between the parties other than pro rata. The COAP can provide, for example, that the spouse will bear all of the cost of the survivor annuity, or the COAP could provide that each party will bear 50 percent of the cost (even though the pension may not be divided equally). When the COAP identifies the pension to be divided as the self-only annuity, and provides for the survivor annuity, silence in the COAP means the annuitant will bear 100 percent of the cost. Unless the employee intends to bear all of the cost of the survivor annuity, the COAP must provide explicitly for who will bear the cost of the survivor annuity.

8.7 Advise the Client of the Effect of Remarriage

The lawyer for the former spouse should advise the client of the effect of remarriage on his or her pension rights.

Under both FERS and CSRS, a former spouse who is entitled to a survivor annuity, and who remarries prior to age 55, will lose his or her entitlement to the survivor annuity permanently; it can never be restored. However, if the employee was married to the former spouse for 30 years or more, the former spouse's remarriage before age 55 does not terminate such entitlement.[2] See Sections 7.8 and 7.9.

The former spouse of a CIARDS (Central Intelligence Agency Retirement and Disability System) participant will not be entitled to a survivor annuity if he or she remarries before age 55, except that it may be restored if the remarriage is dissolved by death, annulment, or divorce.[3]

With respect to Foreign Service pensions, a remarriage before age 60 will void both the right to a pension and the right to a survivor annuity. If a former spouse remarries before age 60, but after a survivor annuity has commenced, the survivor annuity is also terminated. See Section 3.7 for information about subsequent restoration of the survivor benefit.

8.8 Timely Entry of COAP

The best practice regarding pension orders is to draft the COAP, or have it drafted, during the settlement negotiations and prior to executing the agreement. For a contested case, draft the proposed COAP and submit it to the trial judge at trial. There are multiple reasons for not waiting until after the agreement is signed or, in a contested case, until after trial to draft the COAP. Making the text of the COAP a part of the settlement agreement reduces the possibility of vagueness in the agreement. Further, it allows disagreements about the text to be hashed out in advance. Preparing the COAP in advance avoids the problem that can occur when the divorce is entered and the lawyer for the former spouse has to chase after the other party, who may no longer have counsel, to get a signature on a COAP. Entry of the COAP at divorce avoids the problem of the federal employee who gets remarried right after divorce and whose new spouse may eventually acquire survivor rights during a period of delay in getting the order entered.

2. 5 U.S.C. §§ 8341, 8445(h)(1).

3. The former spouse of a CIARDS participant will not begin to receive payment of the survivor annuity until reaching age 50.

When the employee is still working, entry of the COAP at divorce may also avoid the problem of the First Order Rule if the employee retires during a period of postdivorce delay. Prior to the employee's retirement, the COAP can be amended as many times as is needed to get the language right, including the revision of the survivor annuity. However, the order in place at the time of the employee's retirement will not be amendable with respect to the level of survivor annuity awarded. See Section 5.4 for an explanation of the First Order Rule.

8.9 Overlooking Benefits

Certain federal employees have additional retirement benefits beyond their pension and TSP. A review of the careers or benefits page of the employing agency website is important.

For example, employees of the Federal Deposit and Insurance Corporation and the United States Institute of Peace have a 401(k). Employees of the National Credit Union Administration have a retirement savings plan. These are only examples. The attorney will need to make the appropriate inquiries and research what benefits are available to the employee.

8.10 Accounting for and Collecting Pension Arrears

A pension may be in pay status at the time a divorce judgment is entered or an agreement is signed. In such a case, there may be a period from the signing of the agreement or entry of judgment until the COAP is given effect and OPM starts to make payments to the former spouse. Parties entering into a settlement should specify the date from which the former spouse's share is due, should address how arrearages will be paid, and should provide for reimbursement of duplicate payments. When the annuitant will make direct payments to the former spouse until OPM implements a COAP, parties could agree that these payments will be net of tax withholding with an obligation to reconcile payments with the annuitant's actual tax liability based on the applicable income tax return.

If an agreement or court order requires the annuitant to make direct payments to the former spouse until a COAP is implemented, and he or she fails to do so, one remedy is for the former spouse to obtain a judgment for the arrears and pursue collection.[4] Other options to collect arrears are discussed below.

Situation Number 1: Arrearage in Payments Not Due to Delay Caused by OPM:
In the event that there is a delay in effectuating payments to the former spouse for reasons that are not the fault of OPM, 5 C.F.R. § 838.234 allows the former spouse to obtain the arrears using an amended COAP.[5] An example of a delay that is not the fault of OPM is where the former spouse submits a COAP that has not been certified, OPM rejects it, and there is a delay while the former spouse corrects the error, during which an arrearage accrues.

5 C.F.R. § 838.234, Collection of arrears, provides:

> Specific instructions are required before OPM may pay any arrearage. Except as provided in §838.225(b), OPM will not increase a former spouse's share of employee annuity to sat-

4. Discussion of the tax consequences to the parties of a judgment for arrears is beyond the scope of this book.

5. Hayward v. Off. of Personnel Mgmt., 578 F.3d 1337 (2009); Schofield v. Schofield, 62 Cal. App. 4th 131 (1998); Harmand v. Harmand, 931 So. 2d 18 (Ala. 2005).

isfy an arrearage due the former spouse. However, under §838.225, OPM will prospectively honor the terms of an amended court order that either increases or decreases the former spouse's entitlement.

The language of the amended COAP should include the following and must be specific, as it qualifies as a garnishment of the pension:

> In addition to the payment to Former Spouse of retirement annuity benefits as set forth elsewhere in this Order, acting pursuant to the provisions of 5 C.F.R. § 838.234, the Former Spouse is entitled to an additional sum of $_________ per month for a period of ______ months for the purpose of discharging an arrearage due to the Former Spouse.

OPM will honor the amended COAP only if it provides the amount of the arrearage and the incremental payments necessary to satisfy it. OPM cannot be compelled to make these calculations.

Situation Number 2: Arrearage in Payments Due to Delay Caused by OPM:
Parties may divorce and may timely submit the COAP and all other necessary documents to OPM. However, due to an OPM delay in accepting and implementing the COAP, the former spouse has not received his or her share of the pension payments for a period of time. In such case, OPM will compute the arrears, pay the former spouse in a lump sum, and withhold an amount from the annuitant's future payments in monthly installments to recoup. There is no rule of thumb utilized by OPM to determine the rate of the recoupment from the annuitant. Reportedly, the amount of the recoupment is one of the biggest complaints raised by annuitants to OPM.

Part II

Thrift Savings Plan

Chapter Nine

Thrift Savings Plan Accounts

Chapter 9 describes the features of the Thrift Savings Plan (TSP), the largest defined contribution plan for federal government employees, administered by the Federal Retirement Thrift Investment Board. The TSP is offered to government employees who are covered by the Federal Employees' Retirement System (FERS), Foreign Service Pension System (FSPS), Civil Service Retirement System (CSRS), CSRS O ffset, Foreign Service Retirement and Disability System (FSRDS), and FSRDS Offset. Other smaller federal government defined contribution plans exist and are outside the scope of this book.[1]

9.1 Overview

The TSP is a defined contribution plan sponsored by the federal government, similar to a 401(k). The TSP is established under the Federal Employees' Retirement System Act of 1986 (FERSA). The assets in the TSP are held in trust for each individual participant. The

1. Retirement Savings Plan and Trust for Employees of the Army and Air Force Exchange Service 401(k) Savings Plan, Tennessee Valley Authority Savings and Deferral Retirement Plan (401(a) Plan), Farm Credit Foundations Defined Contribution 401(k) Plan, National Bank for Cooperatives (CoBank) Retirement Savings Plan, Uniformed Services University of the Health Sciences 401(k), Smithsonian Institution Defined Contribution Retirement Plan, and USDA Graduate School Plan. PUBLIC PENSIONS: SUMMARY OF FEDERAL PENSION PLAN DATA, LETTER REPORT, GAO/AIMD-96-6 (Feb. 16, 1996).

TSP is treated as a qualified trust, which is exempt from taxation.[2] The Federal Retirement Thrift Investment Board (the TSP Board) administers the TSP for federal employees. As of December 31, 2019, there was approximately $495,351,668 held in the fund, which comprised employee and employer contributions, notes receivable (TSP loans), and earnings.[3]

Where to Find the Law

The TSP is codified primarily under chapter 84 of title 5, United States Code. The regulations are published in chapter VI, title 5 of the Code of Federal Regulations. The TSP Board's regulations governing court orders are in subparts G and I, part 1650, title 5, Code of Federal Regulations.

The lawyer should assume that a TSP is an asset in a federal employee divorce case. It is rare to encounter a federal employee who has no funds in his or her TSP account. Funds contributed by the employee immediately vest.[4] Employees of quasi-governmental agencies may have other retirement accounts instead of or in addition to the TSP.

Changes in law effective in 2010 changed the TSP for FERS participants from an opt-in plan to an opt-out plan. A FERS employee hired after July 31, 2010, is automatically enrolled in the TSP, and 3 percent of his or her basic pay is deducted every pay period and deposited in his or her account. Participation in the TSP is not mandatory; the FERS participant can opt out of contributing.

CSRS participants can participate in the TSP but do not receive any employer contribution.

The vast majority of federal employees participate in the TSP. See the table below for figures as of 2012. More recent figures show even greater participation. As of December 31, 2019, there were approximately 5 million participants in the TSP, with approximately 3.3 million contributing their own funds.

The TSP account consists of employee contributions, the growth thereon, employer contributions, and the growth thereon. The federal government will match at different levels based on the employee contribution and pension system participation. FERS participants are entitled to receive agency matching contributions on the first 5 percent of basic pay that they contribute each pay period, according to a formula prescribed by FERSA.[5]

---

2. *See* 26 U.S.C. § 7701(j)

3. *Thrift Savings Fund Financial Statements, December 31, 2016 and 2015*, Fed. Retirement Thrift Inv. Board, *available at* https://www.frtib.gov/ReadingRoom/FinStmts/TSP-FS-Dec2016.pdf.

4. Central Intelligence Agency employees contribute to a Voluntary Investment Plan account (discussed in Section 1.9.5) in addition to the TSP.

5. Federal Employees Retirement System Act, 5 U.S.C. § 8432(c). The following graphic is from OPM Publ'n: Summary of the Thrift Savings Plan, TSPBK09 (Oct. 2020).

Table 1. Summary Statistics of TSP Participation by Retirement System[6]

Statistics	All	CSRS	FERS
Number of Active Employees	2,322,564	186,239	2,136,325
Percent	100%	8.0%	92%
Participation Rate	88.5%	85.5%	88.8%
Ever Participate	94.8%	100.0%	94.4%
Average Salary	$73,872	$87,536	$72,680
Average Deferral (Participants)	$6,390	$7,722	$6,279
Average Deferral Rate (Participants)	7.9%	8.3%	7.9%
Average TSP Balance	$95,977	$94,987	$96,063
Average Age (years)	47.8	58.4	46.9
Average Length of Service (years)	14.5	33.6	12.9
G Fund Only	39.6%	27.7%	40.7%
Above Agency Match	49.0%	50.1%	48.9%

Full-time employees as of December 31, 2012

TSP CONTRIBUTIONS
come from 2 sources:

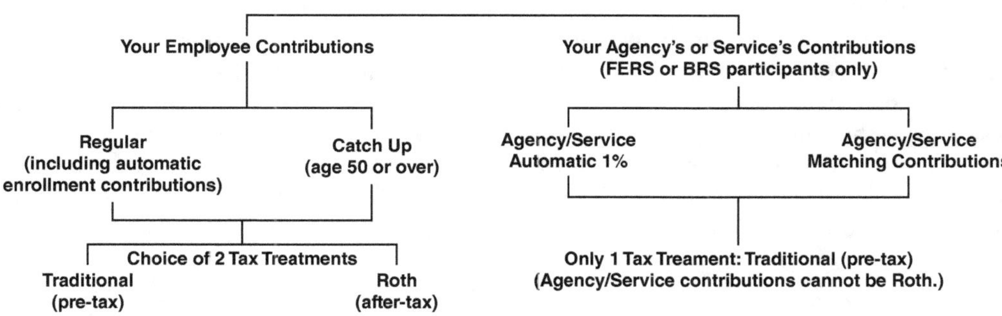

For a FERS participant hired before August 1, 2010, the employing agency will automatically contribute 1 percent of basic pay to the TSP account whether or not the employee contributes. This is referred to as the Agency Automatic Contribution. The 1 percent contribution is not taken out of the employee's pay as a deduction.

6. OPM Publ'n: Federal Employee Participation Patterns in the TSP 2008–2012 (PPA/DAG/09-2015).

The other component is the Agency Matching Contribution. A FERS participant who contributes to his or her TSP account receives Agency Matching Contributions on the first 5 percent of pay contributed every pay period. The agency matches the first 3 percent dollar for dollar; the next 2 percent is matched at 50 cents on the dollar. This means that when the employee contributes 5 percent of his or her basic pay, the agency contributes an amount equal to 4 percent. There is no matching beyond the employee's 5 percent contribution.

Table 2. Agency/Service Contributions to TSP Account (FERS Only)[7]

	Your agency/service puts in:		
Employee puts in:	Automatic (1%) Contribution	Matching Contribution	And the total contribution is:
0%	1%	0%	1%
1%	1%	1%	3%
2%	1%	2%	5%
3%	1%	3%	7%
4%	1%	3.5%	8.5%
5%	1%	4%	10%
More than 5%	1%	4%	Employee contribution + 5%

The TSP statement is generated quarterly and is packed with valuable information. Newer TSP statements include account numbers. Older statements do not have account numbers. The statement shows the date of birth of the plan participant and whether he or she is working or retired. It also has the service date, which is most likely when he or she commenced employment with the federal government. However, in some cases, the service date is the date the employee became entitled to participate in the TSP; he or she may have commenced on an earlier date on a part-time or student basis without entitlement to participate in retirement benefits. The TSP statement also identifies the employee's pension system and the number of years necessary for vesting in the pension plan.

PRACTICE TIP

A person with both a civilian and a military TSP will have two different TSP accounts and therefore will have two account numbers. When preparing a Court Order Acceptable for Processing (COAP) for a person who has both a civilian and a military TSP, be sure to specify which plan the COAP applies to.

7. OPM PUBL'N: 2018 SUMMARY OF THE THRIFT SAVINGS PLAN.

The TSP statement will look something like this:

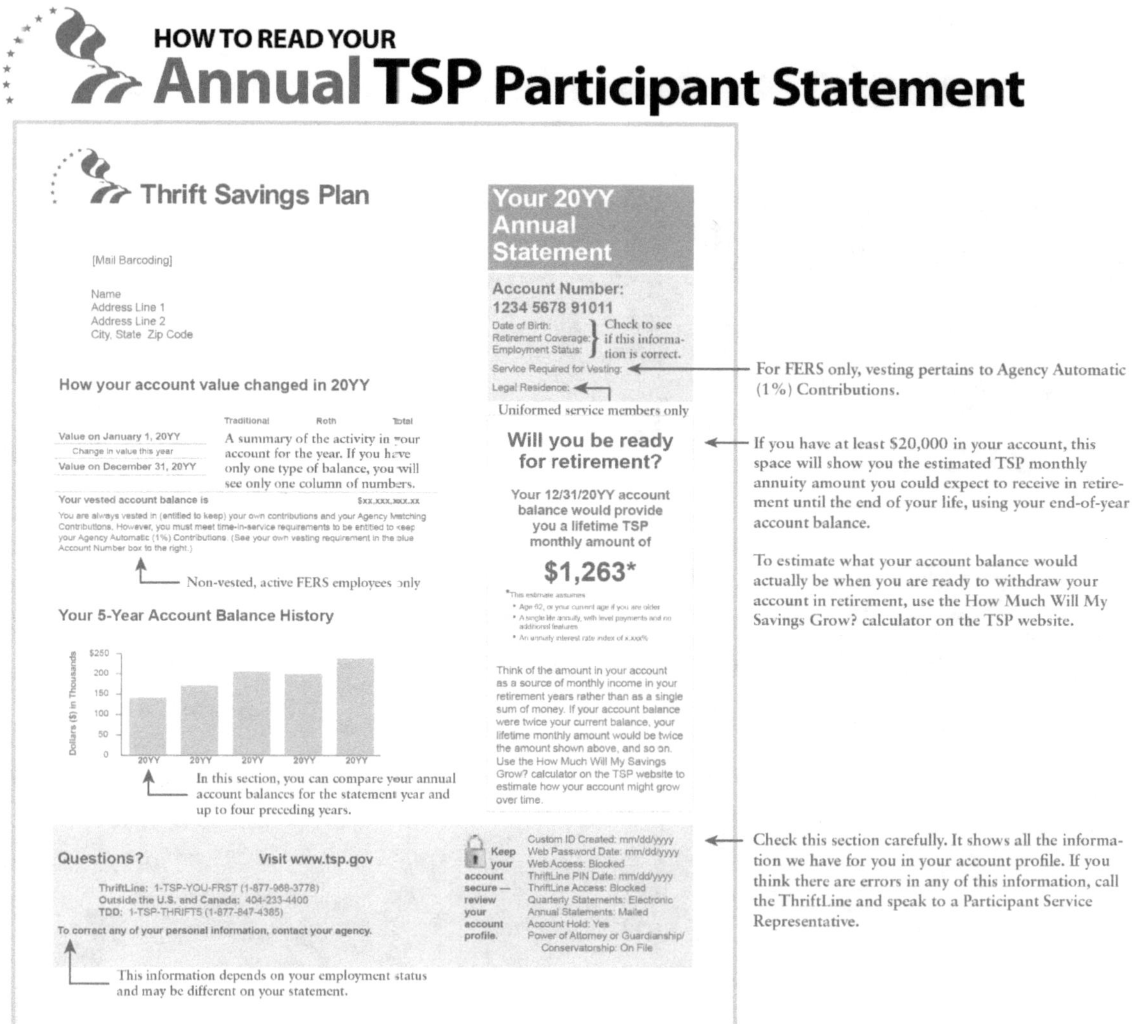

JANE G. DOE
Account Number: 1234 5678 91011

Page 2 of 4

A summary of the transactions that added money to or deducted money from your account during the statement year. (Your quarterly statements show the dates and specific nature of each transaction.)

If you have only one type of balance (traditional or Roth), you will only see one column of numbers in this section. A traditional (pre-tax) balance includes all employee contributions (regular and tax-exempt) that you elected as "traditional," all agency contributions, and any traditional money you transferred into the plan. A Roth (after-tax) balance includes employee contributions you elected as Roth and any Roth money you transferred into the plan.

A Summary of Your Account Activity in 20YY

	Traditional	Roth	Total
Beginning Balance as of January 1, 20YY	$xx,xxx,xxx.xx	$xx,xxx,xxx.xx	$xx,xxx,xxx.xx
Contributions			
Transfers/Rollovers			
Loan Disbursements			
Loan Payments			
Loan Overpayment Refunds			
In-Service Withdrawals[1]			
Forfeitures			
Death Benefit Payment			
Court Order Payments			
Excess Deferrals			
Adjustments[2]			
Redesignations			
Required Minimum Distribution			
Investment Gain/Loss			
Post-Separation Withdrawals			
Ending Balance as of December 31, 20YY	$xx,xxx,xxx.xx	$xx,xxx,xxx.xx	$xx,xxx,xxx.xx

You may not see all of these types of transactions on your own statement.

"Transfers/Rollovers" are money coming into your TSP account from an eligible retirement plan, or from a TSP-to-TSP transfer when you combine uniformed service and civilian TSP accounts. Transfers out of the TSP are shown as "Post-Separation Withdrawals."

"Adjustments" reflect the net amount of reversals of certain transactions (which are detailed on quarterly statements).

"Redesignations" refer to contributions that have been removed from your traditional balance and put in your Roth balance, and vice versa, to correct agency or service contribution submission errors.

Visit www.tsp.gov for definitions of other terms.

A summary of all contributions made to your account during the statement year by type of contribution. You will see only the contribution types that relate to your account. The activity reflected here is the complete summary of what is shown on your four quarterly statements for the year. Employee contributions include catch-up, makeup, and late contributions.

Contributions to Your Account in 20YY (Without Adjustments)

Employee Contributions[3]			Agency Contributions		Transfers/Rollovers Into the TSP		
Traditional	Tax-Exempt	Roth	Automatic 1%	Matching	Traditional	Roth	Total
$xx,xxx.xx	$xx,xxx.xx	$xx,xxx.xx	$xx,xxx.xx	$xx,xxx.xx	$xx,xxx,xxx.xx	$xx,xxx,xxx.xx	$xx,xxx,xxx.xx

This space shows your gross cumulative employee contributions, by type, since you began participating in the TSP.

Your Lifetime TSP Contributions

Traditional	Tax-Exempt	Roth	Catch-Up	Total
$xx,xxx,xxx.xx	$xx,xxx,xxx.xx	$xx,xxx,xxx.xx	$xx,xxx,xxx.xx	$xx,xxx,xxx.xx

This section reflects your contributions from all periods of service.

The Federal Retirement Thrift Investment Board submits an annual report to Congress each year on the operations of the Thrift Savings Plan, including participant demographics and contribution information. To read the report, visit www.frtib.gov, or scan the code to the right.

The percentage of your TSP account balance that was invested in the 10 TSP funds as of December 31 of the statement year. The pie chart shows how your account balance was distributed among the three fund categories. The L Funds are target date funds that offer an optimal mix of the G, F, C, S, and I Funds to provide the highest expected return for a given risk level and time horizon.

This is how you have told the TSP you want to invest all future contributions and additions to your account (such as loan payments, transfers, and rollovers) as of December 31 of the statement year. The pie chart shows your allocation by fund category.

This section shows the 1-year, 3-year, and 5-year performance for all 10 TSP funds, alongside your own personal returns for those periods.

The net expense ratio is the amount that participants' investment returns are reduced by TSP expenses.

TSP expenses include management fees for each investment fund, the cost of operating and maintaining the TSP's recordkeeping system; participant services; and printing and mailing notices, statements, and publications.

Expenses are reduced by forfeitures of Agency Automatic (1%) Contributions of FERS employees who leave Federal service before they are vested; other forfeitures; and loan fees.

JANE G. DOE
Account Number: 1234 5678 91011

Page 3 of 4

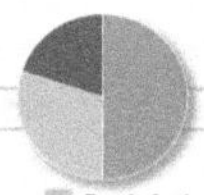

Your Account Distribution on 12/31/20YY

Funds for Diversified Growth and Stability

L 2050 Fund 20%
L 2040 Fund 0%
L 2030 Fund 0%
L 2020 Fund 0%
L Income Fund 0%

Funds for Stability

G Fund — Government Securities Investment Fund 25%
F Fund — Fixed Income Index Investment Fund 25%

Funds for Long-Term Growth

C Fund — Common Stock Index Investment Fund 10%
S Fund — Small Capitalization Stock Index Investment Fund 10%
I Fund — International Stock Index Investment Fund 10%

Your Investment Allocation for Future Contributions

Funds for Diversified Growth and Stability

L 2050 Fund 0%
L 2040 Fund 100%
L 2030 Fund 0%
L 2020 Fund 0%
L Income Fund 0%

Funds for Stability

G Fund — Government Securities Investment Fund 0%
F Fund — Fixed Income Index Investment Fund 0%

Funds for Long-Term Growth

C Fund — Common Stock Index Investment Fund 0%
S Fund — Small Capitalization Stock Index Investment Fund 0%
I Fund — International Stock Index Investment Fund 0%

TSP Fund Performance (As of 12/31/20YY)

	Lifecycle (Target Date) Funds					Individual TSP Funds					
	L 2050	L 2040	L 2030	L 2020	L Income	G Fund	F Fund	C Fund	S Fund	I Fund	Your Rates of Return[4,5]
1-Year	xx.xx%	xx.xx%	xx.xx%	xx.xx%	xx.xx%	xx.xx%	xx.xx%	xx.xx%	xx.xx%	xx.xx%	**xx.xx%**
3-Year	xx.xx	xx.xx	xx.xx	xx.xx	xx.xx	xx.xx	xx.xx	xx.xx	xx.xx	xx.xx	**xx.xx**
5-Year	xx.xx	xx.xx	xx.xx	xx.xx	xx.xx	xx.xx	xx.xx	xx.xx	xx.xx	xx.xx	**xx.xx**

TSP Administrative Expenses for 20YY

	G Fund	F Fund	C Fund	S Fund	I Fund
Net Expense Ratio					
Cost Per $1,000 in Your Account					

JANE G. DOE
Account Number: 1234 5678 91011 Page 4 of 4

Activity Summary by Fund

Fund	Beginning Balance	Contributions and Additions	Withdrawals and Deductions	Interfund Transfers	Investment Gain/Loss	Ending Balance
G Fund	$xx,xxx,xxx.xx	$xx,xxx,xxx.xx	−$xx,xxx,xxx.xx	$xx,xxx,xxx.xx	$xx,xxx,xxx.xx	$xx,xxx,xxx.xx
F Fund	xx,xxx,xxx.xx	xx,xxx,xxx.xx	−xx,xxx,xxx.xx	−xx,xxx,xxx.xx	xx,xxx,xxx.xx	xx,xxx,xxx.xx
C Fund	xx,xxx,xxx.xx	xx,xxx,xxx.xx	−xx,xxx,xxx.xx	−xx,xxx,xxx.xx	xx,xxx,xxx.xx	xx,xxx,xxx.xx
S Fund	xx,xxx,xxx.xx	xx,xxx,xxx.xx	−xx,xxx,xxx.xx	xx,xxx,xxx.xx	xx,xxx,xxx.xx	xx,xxx,xxx.xx
I Fund	xx,xxx,xxx.xx	xx,xxx,xxx.xx	−xx,xxx,xxx.xx	xx,xxx,xxx.xx	xx,xxx,xxx.xx	xx,xxx,xxx.xx
L 2050 Fund	xx,xxx,xxx.xx	xx,xxx,xxx.xx	−xx,xxx,xxx.xx	xx,xxx,xxx.xx	xx,xxx,xxx.xx	xx,xxx,xxx.xx
L 2040 Fund	xx,xxx,xxx.xx	xx,xxx,xxx.xx	−xx,xxx,xxx.xx	xx,xxx,xxx.xx	xx,xxx,xxx.xx	xx,xxx,xxx.xx
L 2030 Fund	xx,xxx,xxx.xx	xx,xxx,xxx.xx	−xx,xxx,xxx.xx	xx,xxx,xxx.xx	xx,xxx,xxx.xx	xx,xxx,xxx.xx
L 2020 Fund	xx,xxx,xxx.xx	xx,xxx,xxx.xx	−xx,xxx,xxx.xx	xx,xxx,xxx.xx	xx,xxx,xxx.xx	xx,xxx,xxx.xx
L Income Fund	xx,xxx,xxx.xx	xx,xxx,xxx.xx	−xx,xxx,xxx.xx	xx,xxx,xxx.xx	xx,xxx,xxx.xx	xx,xxx,xxx.xx
Total	**$xx,xxx,xxx.xx**	**$xx,xxx,xxx.xx**	**−$xx,xxx,xxx.xx**	**$0.00**	**$xx,xxx,xxx.xx**	**$xx,xxx,xxx.xx**

This section shows the dollar amounts that went into or were deducted from your balance in each of the funds in which you were invested during the statement year. The section also shows your annual gain (or loss) in each of the funds, and the net effect of any interfund transfers.

Share Summary by Fund

Fund	Beginning Balance	Investment Gain/Loss	Ending Balance	Beginning Shares Price	Beginning Shares Number	Ending Shares Price	Ending Shares Number
G Fund	$xx,xxx,xxx.xx	$xx,xxx,xxx.xx	$xx,xxx,xxx.xx	$xx.xxxx	xxx,xxx.xxxx	$xx.xxxx	xxx,xxx.xxxx
F Fund	xx,xxx,xxx.xx	xx,xxx,xxx.xx	xx,xxx,xxx.xx	xx.xxxx	xxx,xxx.xxxx	xx.xxxx	xxx,xxx.xxxx
C Fund	xx,xxx,xxx.xx	xx,xxx,xxx.xx	xx,xxx,xxx.xx	xx.xxxx	xxx,xxx.xxxx	xx.xxxx	xxx,xxx.xxxx
S Fund	xx,xxx,xxx.xx	xx,xxx,xxx.xx	xx,xxx,xxx.xx	xx.xxxx	xxx,xxx.xxxx	xx.xxxx	xxx,xxx.xxxx
I Fund	xx,xxx,xxx.xx	xx,xxx,xxx.xx	xx,xxx,xxx.xx	xx.xxxx	xxx,xxx.xxxx	xx.xxxx	xxx,xxx.xxxx
L 2050 Fund	xx,xxx,xxx.xx	xx,xxx,xxx.xx	xx,xxx,xxx.xx	xx.xxxx	xxx,xxx.xxxx	xx.xxxx	xxx,xxx.xxxx
L 2040 Fund	xx,xxx,xxx.xx	xx,xxx,xxx.xx	xx,xxx,xxx.xx	xx.xxxx	xxx,xxx.xxxx	xx.xxxx	xxx,xxx.xxxx
L 2030 Fund	xx,xxx,xxx.xx	xx,xxx,xxx.xx	xx,xxx,xxx.xx	xx.xxxx	xxx,xxx.xxxx	xx.xxxx	xxx,xxx.xxxx
L 2020 Fund	xx,xxx,xxx.xx	xx,xxx,xxx.xx	xx,xxx,xxx.xx	xx.xxxx	xxx,xxx.xxxx	xx.xxxx	xxx,xxx.xxxx
L Income Fund	xx,xxx,xxx.xx	xx,xxx,xxx.xx	xx,xxx,xxx.xx	xx.xxxx	xxx,xxx.xxxx	xx.xxxx	xxx,xxx.xxxx
Total	**$xx,xxx,xxx.xx**	**$xx,xxx,xxx.xx**	**$xx,xxx,xxx.xx**				

This section shows how your annual gain (or loss) in each of your investment funds affected the number of shares you held in each of those funds. You will see the price of one share and the number of shares you held in each fund at the beginning of the year, compared to the price of one share and the number of shares you held at the end of the year.

Your 20YY Loan Summary

	Loan Number 0000001G	Loan Number 0000002G	Loan Number 0000003R
Loan Issue Date	mm/dd/yyyy	mm/dd/yyyy	mm/dd/yyyy
Beginning Principal	**$xx,xxx,xxx.xx**	**$xx,xxx,xxx.xx**	**$xx,xxx,xxx.xx**
Amount of New Loan	xx,xxx,xxx.xx	xx,xxx,xxx.xx	xx,xxx,xxx.xx
Principal Repaid[6]	xx,xxx,xxx.xx	xx,xxx,xxx.xx	xx,xxx,xxx.xx
Nontaxable Distribution	xx,xxx,xxx.xx	xx,xxx,xxx.xx	xx,xxx,xxx.xx
Taxable Distribution	xx,xxx,xxx.xx	xx,xxx,xxx.xx	xx,xxx,xxx.xx
Reversal of Distribution (Traditional)	xx,xxx,xxx.xx	xx,xxx,xxx.xx	xx,xxx,xxx.xx
Reversal of Distribution (Roth)	xx,xxx,xxx.xx	xx,xxx,xxx.xx	xx,xxx,xxx.xx
Ending Principal	**$xx,xxx,xxx.xx**	**$xx,xxx,xxx.xx**	**$xx,xxx,xxx.xx**
Interest Paid	xx,xxx,xxx.xx	xx,xxx,xxx.xx	xx,xxx,xxx.xx
Interest in Arrears	xx,xxx,xxx.xx	xx,xxx,xxx.xx	xx,xxx,xxx.xx

This section will appear on your statement only if you had a TSP loan (or loans) during the statement year, and you will only see those categories that apply to your loans. If you had more than four loans during the year, this section will show the total of the combined loans for each loan type (i.e., general purpose or residential), and no issue date(s) or loan number(s) will be displayed.

[1] Includes an Automatic Enrollment Refund if one was requested during the statement period
[2] Adjustments reflect the net amount of corrections (i.e., reversals) of any transactions shown in this section (see your Quarterly Participant Statement).
[3] Includes catch-up, makeup, and late contributions
[4] Your personal rates of return are calculated with a time-weighted formula, widely used by financial analysts to calculate investment earnings. They reflect the results of your investment selections as well as activity in your account. There are other personal rate of return formulas used that may yield different results. Remember that past performance is no guarantee of future results.
[5] Your personal rates of return could not all be calculated because you did not have an account balance for all of the periods.
[6] Principal repaid includes correction to any loan disbursements or loan payments.

TSPLF23 (1/2013)
PREVIOUS EDITIONS OBSOLETE

TSP participants are immediately vested in their own contributions. However, most employees must be employed for three years to vest in Agency Automatic Contributions (the automatic 1 percent contribution) and associated earnings. Some special groups of federal employees need only two years to be vested in the agency contributions. If an employee separates from federal service before meeting the TSP vesting requirement, he or she forfeits the Agency Automatic Contributions, but if he or she dies in service before being fully vested, then he or she is deemed to be vested, and his or her beneficiaries are entitled to the agency contributions.[8]

9.2 Investment Options under the TSP

FERSA provides a number of mutual funds from which the employee may choose for investment of TSP funds.[9] The TSP does not allow the purchase of individual stocks or bonds. Page 3 of the TSP statement shows the investment options available to the participant. Currently, they are as follows:

L 2050 L 2040 L 2030 L 2020 L Income	L Lifecycle
G Fund	G Government Securities
F Fund	F Fixed Income
C Fund	C Common Stock
S Fund	S Small Cap
I Fund	I International Stock

As of this writing, OPM has contracted with BlackRock, Inc., an American global investment management corporation, to act as investment manager, custodian, and securities lending agent for the C (common stock), F (fixed income), S (small cap), and I (international stock) Funds. The L Funds are lifecycle funds, which base investments on the employee's targeted retirement date. A statement of an employee mostly invested in the 2020 fund suggests that the employee at some point targeted his or her retirement date as during or before 2020. As the retirement date of an employee in an L Fund approaches, the funds are automatically moved to the L Income Fund, which focuses on capital preservation.

The G Fund is a popular investment choice because there is no risk of investment loss. The G Fund invests exclusively in a nonmarketable short-term U.S. Treasury security that is only issued to the TSP. The U.S. government guarantees the payment of G Fund principal and interest.[10]

8. *TSP Bulletin for Agency TSP Representatives: Thrift Savings Plan Vesting Requirements and the TSP Service Computation Date*, Thrift Savings Plan (July 9, 2015), https://www.tsp.gov/bulletins/15-1/.
9. 5 U.S.C. § 8438.
10. 5 U.S.C. § 8438(a)(4).

The F Fund and the C Fund have the objective to match the Bloomberg Barclays U.S. Aggregate Bond Index and the S&P 500, respectively. The S Fund tracks the Dow Jones. The I Fund tracks the MSCI EAFE (Europe, Australasia, Far East) Index.[11]

TSP Fund	Index TSP Fund Tracks
F Fund	Bloomberg Barclays U.S. Aggregate Bond Index (www.bloombergindices.com)
C Fund	Standard & Poor's 500 Stock Index (www.standardandpoors.com)
S Fund	Dow Jones U.S. Completion Total Stock Market (TSM) Index (www.djindexes.com)
I Fund	MSCI EAFE Index (www.msci.com)

PRACTICE TIP

Some investment options are subject to more market risk than others. Parties may want to consider market risk during the pendency of a divorce or while negotiating a settlement and to move TSP funds into a more conservative allocation pending entry and submission of a COAP. If you represent the employee's spouse, you may consider negotiating a change in the asset allocation. However, OPM will not honor a court order that purports to require the TSP Board to change the allocation.

9.3 Roth versus Pretax Contributions

TSP participants may make traditional (pretax)[12] or Roth (after-tax)[13] contributions to their TSP account. The traditional contribution is tax-deferred, meaning the deduction from pay is a pretax deduction, and the contributions to the account grow tax-deferred. When the employee takes distributions from the traditional part of the account, the distributions are taxable as ordinary income. By contrast, the Roth account contributions are taxed to the employee as ordinary income in the year of the contribution. The growth on these contributions is tax-free, not merely tax-deferred. The employee choosing between making contributions to a Roth or a traditional investment must decide whether he or she is better served by paying taxes on the contributions when made or later when he or she takes distributions. As of December 2019, federal employees can make contributions to a Roth TSP only if they earn less than $124,000 (if unmarried) or $196,000 (if married).[14] The TSP statement will show what funds in the account are Roth and what funds are traditional.

It is important to note the tax character of traditional (non-Roth) and Roth contributions when dividing TSP assets in divorce. Because Roth funds have already been taxed, they are worth more. The tax treatment of Roth earnings depends on whether those

11. The following table is from OPM Publ'n: Summary of the Thrift Savings Plan, TSPBK09 (Oct. 2020).
12. 26 U.S.C. § 408(e).
13. 26 U.S.C. §§ 408A, 219.
14. I.R.S. Publ'n 590-A, Cat. No. 66302J (Feb. 24, 2020).

earnings are qualified. Roth earnings become qualified, and are therefore paid tax-free, when two conditions have been met: (1) five years have passed since January 1 of the calendar year in which the first Roth contribution was made, and (2) the participant has reached age 59½, has a permanent disability, or has died.[15] TSP Roth contributions, if rolled over to another retirement account,[16] should be rolled into a Roth IRA, preserving the potential for tax-free growth.

When a TSP account that has both Roth and traditional components is divided pursuant to a COAP, the withdrawals will be taken from the participant's account pro rata, meaning proportionally from all investments, both Roth and traditional. OPM will not accept a COAP specifying which funds are to be withdrawn pursuant to the COAP; it must be pro rata across the entire account. Language that says that all the funds, or a specific amount, must be taken from either the Roth or traditional funds will be rejected.

Compare the Effects of Traditional and Roth Contributions[17]

The Treatment of . . .	Traditional	Roth
Contributions	**Pre-tax**	**After-tax**
Your Paycheck	**Taxes are deferred,*** so less money is taken out of the employee's paycheck.	**Taxes are paid up front,*** so more money comes out of the employee's paycheck.
Transfers In	**Transfers** allowed from eligible employer plans and traditional IRAs	**Transfers** allowed from Roth 401(k)s, Roth 403(b)s, and Roth 457(b)s
Transfers Out	**Transfers** allowed to eligible employer plans, traditional IRAs, and Roth IRAs	**Transfers** allowed to Roth 401(k)s, Roth 403(b)s, Roth 457(b)s, and Roth IRAs
Withdrawals	**Taxable** when withdrawn	**Tax-free earnings** if 5 years have passed since January 1 of the year employee made his/her first Roth contribution, AND employee is age 59½ or older, permanently disabled, or deceased

*If the employee is a member of the uniformed services receiving tax-exempt pay (i.e., pay that is subject to the combat zone tax exclusion), contributions from that pay will also be tax-exempt.

9.4 Death Benefits

In the event of an employee's death, his or her TSP account will be distributed to the beneficiary or beneficiaries the employee designated on Form TSP-3, Designation of Beneficiary. If the employee and spouse divorce and the employee fails to update the designation form to remove his or her now-former spouse and then dies, the TSP will make the distribution to the now-former spouse. The attorney should therefore advise his or her client to update the beneficiary designation. It is also advisable to include a provision in a settlement agreement waiving rights under a previous beneficiary designation and providing that if any funds are distributed to the former spouse, they will be returned to the estate of

15. 26 U.S.C. § 408A(d)(2).
16. 26 U.S.C. § 408(d)(3).
17. OPM Publ'n: Summary of the Thrift Savings Plan, TSPBK09 (Oct. 2020).

the employee net of any income taxes payable by the former spouse as a result of receiving the distribution.

If no beneficiary is designated and the employee dies, the TSP account will be disbursed according to the following statutory order of precedence:[18]

1. To a spouse
2. If none, to a child or children equally, with the share due any deceased child divided per stirpes
3. If none, to his or her parents equally or to a surviving parent
4. If none, to the appointed executor or administrator of the estate
5. If none, to the next of kin according to local intestacy laws

A will or prenuptial agreement will not supersede the above order of precedence, as the statute explicitly states that "the payment bars recovery by any other individual."[19]

Death benefit payments made from a deceased employee's TSP account will be paid directly to the beneficiary and cannot be transferred or rolled over into an IRA.[20] The beneficiary will have to pay the full amount of income taxes due in the year of receipt.

9.5 TSP Loans

Only current federal government employees who are receiving pay (not in nonpay status or furlough) may take a loan against a TSP account and only in an amount up to the total of his or her contributions and the growth thereon. Loans are not available to retirees.

The participant must repay the loan with interest via payroll deductions. This can be very helpful to a divorcing couple who may need funds to pay marital debt or legal fees because the interest rate is usually quite favorable. At this writing, the rate was 2.75 percent (the G Fund rate). The loan rate is the interest rate that is in effect on the date the loan agreement is generated and is fixed for the life of the loan.

The loan funds are disbursed from the TSP proportionally from all the traditional and Roth investments in the account, and repayments are deposited back in a similar manner. The employee may make additional loan payments via check or money order and can prepay without penalty.

The process begins by submitting a loan application. The process may usually be done on the TSP.gov website or by completing Form TSP-20. If the application is completed on the website, funds can be disbursed as quickly as within three days. Paper applications can take several weeks. Repayments begin 60 days after disbursement.

The taking of a TSP loan is not a taxable event, unless the loan is not paid back. If the employee separates from federal service, he or she must repay the loan in full. If the loan is not repaid, any pretax amount is taxable, and the employee will also become subject to the 10 percent penalty for early withdrawal. If any of the funds were Roth funds, they may be given more favorable treatment. The employee will not be subject to income taxes on the withdrawal of any portion that consists of tax-exempt contributions, Roth contributions, or qualified Roth earnings; however, even for such funds, the 10 percent penalty still applies unless the employee is older than 59½.

18. 5 U.S.C. § 8424(d).

19. *Id.*

20. Thrift Savings Plan Tax Notice: Important Tax Information about Thrift Savings Plan Death Benefit Payments, TSP-583 (Oct. 2015).

Loans are reflected on the quarterly TSP statement. The attorney should review these statements carefully to identify any outstanding loans.

A FERS participant must obtain spousal consent to a TSP loan by having the spouse sign the loan agreement (signing does not make him or her liable on the loan). The employee may request a waiver of spousal consent by completing Form TSP-16, Exception to Spousal Requirements. The waiver may be granted if the spouse cannot be located or if special circumstances apply. The employee must provide documentation substantiating the allegations. Form TSP-16 gives the following example of one type of documentation that could substantiate an exception:

> For example, a court order could indicate that you and your spouse have been maintaining separate residences with no financial relationship for three or more years; or indicate that your spouse abandoned you, but for religious or other compelling reasons, you chose not to divorce; or state that you may borrow money from or withdraw all or a portion of your TSP account notwithstanding the absence of your spouse's signature.

No spousal consent is required for a loan from a CSRS employee's TSP account. The TSP Board merely informs the participant's spouse about the TSP loan after the fact.

There are two types of loans that the employee may take:

- A general-purpose loan, which has a repayment period of one to five years, with no documentation required.
- A residential loan with repayment of one to 15 years that requires documentation for purchase or construction of a primary residence. While the interest rate is quite reasonable, the interest is not deductible as mortgage interest. Such a loan is not available for a refinance of an existing mortgage. A residential loan requires sufficient documentation to obtain approval from OPM.[21]

An employee may only have one general-purpose loan and one residential loan outstanding at any one time. The minimum loan amount for either type of loan is $1,000. The maximum possible loan amount for either type of loan is $50,000 but is calculated as the smallest of the following:

1. The participant's contributions and earnings on those contributions in the TSP account, not including any outstanding loan balance.
2. 50 percent of the total vested account balance (including any outstanding loan balance) or $10,000, whichever is greater, minus any outstanding loan balance.
3. $50,000 minus the highest outstanding loan balance, if any, during the last 12 months. Even if the loan is currently paid in full, it will still be considered in the calculation if it was open at any time during the last 12 months.[22]

PRACTICE TIP

If a court enters an order affecting a TSP account, such as an order to enforce child support or alimony or awarding a portion of the account to a former spouse, there will be a hold against the account, preventing any loans or withdrawals thereafter until the hold is lifted.

---

21. *Loans*, Thrift Savings Plan (Jan. 2018), https://www.tsp.gov/publications/tspbk04.pdf.
22. *Id.*

9.6 Financial Hardship In-Service Withdrawals

The TSP offers the employee the ability to take a hardship withdrawal under certain circumstances, one of which is to pay attorney's fees related to divorce or separation. Other circumstances under which a hardship withdrawal is allowed include recurring negative monthly cash flow, noncovered medical expenses, and personal casualty losses not covered by insurance. Only the employee contributions plus earnings can be withdrawn, not the employer contributions, and the amount requested must be more than $1,000 and less than the total amount of the hardship. Withdrawals are subject to federal and state income tax, as well as a 10 percent penalty. Application for withdrawal can be made online at TSP.gov or by using Form TSP-76 and may take up to several weeks.

PRACTICE TIP

A client with negative cash flow or without the funds to pay the cost of his or her divorce may ask whether he or she should take a hardship withdrawal or a loan from his or her TSP. You can add value by helping the client compare the two options and weighing the pros and cons of each. Be sure to reference your state case law with respect to how either option could impact the distribution of assets in the divorce.

The chart below compares how taking a TSP loan or making an in-service withdrawal would affect the employee's account.[23]

	Loan	In-Service Withdrawal
Cost to Employee	$50 loan fee	Retirement savings permanently reduced by amount of withdrawal No future earnings on amount withdrawn
Effect on Taxes	None (unless loan is not paid back and a taxable distribution is declared*)	Immediate tax liability (unless age-based withdrawal is transferred to an IRA or eligible employer plan) Possible additional 10% early withdrawal penalty tax
Effect on Earnings	No earnings on amount of loan until funds are repaid	No earnings on amount withdrawn

*When a taxable distribution is declared, the Internal Revenue Service (IRS) considers the unpaid balance (including any accrued interest) of the loan to be taxable income.

9.7 Active Employee Age-Based Withdrawals

If an active employee wishes to withdraw funds from his or her TSP, the employee may be eligible for an age-based withdrawal. An age-based withdrawal is a lump-sum withdrawal that can be made after age 59½ while still employed. An age-based withdrawal can be rolled over to an IRA or an eligible employer plan. Such a withdrawal is taxable if not

23. *In-Service Withdrawals*, Thrift Savings Plan Pamphlet TSPBK12 (Sept. 2019).

rolled over to a traditional IRA, a Roth IRA (as applicable), or an eligible employer plan. The age-based withdrawal is not subject to the 10 percent withdrawal penalty, even if the funds are not rolled over. The employee can make up to four age-based in-service withdrawals per calendar year.

PRACTICE TIP

Age-based withdrawals are subject to spouse's rights. FERS participants must obtain spousal consent. CSRS participants must notify their spouse. See Section 9.5 for more information.

9.8 Full and Partial Withdrawal Options after Leaving Federal Service

After leaving federal government service, whether by separating from service before retirement or at retirement, the participant has several options to withdraw his or her TSP funds: he or she may elect benefit withdrawals in the form of a partial withdrawal or may choose a full withdrawal as a single payment (also referred to as a lump-sum payment), a series of monthly payments, or a life annuity. Participants may combine any of the foregoing withdrawal options. Prior law allowed only one partial withdrawal after separation from service, with a subsequent withdrawal having to cover the remaining balance. This policy changed beginning in late 2019 so that the number of postseparation withdrawals is now unlimited. If the participant wishes to move the funds out of the TSP entirely, he or she may also roll the funds into an IRA or another employer-sponsored plan.

A distribution from a TSP prior to age 59½ incurs a 10 percent early-withdrawal penalty, and pretax funds, or nonqualified Roth funds (see Section 9.3), are subject to income tax; however, in general, if the employee leaves federal service during or after the year he or she reaches age 55, the penalty does not apply.[24]

After retirement or otherwise separating from service, the employee must make a withdrawal choice by April 1 in the year following the year he or she reaches age 72.[25] The withdrawals will be subject to IRS required minimum distribution rules based on life expectancy.

PRACTICE TIP

When you encounter a party with prior federal employment, inquire about the TSP and whether the funds were rolled over or left in the plan. A participant could have left money in the TSP, withdrawn it, or rolled it over to another eligible plan.

24. I.R.C. 72(t)(2)(A)(v), 72(t)(10).
25. 26 U.S.C. § 401(a)(9)(c).

Notwithstanding the foregoing options, after the employee separates from federal service, if the employee's vested account balance is $3,500 or less, the employee's entire account will be paid to the employee automatically in a single payment unless the employee elects another withdrawal option or chooses to leave the money in the TSP. This is known as the automatic cash-out.

9.9 Annuitizing the TSP at Retirement

There are two ways to annuitize a TSP account at retirement. One way is for the employee to simply request a series of monthly payments of a specific dollar amount, or the employee can request that the TSP calculate a monthly payment based on the employee's life expectancy.

Another option is purchasing an annuity. The annuity will pay a fixed benefit to the employee or to his or her survivor every month for life. These payments are made from a private insurance company, not the TSP.[26] The annuity is purchased using all or part of the funds in the TSP account, and once this is done, it cannot be undone. The annuity types are as follows:[27]

- Single-life annuity—paid to the employee until he or she dies
- Joint life annuity with a spouse—paid to the employee until he or she dies and then to his or her survivor until he or she dies
- Joint life annuity with someone else—same as above; however, that person must have an insurable interest in the employee

A joint life annuity can provide a 50 percent or 100 percent survivor annuity, as well as other features such as a cash refund, ten-year certain, or increasing payment features.

Once the funds have left the TSP account, all communications concerning the annuity (including subpoenas) should be directed to the annuity provider.

9.10 Spousal Rights regarding the TSP

Various notification and consent requirements protect the spouse of an employee who seeks to withdraw funds from the TSP, provided the TSP account is vested with a balance in excess of $3,500. These notification requirements apply to loans, in-service withdrawals, and postseparation withdrawals.[28] A married FERS participant must obtain written consent before obtaining a TSP loan and must obtain notarized written consent to an in-service or partial withdrawal. A married CSRS participant need not obtain consent, but the TSP Board will notify his or her spouse of a loan application or request for a partial or in-service withdrawal.[29]

After separation from employment, full withdrawals or transfers are treated slightly differently. The spouse of a FERS employee is entitled to a joint life and survivor annuity

---

26. Note that if the participant retired and requested a series of monthly payments, the TSP funds are still intact in the account, and the spouse can still receive a lump sum by COAP. However, if the TSP is annuitized, it is no longer in trust with the TSP Board, and a COAP cannot be submitted to TSP dividing the TSP account. It must be divided through the private company that now has custody of the funds. The logistics of such a division is outside the scope of this book.

27. *Annuities*, Thrift Savings Plan Fact Sheet TSPFS24 (Mar. 2020).

28. OPM Publ'n: Withdrawing Your TSP Account after Leaving Federal Service 21, TSPBK02 (Jan. 2018).

29. OPM Publ'n: 2018 Managing Your Account for Civilian Federal Employees in OPM Pamphlets 21, TSPBK30 (Jan. 2018).

with a 50 percent survivor benefit, level payments, and no cash refund feature; in order for the employee to make a rollover to a qualified retirement account, or elect any alternative type of annuitization, the spouse must first waive his or her right to the prescribed annuity.

The spouse of a CSRS participant has no statutory entitlement to a share of an annuitized TSP account. He or she will only be notified of the withdrawal after the fact.

An exception to these spousal notification and consent requirements may be granted under certain circumstances.[30] The TSP participant must prove exceptional circumstances or that the spouse's whereabouts are unknown. These requirements are strictly enforced. The existence of a separation agreement, a prenuptial agreement, or a protective order, or the fact of litigation pending, does not alone constitute exceptional circumstances.

Spouses' Rights

Retirement System	Withdrawal Type	Requirement	Exceptions*
FERS or uniformed services (including BRS)	Full**	Spouse is entitled to a joint life annuity with 50% survivor benefit, level payments, and no cash refund feature, unless he or she waives this right.***	Whereabouts unknown or exceptional circumstances
FERS or uniformed services (including BRS)	Partial	Spouse must give written consent to the withdrawal.	Whereabouts unknown or exceptional circumstances
CSRS	Full**	TSP must notify the spouse of the participant's withdrawal request.	Whereabouts unknown
CSRS	Partial	TSP must notify the spouse of the participant's withdrawal request.	Whereabouts unknown

* **The criteria for supporting a claim on the basis of exceptional circumstances or whereabouts unknown are strict.** The fact that there is a separation agreement, a prenuptial agreement, a protective order, or a divorce petition does not in itself support a claim of exceptional circumstances. When requesting an exception because employee does not know the whereabouts of his or her spouse, the Board will require information and documentation on efforts the employee has undertaken to locate him or her.

** For full withdrawals (including mixed withdrawals), spouses' rights requirements apply only if the account balance is more than $3,500.

*** Unless the **entire** account balance is used to purchase the prescribed survivor annuity, the spouse must waive his or her right to that annuity.

The TSP may prosecute a participant who attempts to defraud his or her spouse by forging a signature, lying about his or her marital status, or other similar acts.

The TSP will honor a retirement benefits court order to freeze a TSP account during a divorce action.[31] As soon as possible after receiving a court order that is issued in an action for divorce, annulment, or legal separation, the TSP will freeze a participant's account if

- the court order names the TSP and provides that the participant may not obtain a TSP loan or withdrawal; or
- the court order purports to divide a participant's TSP account.

30. *See* Form TSP-16, Exception to Spousal Requirements.
31. 5 C.F.R. § 1653.2(a)(2).

PRACTICE TIP

When you are representing the nonemployee spouse and if there is a bona fide concern that the employee may take actions to decrease the amount of funds in the TSP account, a COAP can be entered to freeze the account and prevent dissipation on the part of the employee. Note that for a FERS participant to take such an action would also require forging the nonemployee spouse's signature on the consent forms for a withdrawal or a loan or lying to establish an exception. However, the CSRS participant with a TSP does not need such spousal consent and could take such action without forging the nonemployee spouse's signature.

Once an account is frozen, no new loans or withdrawals are permitted from the account until the action is resolved. All other account activity will be permitted, including investment decisions and payments on existing loans.[32] If the account is frozen in response to a court order issued to preserve the status quo, the freeze will be removed when the TSP receives a court order that removes the freeze or when the TSP receives a court order dividing the account.

9.11 Marital and Prenuptial Agreements and the TSP

A prenuptial agreement may include mutual waivers of retirement interests and, in the case of a federal employee, could include a waiver of the TSP. The waiver should conform to the spousal consent requirements of federal law so that the employee has full control of his or her TSP account. The agreement should specify that in the case of a FERS participant, the nonemployee spouse consents to any and all elections or withdrawals that the employee may make, including partial withdrawal, full withdrawal, rollover, single-life annuity, and/or joint life annuity with a person other than the spouse. It should require the spouse to sign any consent required by federal law to make the waiver effective.

A waiver of a future spouse's interest in a TSP account in a prenuptial agreement is not valid without a completed Form TSP-3 on file with OPM. The TSP-3 form designates a beneficiary and must be signed and notarized by the employee and spouse. It must be received by the TSP Board on or before the day of the death of the employee in order to be honored.

Sample language for a prenuptial agreement waiver is as follows, in which Shane is the federal employee and Alex, his fiancée, is waiving interest:

> *Shane, as a federal employee, has a Thrift Savings Plan (TSP). The parties agree that Shane shall retain all right, title, and interest in his TSP, including all premarital interest and any earnings, gains, and/or losses thereon, as well as any contributions made during or after the marriage (whether by Shane or by his employer) and any earnings, gains, and/or losses thereon and the repayment of any loans. As such, Alex waives any right, title, or interest she may acquire in Shane's TSP as a result of their marriage. Alex hereby agrees to execute Form TSP-3, or any other form required for Shane to exercise control over the TSP as he desires, including, but not limited to, to designate beneficiaries or take out loans.*

32. OPM Publ'n: Court-Ordered Benefits for Former Spouses, RI 84-1 (rev. July 2014).

Sample language for a marital agreement waiver is as follows, in which Tanvi is the federal employee and Dhruv, her husband, is waiving his interest:

> *Tanvi has a Thrift Savings Plan (TSP) as a result of her employment with the federal government, with a current balance of $50,000. The parties agree that Tanvi shall retain the TSP as her sole and separate property, and Dhruv waives all interest therein.*

Chapter Ten

Dividing a TSP Account in Divorce

Chapter 10 will review the ways in which a Thrift Savings Plan (TSP) account can be divided in divorce, from how to value the account to what to do with the funds next. It will also review potential mistakes and pitfalls and how to avoid them.

10.1 Requirements for the Order Dividing a TSP

A TSP account can be divided at divorce by means of "a court decree of divorce, annulment, or legal separation; or a court order or court-approved property settlement agreement incident to such a decree."[1] The Internal Revenue Code permits the transfer to the

1. 5 U.S.C. § 8467.

former spouse to be tax-free when it is made incident to a divorce.[2] Division of a TSP is governed by provisions of the U.S. Code and Code of Federal Regulations[3] specific to TSP accounts.[4] An order dividing a TSP account may be referred to as a Court Order Acceptable for Processing (COAP), Retirement Benefits Court Order (RBCO), or Qualifying Court Order (QCO). The court order must meet the requirements of 5 U.S.C. §§ 8435(c) and 8467 and 5 C.F.R. part 1653, subpart A:

(1) It must be issued by a court in any of the 50 United States, the District of Columbia, the Commonwealth of Puerto Rico, Guam, the Northern Mariana Islands, or the Virgin Islands, or by any [Native American] court as defined by 25 U.S.C. § 1301(3).

(2) It must specifically identify the TSP and, if the employee also has a uniformed service TSP account, identify the TSP to which the order refers

(3) It must use language appropriate to a defined contribution account

(4) It must either require the TSP to freeze the participant's account to preserve the *status quo* pending final resolution of the parties' rights to the participant's TSP account, or to make a payment from the participant's account to a permissible payee.

(5) It must clearly set forth the former spouse's entitlement

(6) If the order requires a payment from the participant's account, the award can only be described in one of the following terms:
(i) A specific dollar amount;
(ii) A stated percentage or fraction of the account as of a date certain; or
(iii) a stated percentage or fraction of the amount accrued in the account between two dates.[5]

The TSP Board does not review draft orders. The TSP Board will only review a complete copy of the order, as entered, and it must be accompanied by

- the participant's TSP account number or Social Security number (SSN);[6]
- the name and mailing address of each payee;
- if the current or former spouse of the participant is a payee, the SSN of the spouse-payee; and
- if the court order is written in a language other than English, a certified English language translation of the entire court order.

The TSP accepts electronic and remote notarization in addition to traditional, in-person notarization for TSP forms that require a notarized signature.

The following language will cause the TSP to reject the order:[7]

(1) An order requiring payment to anyone other than a spouse, former spouse, child or dependent of a participant.
(2) An order requiring that certain funds be taken from a Roth or Traditional Balance other than pro rata. Any payment made under a qualifying order will

2. 26 U.S.C. § 408(d)(6).
3. 5 C.F.R. § 1653.1.
4. The TSP is not covered by the Employee Retirement Income Security Act of 1974 (ERISA), so rules for Qualified Domestic Relations Orders (QDROs) that apply to private-sector retirement plans do not apply to the TSP.
5. 5 C.F.R. § 1653.4.
6. OPM Publ'n: 2014 Court Orders and Powers of Attorney (Sept. 2014).
7. *See* 5 C.F.R. § 1653.2.

be disbursed proportionally from any traditional and Roth balances in the participant's account.

(3) An order requiring the return to the TSP of money that was properly paid pursuant to an earlier court order or relating to a TSP account that has been closed;
(4) An order relating to a TSP account that contains only non-vested money, unless the money will become vested within 30 days of the date the TSP receives the order if the participant were to remain in Government service;
(5) An order requiring the TSP to make a payment in the future, unless the present value of the payee's entitlement can be calculated, in which case the TSP will make the payment currently;
(6) An order that does not specify the account to which the order applies, if the participant has both a civilian TSP account and a uniformed services TSP account;
(7) An order that requires the TSP to calculate the payee's entitlement or earnings in a manner that is inconsistent with CFR §1653.4;
(8) An order that designates the TSP Fund, from which the payment or portions of the payment shall be made.
(9) An order asking that a single payment be made jointly (for example, $10,000 to be divided among the former spouse and dependents). The court order must separately specify the dollar amount, percentage, or fraction of the award made to each person.

OPM explains the steps in its processing of a court order to divide a TSP account:[8]

Step 1. As soon as possible after the TSP Board receives a document that purports to be a qualifying RBCO, the participant's account will be frozen.

Step 2. The TSP Board will then evaluate whether the court order is complete. If the court order is not complete, the TSP Board will request that the parties submit a complete copy of the order. If a complete copy is not received within 30 days of the date of that notification, the participant's TSP account will be unfrozen, and no further action based on that court order will be taken until a complete court order is received.

Step 3. When the TSP Board receives a complete court order, the TSP Board will freeze (or retain the freeze on) the participant's account and evaluate the court order to determine whether it is a qualifying RBCO and how the account should be divided.

Step 4. The TSP Board will mail a decision letter to the participant and provide a copy to the spouse and attorneys on record. The decision letter will describe the effect the order will have on the participant's account and will state when the freeze will be removed from the account.

If the court order is not qualifying, the decision letter will explain why. If the order requires a payment, the letter will also explain how the payment amount will be calculated and when the payment will be made. The party who must pay federal income tax on the distribution will receive tax reporting and withholding information from the TSP.

If the payee is the current or former spouse of the participant, the payee will also receive information about the option to transfer the payment to a traditional IRA, a Roth IRA, or an eligible employer plan.

8. OPM Publ'n: 2014 Court Orders and Powers of Attorney 5 (Sept. 2014).

The lawyer should let the client know that he or she must forward to the lawyer a copy of correspondence from the TSP Board. If the TSP Board isn't aware that a party is represented, his or her counsel may not be copied. The lawyer should not close the file until receipt of the letter from the TSP Board.

10.2 How the TSP Board Calculates the Amount of the Former Spouse's Entitlement

The court order dividing the TSP as part of a property division at divorce should specify the former spouse's entitlement, including whether it is a percentage or a fixed dollar amount, the date as of which the percentage or fixed amount is determined, and whether the former spouse's share will be adjusted for gains and losses from the valuation date to the date of division. The order may also specify that the spouse receive a stated percentage or fraction of the amount accrued in the account between two dates. The TSP Board follows certain rules in interpreting a court order awarding a spouse an entitlement from a participant's TSP:

How the Amount of an Entitlement Is Calculated for an RBCO[9]

If a court order awards a percentage or fraction of a TSP account as of a specific day	→	the payee's entitlement is determined based on that day's total account balance.
If a court order awards a percentage or fraction of a TSP account and does not specify a date for calculating the award	→	the payee's entitlement is determined based on the effective date of the order.
If a court order awards a fixed dollar amount	→	the payee's entitlement is that dollar amount.
If a court order describes a payee's entitlement as a fixed dollar amount and as a percentage or fraction of the account	→	the payee's entitlement is the specified dollar amount, even if the percentage or fraction, when applied against the total account balance, yields a different amount.

A court order cannot require the TSP to pay more than the participant's total vested account balance. Therefore, if the court order purports to entitle the former spouse to an amount that exceeds the participant's vested account balance when the TSP pays the award, the TSP will only pay the vested account balance.

PRACTICE TIP

A pamphlet, *Court Orders and Powers of Attorney*, TSP BK 11, is available for download from the TSP and is very informative.

General questions can be directed to ThriftLine at 877-968-3778.

The website for the TSP is www.tsp.gov.

9. *Id.* at 11.

10.3 Providing for Investment Earnings, Gains, and Losses on the Former Spouse's Share

In preparing the COAP, the lawyer for the spouse has three options regarding treatment of earnings, gains, and losses on the share being transferred to the spouse:

1. Do not apply earnings, gains, and losses. In such case, the order may state the amount to be transferred as a flat sum and state explicitly that earnings, gains, and losses are not to be applied to the spouse's share. The TSP does not automatically apply earnings, gains, and losses to the spouse's share of the TSP account. Rather, the COAP must expressly provide for it if that is what parties intend.
2. Provide for the application of earnings at a stated annual percentage rate or the addition of a per diem dollar amount to the spouse's entitlement. The order cannot reference a TSP fund as an interest or earnings rate.
3. Provide for application of earnings, gains, and losses to the amount being transferred. If only the term "earnings" is used, the TSP Board will interpret it to include losses. In such case, the TSP will do the following: "If the court order provides for earnings, but does not specify a rate or a per diem dollar amount, the TSP will calculate earnings based on the type of TSP funds the participant was invested in on the date used to calculate the payee's entitlement, the number of shares the participant had in each fund on the date used to calculate the payee's entitlement, and the share price of those TSP funds up to two days prior to disbursement."[10]

The lawyer should advise the client of the risks and potential benefits of each approach.

PRACTICE TIP

Once you determine how much the spouse will receive from the TSP, clarify in the agreement or court order if the amount will be credited with

1. a rate of interest (annual percentage rate or a per diem interest rate),
2. actual earnings, gains, and losses, or
3. nothing.

Explain these options to your client and the possible risks and benefits of each. If a flat sum is transferred that was calculated as of a certain date, and the market takes a downward turn, the sum transferred could result in a windfall for the spouse. Providing for earnings, gains, and losses to be applied to the spouse's share means parties share the risks and rewards of market fluctuations.

10. 5 C.F.R. § 1653.4.

10.4 Accounting for Roth and Pretax Funds Separately

A COAP cannot provide that the former spouse's share of the TSP be drawn only from Roth funds or only from traditional pretax funds. The former spouse's share can only be drawn pro rata. An order stating otherwise will be rejected. For example, suppose a federal employee has a TSP account worth $100,000, of which $75,000 is pretax and $25,000 is in Roth funds. An equal division will result in each party getting $37,500 in pretax funds and $12,500 in Roth after-tax funds.

What if both parties have marital retirement accounts, they intend to equalize accounts and the tax burdens, and only the federal employee spouse has Roth funds while the other spouse has a 401(k) with only pretax funds? See the following example:

> *Joanna and George are negotiating a settlement. Joanna has $150,000 in her TSP. $100,000 is pretax and $50,000 is Roth funds. George has a 401(k) with all pretax, traditional funds, with a balance of $100,000.*

If Joanna and George sign an agreement to equalize their accounts, without taking into account the Roth funds separately, Joanna would agree to transfer to George $25,000 from her TSP. However, the funds would be taken from her TSP account pro rata: specifically, $16,667 of the pretax funds and $8,333 of the Roth funds would be transferred to George's 401(k).

They would then have the following distribution of funds:

	Joanna:	George:
Pretax:	$83,333	$116,667
Roth:	$41,667	$8,333

Although it appears that they have the same amount of total funds postequalization, Joanna kept far more of the Roth funds, so her account is worth more than George's.

In a settlement negotiation, parties can account for the difference in a variety of ways, such as through the allocation of other assets. In a contested matter, the lawyer for the party who will be disadvantaged by a straight equalization will need to present evidence to the court of the tax consequences as a basis for asking for an award to account for the difference.

10.5 Accounting for Loans

A divorcing federal employee may have an outstanding TSP loan. The lawyer for the spouse will need to review the TSP statements to determine whether there is such a loan.[11] A loan balance cannot be transferred to a spouse or former spouse; the participant will remain solely responsible for paying the loan after divorce. Therefore, parties will need to address the loan balance when providing for a division of the TSP account. An order dividing a TSP account that purports to divide it equally will not accomplish that purpose without accounting for the loan. Doing so would shortchange the TSP account holder. If the parties intend to share the loan as a marital debt, the TSP order should make that clear.

To illustrate the options: Assume a TSP account with a balance of $20,000 but with an outstanding loan balance of $5,000 so that the net value of the account is $15,000.

---

11. The TSP statement will show how much of the loan remains outstanding. A review of the employee's pay statements will also show whether a loan exists, because it will show the payments as deductions from the employee's pay.

Option A: If the parties intend the valuation to take account of the loan balance so that each party will have half of the net value of the account, the settlement agreement or COAP would say:

"For purposes of valuing the account, the loan balance will be taken into account."

$20,000	Total TSP balance **including** the loan balance
– $5,000	Outstanding loan balance
$15,000	Account balance net of loan
$15,000 / 2 = $7,500	Equal division of net TSP balance value after taking loan into account
$7,500	Transfer to spouse
$12,500	Retention of account balance by participant
– $5,000	Retention of loan balance to be repaid by participant
$7,500	Net value retained by participant

Option B: If parties intend to disregard the loan balance in valuing the account, meaning that the TSP participant will bear the loan balance and it will decrease only the value of his or her share, the agreement or COAP would say:

"For purposes of valuing the account, the loan balance will be disregarded."

$20,000	Account balance
$20,000 / 2 = $10,000	Equal division of account balance
$10,000	Transfer to spouse
$10,000	Retention of account balance by participant
– $5,000	Loan balance to be repaid by participant
$5,000	Net value of participant's share after loan repayment

10.6 The Valuation Date

A COAP or settlement agreement dividing a TSP account should always include a valuation date. In some jurisdictions, state law defines the valuation date as the date of divorce. In others, it will be the date of separation. Parties entering into a settlement may use yet another valuation date, such as the date of the agreement or another compromise date. Whatever date the parties choose should be stated explicitly in the agreement and COAP. The following examples properly express a valuation date that can be used in a settlement agreement or COAP:

Brian's TSP will be divided equally as of the date of this agreement, with earnings, gains, and losses thereon, to the date of distribution.

Anthony will be entitled to receive 25 percent of Leslie's TSP as of 12/31/20, with earnings, gains, and losses thereon to the date of distribution.

Marie will receive $50,000 from Max's TSP as of 1/13/20 ("Marie's Share"). Marie's Share shall be credited with earnings, gains, and losses from 1/13/20 to the date of distribution.

By contrast, an agreement or COAP may omit a valuation date as follows:

Evan will receive $20,000 from Jillian's TSP account.

In such case, because no valuation date is expressed, OPM presumes the $20,000 is a flat sum, as of the date the COAP is processed and implemented. If $20,000 represented half the account at the time the agreement was reached and the market fluctuates between the date of the agreement and the date of distribution, Evan may receive a windfall or may receive significantly less than he bargained for. Rarely will it be appropriate to omit a valuation date.

10.7 Obtaining TSP Account Statements

Certain TSP account information is available to the nonemployee spouse without the need for a subpoena. The TSP Board will provide the spouse and the spouse's attorney upon written request with the following information: account balance, transaction history, outstanding loan balance if any, and annual or quarterly statements. The TSP Board will not provide an address, date of birth, or SSN for the plan participant.

Requests for such information must be directed to the TSP legal processing unit (PO Box 4390, Fairfax, VA 22038-4390 or fax number 1-866-817-5023). The request must provide the participant's name and TSP account number or SSN, identify the spouse, and describe the information and documentation requested and the purpose for which it is being requested.[12] There is no cost for this service. The requester can use Form TSP-92D (Request for Participant Account Information), included in the downloadable resources provided with this book, available at https://ambar.org/RepFed.

10.8 Accounting for Nonmarital Contributions to the TSP

Whether, and to what extent, a TSP account is divisible property at divorce is a matter of state law. A TSP participant may have premarital contributions that are defined as nonmarital property under state law. Similarly, he or she may have postseparation contributions that are defined under state law as nonmarital property. Or he or she may have rolled a premarital private-sector account, such as a 401(k), into his or her TSP.

Even when state law defines all contributions made during the marriage through the date of divorce as marital property, or allows a court to make an award of any property held by a party without regard to when acquired, a party may want to negotiate or ask a court for a division that allocates certain contributions (along with earnings, gains, and losses thereon) to him or her and divide the balance of the account.

To pursue such an objective, the participant will need to produce account statements. To establish a premarital value, for example, the participant must be able to prove the balance as of the date of marriage; to prove the premarriage value adjusted for earnings, gains, and losses, he or she must have every account statement beginning with the date of marriage. It is relatively easy to obtain even very old account statements from the TSP Board. Any calculation should also take into account rollovers from another employer's plan, loans, loan repayments, and withdrawals.

---

12. *See* U.S.C. § 552(a).

Alternatively, the TSP Board does allow for unique division language to purposely include in the divisible portion of the account the increase in the value of funds between two specific dates. This approach could be used to allocate to the participant the premarriage account balance but divide the increase in the TSP account's balance from the date of marriage through the date of divorce. Note, however, that this will include in the division any earnings, gains, and losses on any premarital contributions. See Section 10.10 for sample language.

10.9 Calculating the Premarital Portion of the TSP

With TSP statements from the date of marriage forward, the lawyer can determine the account balance as of the date of marriage. The lawyer, the client, or an accountant can do the math to apply the earnings, gains, and losses attributable to that premarital balance for each reporting period up to the date of divorce or other appropriate date. For long marriages, this can be a laborious chore.

Deciding how to treat rollovers from another retirement account, withdrawals, loans, and loan repayments can be challenging. Threshold questions are whether the loan or withdrawal should be deducted from the marital or the nonmarital share and whether the loan repayments or withdrawal repayments should be considered marital property, nonmarital property, or a combination thereof. This determination is primarily based on the facts and circumstances of the particular case and the law in that jurisdiction. Loans and withdrawals can be deducted from either the marital or nonmarital share of the account or from each account proportionately.

There are two options to present the calculation of the nonmarital share:

1. The attorney (or the client or the attorney's staff) may prepare the calculations. It will be necessary to show the work using Microsoft Excel or a similar program. This is more achievable in cases where there have been no rollovers, withdrawals, or loans and in short-term marriages. The lawyer may request that the judge or magistrate take judicial notice of the math.
2. The lawyer may retain an expert to do the calculation and present it on a spreadsheet. The expert may be an actuary, accountant, or other qualified financial professional.

Either way, the most commonly accepted process is described below:

1. Start with the statement that indicates the account balance as of or near to the date of marriage.
2. By referencing the statement that is next available chronologically, determine the earnings, contributions, rollovers, loans, loan repayments, and withdrawals that occurred during the period. Earnings are prorated between the marital and nonmarital interest in proportion to the account balance, generally at the beginning of the period. Contributions during the period are generally allocated to the marital interest. Rollovers are allocated to the marital or nonmarital interest based on their marital/nonmarital character prior to the rollover. Loans, loan repayments, and withdrawals are allocated based on the facts and circumstances of the particular case.
3. The above process is repeated for each statement period with the ending balance of any prior period used as the beginning balance of the next period.

10.10 Sample Language to Divide a TSP Account

The following sample language may be used in a marital settlement agreement or order to divide a TSP. In the following examples, assume that Bob is the federal employee and Linda is the spouse. Bob is the owner of a TSP account, and Linda is to receive a transfer of funds from Bob's TSP. The date of the agreement is April 15, 2019. The date of divorce is April 2020.

10.10.1 Flat Sum

As discussed in the foregoing sections, the participant's TSP balance will have a specific balance as of a date certain. One manner of dividing the account is by allocating a specific sum certain to the former spouse. The following model language would accomplish that:

> *Bob has a balance of $150,356 in his TSP account as of the date of this agreement. The parties agree that Linda shall receive $50,000 as a flat sum from Bob's TSP.*

There are advantages and disadvantages to this language. If Bob's TSP balance drops after the agreement is executed, Linda will receive more than one-third of his account, the proportion her $50,000 originally represented. If his balance drops to $120,000 due to market forces, Linda will still receive $50,000, which is closer to 42 percent of his account. The advantage to expressing the spouse's share in this manner is that both parties know exactly how much Linda will receive. Some parties may prefer this and are willing to take a chance on changes in the market. Alternatively, the agreement can provide that earnings, gains, and losses will be applied to the flat sum from the date of agreement (or date of divorce) to the date of distribution (see Section 10.10.4).

> **PRACTICE TIP**
>
> One instance where parties might want to agree to a flat sum would be where they agree to pay off their marital credit-card debt with TSP funds. Using the above example, if Bob is in a higher tax bracket, if he takes a distribution, he pays income taxes on that distribution at his higher rate, and he pays a 10 percent penalty. If Linda is in a lower bracket, she can take the distribution from Bob's TSP at her lower tax rate, without the 10 percent penalty, and they end up with more after-tax money to pay their debt. The TSP is required to withhold 20 percent of the amount distributed to cover the estimated taxes.

10.10.2 Percentage

Another option is to assign a percentage of Bob's account to Linda as follows:

> *Linda shall be entitled to receive, via COAP, 33 percent of Bob's TSP account valued as of April 15, 2019, plus earnings, gains, and losses on such amount to the date of distribution.*

The above language would cut off Linda's rights as of the date specified so that she would not receive any of Bob's subsequent contributions to the account. It also would mean that Linda and Bob would each experience earnings, gains, and losses on his or her share. When the former spouse's share is expressed as a percentage as of a given date, it will receive earnings, gains, and losses to the date of distribution even if the agreement or court order does not say so expressly. The better practice when negotiating a settlement is to provide expressly in the settlement agreement for each party's share to experience earnings, gains, and losses. Doing so can head off a potential dispute about the terms of the COAP and whether the parties intended that the former spouse benefit from postsettlement earnings and gains or share postsettlement losses.

An agreement that expresses the spouse's share as a percentage of the account without a valuation date and that is silent as to application of earnings, gains, and losses (*The parties agree that Linda shall receive 33 percent of Bob's TSP account.*) is problematical. Such language would mean that Linda would share in all new contributions to the TSP from the date of the settlement agreement through the date the TSP is divided. Parties may intend that she share new contributions made after settlement and before divorce; if so, the agreement should say so expressly. Moreover, without a valuation date, arguably Linda will receive 33 percent of postdivorce contributions. If there is a delay after the divorce in submitting the COAP to the court for entry, delay in submitting it to the TSP Board, or delay after submission, Linda may receive a windfall to Bob's disadvantage.

10.10.3 Amount Accrued between Two Dates

For parties who are unable to determine the value of the benefit accrued during the marriage, or other relevant time period, so as to express an award of a stated flat amount or percentage of a known value, the TSP Board will accept language dividing an amount accrued between two dates.

> *Bob has a Thrift Savings Plan (TSP) account. The parties agree that Linda shall be entitled to 50 percent of the amount accrued in Bob's TSP between the date of marriage (June 11, 1991) and the date of this agreement (April 15, 2019). The amount allocated to Linda shall be credited with earnings, gains, and losses thereon from the date of divorce through the date of distribution to Linda.*

Note that because the sample language does not state the amount accrued between these two dates, and parties must wait for the TSP Board to calculate it, Linda will not know the base amount that she will receive nor the value of earnings, gains, and losses on her share. The advantage of this provision is that it requires less document collection from the attorney. The disadvantage is that the lawyer may not be able to answer Linda's question if she asks, "What am I getting?"

10.10.4 Application of Earnings, Gains, and Losses

Parties entering into a settlement to divide a TSP account may expect to benefit from the appreciation and reinvested income on his or her share that occurs from the agreed valuation date; similarly, parties may expect that each party will bear the consequences of a reduction in value of his or her share resulting from a market dip. Best practice is to be explicit about that intention in the settlement agreement and in the COAP. That can be achieved with the following language:

> *Bob has a balance of $150,356 in his TSP account as of the date of this agreement. The parties agree that Linda shall receive $50,000 of Bob's TSP as of the date of this agreement ("Linda's share"). Linda's share shall be credited with earnings, gains, and losses from the date of this agreement to the date of distribution to Linda.*

Here is another way to express the same concept:

Bob has a balance of $139,124 in his TSP account as of the date of this agreement. The parties agree that Linda shall receive $50,000 of Bob's TSP as of April 15, 2020 ("Linda's share"). Linda's share shall be credited with earnings, gains, and losses from April 15, 2020, to the date of distribution to Linda.

In both of the above examples, Linda's share is valued as of a certain date, and her share will experience the earnings, gains, and losses that will be accounted for when the TSP Board calculates her share as of the date of distribution. The parties and their attorneys do not need to calculate the earnings, gains, and losses themselves.

10.11 Tips for Avoiding the Delay or Denial of a TSP Award

The following comes from TSP pamphlet *Court Orders and Powers of Attorney* (2014) and distills points that will help ensure acceptance of a COAP for division of a TSP:

- The order should include the signature of the appropriate judicial official. The TSP will not review draft court orders or legal processes; it will treat any order or process submitted without the appropriate judicial signature as a draft.
- Include the payee's current address and, if the payee is a spouse or former spouse, his or her SSN. If the payee's information is not in the court order or legal process, it may be submitted by only the payee or either party's attorney of record.
- Include the participant's TSP account number or SSN and current address.
- The court order or legal process should refer expressly to the "Thrift Savings Plan" by name. No variations will be accepted.
- The dollar amount of the award (or percentage or fraction, if an RBCO) must be clearly stated.
- The court order or legal process may not ask for a share of a stream of future payments even if a retiree elected such a payout. The award must be a one-time payment that can be paid out immediately.[13]
- If the participant has more than one type of TSP account, the court order or legal process must identify the account from which the award is to be paid using the terms "civilian," "uniformed services," and/or "beneficiary participant."
- If eligible, the spouse-payee should submit the forms for transferring the payment to a traditional IRA, a Roth IRA, or an eligible employer plan in a timely manner. Failure to do so will result in the issuance of a check directly to the former spouse, and the mandatory 20 percent tax withholding will apply to any taxable amounts. The TSP will not reverse a properly disbursed payment.

10.12 After the Order—Dividing the TSP Account

Following receipt of the TSP order, the TSP Board will send a decision letter to the attorney who submitted it and both parties, and if it is approved, it will advise the former spouse as to his or her rights and give him or her the opportunity to roll over the funds to an IRA or other eligible retirement account. The decision letter from the Board will also advise that if

13. Note that if the participant retired and requested a periodic stream of payments, the TSP funds are still intact in the account, and the spouse can still receive a lump sum. However, if the participant elected at retirement to have the TSP annuitized, it is no longer in trust with the TSP Board, and a COAP cannot be submitted dividing the TSP account.

the amount in the account is less than the amount ordered to be paid, TSP will pay the full vested portion of the account and that TSP will not segregate the former spouse's share pending transfer.

Upon receipt of this decision letter calculating the entitlement of the former spouse, each party has 25 days to dispute the decision. In some cases, it may be appropriate to seek an amended court order to correct the issue.

Once the TSP accepts the order and issues the decision letter, it will provide instructions as to how the former spouse can transfer or roll over the funds. The TSP sends a TSP Form 13-S-C, which permits the former spouse to direct funds to be rolled over to a traditional IRA, Roth IRA, or employer-sponsored plan or distributed directly to him or her.

PRACTICE TIP

Advise your client to keep an eye out for this letter in his or her mailbox and advise him or her of the 60-day deadline to deposit the funds.

The former spouse has 60 days to send rollover directions to the TSP on TSP Form 13-S-C; if he or she fails to do so, the funds will be distributed by check, less 20 percent withholding for taxes, and it will be a taxable distribution. However, the spouse can request more time to arrange for a rollover and avoid that result. A disbursement is typically made 60 days after the TSP Board issues the decision letter. In some cases, disbursement can be expedited.

Agency Contact Information

The former spouse or his or her lawyer should send the TSP COAP and Form TSP-13-S-C to the address below.

An inquiry regarding these actions should also be sent to one of these addresses.

For submission by fax:
(703) 592-0151
Mailing address:
TSP Legal Processing Unit
P.O. Box 4390
Fairfax, VA 22038-4390

For overnight delivery:
ATTN: TSP Legal
Processing Unit
12210 Fairfax Town Center
Unit 906
Fairfax, VA 22033

10.13 Transferring Funds into the Former Spouse's TSP Account

If the former spouse also owns a TSP account, as would be the case if both parties are federal government employees, and will receive funds pursuant to a COAP, he or she may transfer such funds directly into his or her TSP. The TSP will accept into the traditional balance of the former spouse's TSP account a transfer or rollover of tax-deferred funds from a nongovernmental account (such as an IRA, SIMPLE IRA, or 401(k)). Likewise, TSP will accept into the Roth balance of the TSP account a transfer of qualified and nonqualified Roth distributions from a Roth 401(k), Roth 403(b), or Roth 457(b). If the receiving employee does not have a Roth balance in the TSP, the transfer will create one. However, the TSP does not accept transfers or rollovers from Roth IRAs. The employee receiving funds can use Form TSP 60 to effect a rollover and must do so within 60 days from the date he or she receives funds from the employee's TSP to avoid the funds being distributed directly.

10.14 Cash Distribution to Former Spouse

A former spouse may wish to receive his or her share of the TSP funds as cash, rather than by rollover into an eligible Individual Retirement Arrangement. This has no effect on the employee-spouse. The lawyer for the former spouse should make him or her aware of the tax consequences of a cash distribution or advise the client to consult his or her tax advisor. The tax consequences to the former spouse include the possibility that the 20 percent withholding will be insufficient to pay all of the actual income tax liability with respect to these funds.

10.15 Updating the Beneficiary Designation

When an employee commences employment, he or she typically designates a beneficiary to receive the funds in his or her TSP account in the event of the participant's death. Divorce does not revoke the beneficiary designation. That means that in the event the participant dies and his or her former spouse is still the designated beneficiary, the TSP Board must distribute the funds to the now-former spouse. A settlement agreement may include a provision in which the spouse disclaims the right to such funds. However, best practice is to advise the client to update his or her beneficiary designation using Form TSP-3. See Section 9.4 for more information.

PRACTICE TIP

Advise your client at or before the close of the case to update beneficiary designations. Consider putting this advice in your file-closing letter.

Part III

Other Federal Government Employee Benefits

Chapter Eleven

Federal Employees Health Benefits (FEHB)

Chapter 11 covers the largest employer-sponsored health program in the world, the Federal Employees Health Benefits (FEHB) program, and discusses how the employee's spouse and children can maintain their plan participation after a divorce.

11.1 FEHB Coverage for Employees and Their Families

Most federal employees have available to them, as a perquisite of employment, enrollment in the FEHB program.[1] The FEHB program became effective in 1960. It is the largest employer-sponsored group health insurance program in the world, covering over 8 million federal employees, retirees, former employees, family members, and former spouses.

FEHB coverage is available to most federal government employees, retirees, their spouses and dependents, and their survivors.[2] Many coverage options are available with premiums lower than most private plans. The government subsidizes the cost by contributing up to 75 percent of the employee premium. Coverage is guaranteed; the plan cannot deny or cancel coverage for medical reasons, and there is no waiting period for eligibility, medical examination, or exclusion due to a medical condition. A comparison of plans

1. Members of Congress and congressional employees were formerly covered under FEHB. Under the Affordable Care Act, as of 2013, they are exempt from FEHB coverage. Instead, they have mandatory enrollment in the District of Columbia Health Exchange. Affordable Care Act § 1312(d)(3)(D); 42 U.S.C. § 18032. *See also* Ira Brudnick, Cong. Research Serv., Rep. 7-5700 (RL 30064), Congressional Salaries and Allowances: In Brief (2018).

2. A same-sex domestic partner of a Foreign Service officer is also eligible to enroll in federal health benefits. 3 Dep't of State, Foreign Affairs Manual § 1612, *available at* https://fam.state.gov/searchapps/viewer?format=html&query=3%20FAM%201600&links=3,FAM&url=/FAM/03FAM/03FAM1610.html#M1612 (last visited Nov. 17, 2020).

Where to Find the Law

The law governing FEHB is chapter 89, title 5, United States Code. The regulations are in part 890, title 5, and chapter 16 of title 48, Code of Federal Regulations. The OPM website provides an online FEHB Program Handbook, which is full of useful information. *FEHB Program Handbook Introduction*, OFF. OF PERSONNEL MGMT., https://www.opm.gov/healthcare-insurance/healthcare/reference-materials/fehb-handbook/ (last visited Nov. 17, 2020).

(more than 200) is available on the OPM.gov website. There are fee-for-service plans, Preferred Provider Organizations (PPOs), Health Maintenance Organizations (HMOs), and Point of Service plans. An employee can enroll upon entering federal employment.

If an employee wishes to change his or her plan, he or she must wait until Open Season, which is during November of each year. During Open Season, the employee can change the type of enrollment, change who is covered under the plan, or change plans entirely. The employee can add a current spouse to his or her plan during Open Season. The FEHB program allows only certain limited changes to an employee's enrollment outside of Open Season. Examples of changes that can be made outside of Open Season are adding a new spouse after marriage and adding a child after birth or adoption. These are called Life Events. An employee who wishes to drop his or her spouse from FEHB coverage, even during Open Season, must get the spouse's consent to the loss of coverage, even if the parties are separated.

A former spouse automatically loses FEHB coverage under the employee's self-and-family enrollment 31 days after the divorce decree or annulment is final. However, the former spouse may be able to continue FEHB coverage after the termination of the marriage. There are two ways a former spouse may continue coverage, discussed in Sections 11.3 and 11.4.[3]

PRACTICE TIP

If you represent a spouse who may want FEHB coverage and is not currently covered under the federal employee–spouse's plan, keep your eye on Open Season. You could negotiate adding him or her onto the insurance plan during Open Season to leave open the possibility of continuing Spouse Equity Coverage postdivorce.

3. The Office of Personnel Management (OPM) provides many short publications, called *FastFacts*, on a variety of topics, including federal benefits, Open Season, long-term care insurance, health care reform, life insurance, and flex spending accounts. *Insurance: FastFacts*, OFF. OF PERSONNEL MGMT., https://www.opm.gov/healthcare-insurance/fastfacts/ (last visited Nov. 17, 2020).

Upon retirement, if a married employee is eligible and elects to continue his or her health benefits coverage, and coverage for his or her spouse, into retirement, the premiums for these are withheld from the employee's monthly pension benefit. If the employee's monthly retirement payment does not cover the full premium, the employee can arrange to make direct payment for the premiums to the Office of Personnel Management (OPM).

The employee can continue to receive health insurance after separating from government employment and before going into pay status on his or her pension. The employee may receive extended coverage for up to 18 months under a Temporary Continuation of Coverage (TCC); the employee must pay the full premiums and a 2 percent administrative fee. If the employee defers going into pay status on his or her pension for longer than the 18-month TCC, then the employee must find an alternative source for health insurance coverage. Once the employee goes into pay status on the pension, he or she can reenroll in FEHB if he or she was enrolled in FEHB for at least five years prior to separating from federal government service. OPM will pay the government's share of the premiums.[4]

11.2 Continuation of Spousal Health Insurance Coverage under FEHB after Divorce—Overview

Providing for health insurance for both spouses after divorce, as well as for their children, is a critical issue, especially when a spouse is financially dependent, unemployed, employed without benefits, self-employed, retired, or employed part time. The Civil Service Retirement Spouse Equity Act of 1984 (5 U.S.C. § 8341) allows certain former employees, annuitants, and their spouses to enroll in a health benefits plan under the FEHB program.

There are two types of coverage available to former spouses, discussed below: Spouse Equity Coverage and Temporary Continuation of Coverage (TCC). The former spouse's entitlement depends upon whether he or she meets the eligibility requirements of federal law and whether he or she follows the proper procedures to elect coverage.

OPM cannot honor a court order requiring it to provide FEHB coverage to a former spouse even if such an order is authorized by state law. Because such an order is preempted by federal law, 5 U.S.C. § 8902(m)(1), the former spouse can obtain coverage only by following the procedures mandated by the statutes and regulations discussed below.

The former spouse's FEHB coverage ends 31 days after divorce, giving the former spouse time to submit an application for TCC, discussed below.

PRACTICE TIP

Have your COAP entered at the same time as the divorce to ensure your client's insurance coverage can continue. The former spouse's FEHB coverage ends 31 days after divorce, and the Spouse Equity Coverage is tied to the COAP.

4. *Voluntary Retirement*, Off. of Personnel Mgmt., https://www.opm.gov/retirement-services/fers-information/types-of-retirement/#url=Voluntary-Retirement (last visited Nov. 17, 2020).

11.3 Spouse Equity Coverage

Spouse Equity Coverage is the coverage available to a former spouse that permits him or her to have continued group health insurance coverage through the federal government. To be eligible for Spouse Equity Coverage, he or she must qualify as a former spouse for FEHB purposes under 5 U.S.C. § 8901(10), which defines "former spouse" as a person

> (A) who has not remarried before age 55 after the marriage to the employee, former employee, or annuitant was dissolved,
>
> (B) who was enrolled in an approved health benefits plan under this chapter as a family member at any time during the 18-month period before the date of the dissolution of the marriage to the employee, former employee, or annuitant, and
>
> (C) (i) who is receiving any portion of an annuity under section 8345(j) or 8467 of this title or a survivor annuity under section 8341(h) or 8445 of this title (or benefits similar to either of the aforementioned annuity benefits under a retirement system for Government employees other than the Civil Service Retirement System or the Federal Employees' Retirement System),
> (ii) as to whom a court order or a decree referred to in section 8341(h), 8345(j), 8445 or 8467 of this title (or similar provision of law under any such retirement system other than the Civil Service Retirement System or the Federal Employees' Retirement System) has been issued, or for whom an election has been made under section 8339(j)(3) or 8417(b) of this title (or similar provision of law), or
> (iii) who is otherwise entitled to an annuity or any portion of an annuity as a former spouse under a retirement system for Government employees, except that such term shall not include any such non-remarried former spouse of a former employee whose marriage was dissolved after the former employee's separation from the service (other than by retirement)[.]

There are two key requirements for a former spouse to be eligible for FEHB coverage after divorce:

- The former spouse must have been covered under the employee's FEHB plan as a family member at some point during the 18 months prior to divorce. Therefore, when the spouse is not currently covered and parties want to negotiate to make coverage available to him or her after divorce, the employee will need to add the spouse to his or her plan during the next Open Season and prior to divorce.
- The former spouse must get a COAP entitling him or her to at least one dollar per month of the employee's retirement annuity, the survivor annuity, or both.

PRACTICE TIP

A COAP granting the former spouse a portion of the retiree's annuity qualifies him or her for continued FEHB coverage until the employee dies. A COAP providing both a portion of the retirement annuity and a survivor annuity provides continued FEHB coverage until the former spouse dies. The COAP need only provide for the spouse to receive $1.00 per month to be eligible for FEHB coverage. 5 U.S.C. § 8905.

The former spouse may request self-only, self plus one, or self and family enrollment. However, the former spouse cannot cover a subsequent spouse or child unrelated to the employee.[5] The former spouse can choose a coverage option different from that of the employee.

Time limitations for the former spouse to apply for Spouse Equity Coverage are prescribed by 5 U.S.C. § 8905(c):

- 60 days after the marriage ends; or
- 60 days after the date of OPM (CIA or Foreign Service) notice of his or her eligibility to enroll based on a qualifying court order awarding entitlement to a portion of the employee's annuity or to a former spouse survivor annuity.

PRACTICE TIP

The lawyer for the former spouse should advise the client of the time limitations to apply for Spouse Equity Coverage and that the former spouse will have to bear the full cost of the coverage.

If the former spouse does not apply to the employing office in person, the employing office will use the postmark date on the application to determine if he or she has applied timely.

The former spouse must pay the full monthly premium for the cost of his or her coverage directly to the HR department of the employing agency until the retirement of the federal employee. After retirement, OPM will draw the premium from the annuity, unless the annuity is insufficient to cover the premium, in which case the former spouse must directly pay the cost to OPM.

PRACTICE TIP

It is a good practice for the employee to determine, prior to the divorce, the name of the contact person at his or her agency who will receive the application and payment of Spouse Equity Coverage premiums and his or her contact information, so there is no lag in getting coverage in place. The former spouse should also get this information.

5. 5 U.S.C. § 8905(c)(2). Any child covered by the former spouse's continuation of FEHB coverage must be a natural or adopted child of the employee.

These are the key steps for the spouse's lawyer to secure his or her Spouse Equity Coverage:

1. Draft the appropriate pension COAP prior to entry of the judgment of divorce (preferably when the separation agreement is prepared). Have both parties and/or counsel sign it.
2. Determine the person who handles the processing of Spouse Equity Coverage at the employing agency.
3. Have the spouse fill out Form SP 2809.
4. Have the COAP entered at the time of entry of the judgment of divorce.
5. If the employee is retired and receiving retirement benefits, submit the judgment of divorce and COAP to OPM as soon as possible, including a cover letter (a sample cover letter is provided in the downloadable resources with this book, available at https://ambar.org/RepFed).
6. If the employee is still employed, submit the cover letter and COAP to the employing agency, along with the completed SP 2809 form, as soon as possible and within 60 days of entry of the judgment of divorce.

The former spouse should complete the above steps personally, or through counsel, in the specified timeframes rather than relying on the employee to do it. If the employee submits the enrollment and there is any issue with it, the former spouse will not receive notification, and the time will begin to run; therefore, only the spouse who is enrolling should submit the documentation.

If OPM determines that the former spouse is eligible for health benefits coverage, the employing office will write to him or her confirming its decision, send a premium payment schedule, and provide a certification form to sign and date stating the requirements for continued enrollment. The certification is along the lines of the following:[6]

I understand that I must notify the office maintaining my enrollment within 31 days after the occurrence of any of the following events that would end my eligibility for enrollment in the Federal Employees Health Benefits Program:

(1) The court order ceases to provide my entitlement to a portion of a retirement annuity or a former spouse survivor annuity under a retirement system for government employees.

(2) I remarry before age 55.

(3) The employee on whose service my benefits are based dies and no former spouse survivor annuity is payable.

(4) The separated employee on whose service my benefits are based dies before meeting the requirements for a deferred annuity.

(5) The employee on whose service my benefits are based leaves federal service before establishing title to an immediate annuity or a deferred annuity.

(6) The retirement system pays a refund of retirement contributions to the separated employee on whose service my health benefits are based.

Signature Date

6. *Healthcare Reference Materials: Former Spouses*, Off. of Personnel Mgmt., https://www.opm.gov/healthcare-insurance/healthcare/reference-materials/reference/former-spouses/ (last visited Nov. 17, 2020).

If the former spouse has no present need for health insurance, he or she can defer Spouse Equity Coverage until it is needed. The coverage cannot be turned on and off like a light switch. It can be deferred and started only one time. However, it can be deferred indefinitely.

PRACTICE TIP

The lawyer for the former spouse should advise the client to investigate other options available that may better suit the client's needs or may be cheaper than the continuation of FEHB. For example, the former spouse may obtain coverage under the Affordable Care Act. Alternatively, a client nearing age 65 may qualify for Medicare. The cost of Medicare is determined based on the recipient's income after attaining age 65. The cost for Medicare may be lower than that for FEHB coverage.

As long as the former spouse pays the premiums on time, and remains entitled to a portion of the employee annuity or survivor annuity, Spouse Equity Coverage can be maintained indefinitely.

11.4 Temporary Continuation of Coverage (TCC)

Temporary Continuation of Coverage (TCC) is short-term FEHB coverage that allows a former employee, child, spouse, or former spouse to continue coverage on a temporary basis. TCC is comparable to COBRA coverage.

Where to Find the Law

5 U.S.C. § 8905a provides for TCC under the FEHB program.

A divorcing spouse may want TCC coverage. In order to be eligible for TCC, he or she must have been covered as a family member under the employee's FEHB plan at some time during the 18 months before the marriage ended. Therefore, if the spouse is not covered, parties who agree on affording him or her access to TCC coverage should plan to have the employee add him or her during Open Season. TCC coverage is only available to a former spouse who does not qualify for coverage under the Spouse Equity provisions of the FEHB program because he or she

- remarried before reaching age 55;[7] or
- is not entitled to a portion of the employee's retirement annuity benefits or to a survivor annuity.

7. 5 C.F.R. § 890.807.

As to the latter requirement, the spouse's eligibility for TCC based on the lack of entitlement to a portion of the retirement annuity includes during a period of time before a COAP has been entered or processed. Thus, upon divorce, the former spouse can receive TCC coverage while waiting for the COAP to be approved that will give him or her access to FEHB Spouse Equity Coverage.

A former spouse may receive TCC coverage for up to 36 months or until the former spouse is covered by other health insurance, whichever occurs first. The cost to the former spouse is the full premium (without any government subsidy), plus a 2 percent administrative charge. Premium payments must be made to the employing agency, generally on a monthly basis.

Coverage for a former spouse under the Spouse Equity provisions may be delayed while the retirement system determines whether a court order for division of a federal pension is qualified to be accepted as a COAP. Coverage under the Spouse Equity provisions does not begin until the pay period after the employing office receives the determination that the court order is qualifying (although the former spouse may request retroactive enrollment). The former spouse may be eligible for TCC while waiting for coverage under the Spouse Equity provisions to begin (but not beyond 36 months after the divorce or annulment).[8] To avoid a break in insurance coverage, the former spouse may want to enroll in TCC, pending a decision on eligibility for Spouse Equity Coverage.

According to the OPM FEHB Handbook, a former spouse must submit his or her TCC election to the federal employee's employing office by the later of

- 60 days after the date of divorce or annulment, if you or your former spouse did not notify your employing office within the required 60-day notification period (even if someone else provided notification); or
- 65 days after the date of your employing office's notice, if you or your former spouse notified your employing office within the required 60-day notification period; or
- 60 days after the date he or she lost coverage under Spouse Equity provisions (because of remarriage before age 55 or loss of the qualifying court order), if the loss of coverage is within the 36-month period of TCC eligibility.

If the employee or former spouse does not notify the employee's employing office within the 60-day period, the former spouse's opportunity to elect TCC ends 60 days after the divorce or annulment.[9] To make a TCC election, the former spouse should submit a Health Benefits Election Form (SF 2809) to the employing agency that is servicing the account.

A former spouse who enrolls in TCC may enroll for family coverage that includes the children of the employee (including children the employee has adopted). However, the federal government does not subsidize the premiums for the children when they are covered under the former spouse's plan. Therefore, it will generally be more economical

8. *Healthcare Reference Materials: Termination, Conversion, and Temporary Continuation of Coverage*, Off. of Personnel Mgmt., https://www.opm.gov/healthcare-insurance/healthcare/reference-materials/reference/termination-conversion-and-temporary-continuation-of-coverage/ (last visited Nov. 17, 2020).

9. *Id.*

for the children to stay on the employee's plan. The former spouse may not cover other children or a new spouse under his or her plan.

In the event that a former spouse enrolls in Spouse Equity Coverage and loses that eligibility, he or she may enroll for TCC coverage for up to 36 months. This could occur if he or she remarries before age 55.

11.5 Continuation of Health Insurance for a Child of the Marriage

A child may also be entitled to TCC. For a child, the qualifying events are

- reaching age 26;
- loss of status as stepchild, foster child, or recognized natural child;
- in the case of a child whose coverage has continued beyond age 26 because of his or her inability to support him- or herself due to a disability occurring before he or she reached age 26, recovering from the disability or becoming self-supporting;
- death of the employee or annuitant if the child does not qualify for a survivor annuity; and
- survivor annuity stopping for any reason, including because he or she is no longer a full-time student.

A court order may instruct the employee to provide health benefits coverage for the employee's child.[10] If the employee is subject to such an order, the employee cannot change the employee's coverage from family to a self-only plan. The employee must enroll in a family plan that provides full benefits for the child in the area where he or she lives. This applies to the employee as long as the court order is in effect.

10. Life Events and Your Retirement and Insurance Benefits (for Annuitants), Civil Service Retirement System (CSRS), Federal Employees Retirement System (FERS), RI 38-126 (rev. Sept. 2012).

Chapter Twelve

Federal Employees' Group Life Insurance (FEGLI)

Chapter 12 will review the Federal Employees' Group Life Insurance (FEGLI), the group term life insurance program available to federal employees and retirees. It will also discuss how to assign benefits at divorce.

12.1 The FEGLI Program

FEGLI is the group term life insurance program for federal employees and retirees. It has no cash value, and no loans can be taken out against it. The Office of Personnel Management (OPM) currently has a contract with Metropolitan Life Insurance Company (MetLife) to provide this insurance. The Office of Federal Employees' Group Life Insurance (OFEGLI) administers the program.

Where to Find the Law

8 U.S.C. § 1612 created FEGLI. Regulations governing FEGLI are in part 870, title 5, Code of Federal Regulations.

Federal employees are automatically enrolled in FEGLI Basic Insurance, effective on the first day of employment, unless they opt out. Both active and retired employees can maintain FEGLI coverage. The spouse or former spouse of a federal employee has no entitlement to buy separate FEGLI coverage on his or her own life; however, as discussed below, the employee can opt for coverage on the life of a spouse. Under the basic program, the employee pays two-thirds of the premium and the government pays one-third (however, the U.S. Postal Service pays 100 percent of the cost for its employees). Premiums are withheld from employee pay or annuity payments.

The death benefit (the Basic Insurance Amount, BIA) is the greater of

(1) the employee's annual rate of basic pay, rounded up to the next even $1,000, plus $2,000; or
(2) $10,000.

Premiums are not based on age and do not increase over time; however, employees under age 45 have extra coverage without paying an additional premium. Specifically, they receive double the death benefit otherwise applicable until age 36, decreasing at 10 percent per year until age 45, at which time the extra coverage ends.

The employee's two-thirds share of the premium as of December 31, 2019, is $15 biweekly for each $1,000 of BIA.

The employee may elect additional optional insurance coverage with an additional cost; the government does not share the premiums for these additional benefits:

(a) Option A—Standard: $10,000 benefit
(b) Option B—Additional: One, two, three, four, or five multiples of annual rate of basic pay, rounded up to the next even $1,000
(c) Option C—Family: Insures the lives of spouse and eligible dependent children in one, two, three, four, or five multiples of coverage. Each multiple is equal to $5,000 for a spouse and $2,500 per child. This option does not extend to former spouses.

PRACTICE TIP

OPM provides an online calculator to help employees calculate the premiums for the various coverage levels and options:

https://www.opm.gov/retirement-services/calculators/fegli-calculator/

FEGLI is an appealing option for many federal employees, because the premiums are low as compared to life insurance available in the private market. In addition, FEGLI does not require a medical examination, unless the employee has opted out and seeks to waive back in.

After age 65, or at retirement, if later, the retiree can continue some coverage at no cost. When the employee retires, he or she can continue FEGLI if he or she is entitled to an immediate pension annuity, has been insured for five years prior to retirement, is enrolled in FEGLI on the date of retirement, and has not converted to an individual policy. If the employee elects or is required to defer payment of the pension annuity, the employee's enrollment will terminate during the deferral period. The enrollment can be resumed once the employee goes into pay status with respect to the pension annuity.

When insurance is terminated, the participant has the option to continue coverage by converting it to a private policy and may, but is not required to, undergo a medical exam to potentially lower premiums.

Upon retirement, the amount of coverage is reduced according to a schedule dependent upon age.[1]

When the employee dies, OFEGLI pays benefits by order of precedence as set forth below:

1. If ownership of the life insurance was assigned by filing an *Assignment, Federal Employees' Group Life Insurance* (RI 76-10), OFEGLI will pay benefits:
   - First, to the beneficiary(ies) designated by the employee's assignee(s), if any;
   - Second, if there is no such beneficiary(ies), to the employee's assignee(s).
2. If there has been no assignment of ownership and there is a valid court order on file, OFEGLI will pay benefits in accordance with that court order.
3. If there has been no assignment of ownership and there is *no* valid court order on file, OFEGLI will pay benefits:[2]
   - First, to the beneficiary(ies) validly designated;
   - Second, if no such beneficiary(ies), to a widow or widower;
   - Third, if none of the above, to a child or children in equal shares, and the descendants of any deceased children;
   - Fourth, if none of the above, to parents in equal shares, or the entire amount to the surviving parent;
   - Fifth, if none of the above, to the court-appointed executor or administrator of the estate;
   - Sixth, if none of the above, to other next of kin entitled under the laws of the State where the decedent lived.

Option C benefits provide life insurance for the employee's spouse and eligible dependent children. When an employee elects Option C coverage, all of his or her eligible family members are automatically covered.

Accidental Death and Dismemberment (AD&D) coverage is an automatic part of Basic Insurance and Option A insurance (if elected) for employees. It is free. Accidental death benefits are payable when an employee sustains an injury by accidental means and, within one year afterward, dies as a direct result of that injury. Under Basic Insurance, accidental death benefits are equal to the BIA. Similarly, accidental dismemberment benefits are payable when the employee sustains an injury by accidental means and, within one year afterward, loses a limb or sight in one or both eyes as a direct result of that injury. AD&D insurance coverage stops at retirement.

1. Federal Employees' Group Life Insurance (FEGLI) Program Handbook, Off. of Personnel Mgmt. (Apr. 2014), https://www.opm.gov/healthcare-insurance/life-insurance/reference-materials/handbook.pdf.
2. 5 U.S.C. § 8705.

12.2 Beneficiary Designations

When the employee or retiree dies, the death benefit will be paid in accordance with the employee's beneficiary designation or, if none, in the statutory order of precedence, as described above. It is the employee's responsibility to ensure that his or her designation of beneficiary remains accurate. Benefits will be paid based on a valid designation, regardless of whether that designation still reflects his or her intentions. It is important that the employee or retiree update the designation upon the occurrence of a major life event, such as divorce. A divorce does not invalidate a designation that names an employee's former spouse as beneficiary, nor do state laws invalidate a designation. An employee must complete a new SF 2823 to remove a former spouse.

The employee or retiree can change the FEGLI designation of beneficiary at any time (unless assigned or subject to court order as discussed below).[3] This is true even when a court order or judgment of divorce directs the employee or retiree to name the former spouse as beneficiary unless the court order complies with the requirements of the FEGLI statute, discussed below. The FEGLI law preempts any such noncompliant state court orders; it mandates that benefits be paid in accordance with the statutory order of precedence.[4] Cases have gone both ways on whether federal law preempts a state law remedy, such as a constructive trust to recover benefits after they are paid out and are in the hands of a now-former spouse who waived these benefits in a settlement.[5] The safest course of action is for the employee to file the new designation.

PRACTICE TIP

The lawyer should advise the client to review all beneficiary designations, including life insurance designations, and submit new ones upon divorce.

12.3 FEGLI and Divorce

There are two ways that a federal employee's FEGLI benefits may be made available to a former spouse or child: (1) an irrevocable assignment of ownership; (2) a court order that complies with the statute and mandates a specified beneficiary or incorporates a settlement agreement providing for a beneficiary designation.

---

3. OPM PUBL'N: COURT ORDER HANDBOOK (1997); FEGLI PROGRAM HANDBOOK, *supra* note 1.
4. See *McCord v. Spradling*, 830 So. 2d 1188 (Miss. 2002), and cases cited therein.
5. Sedarous v. Sedarous, 285 N.J. Super. 316 (App. Div. 1995); Kidd v. Pritzel, 821 S.W.2d 566 (Mo. App. 1991); Roberts v. Roberts, 560 S.W.2d 438 (Tex. Ct. Civ. App. 1977); Metropolitan Life Ins. Co. v. Christ, 979 F.2d 575 (7th Cir. 1992); Dean v. Johnson, 881 F.2d 948 (10th Cir. 1989); Metropolitan Life Ins. Co. v. Thompson, 968 F. Supp. 312 (S.D. Miss. 1997); Metropolitan Life Ins. Co. v. Potter, 533 So. 2d 589 (1988).

12.3.1 Irrevocable Assignment of Life Insurance

A federal employee or retiree may irrevocably assign his or her FEGLI coverage to another person by assignment.[6] Such an assignment could be made to a former spouse, current spouse, child, or even a trust or other third party or entity. The assignment must specify the percentage or fraction of the insurance to go to each assignee. Contingent assignees are not allowed. The premium payments will continue to be deducted from the employee's pay or the retiree's annuity.

The employee or retiree may only assign Basic Insurance and Option A and Option B insurance. Dismemberment insurance, the additional death benefit payable with respect to a decedent who is under the age of 45, and Option C are not assignable. The employee or retiree cannot make an assignment of only a portion of a policy or assign only one type of insurance. When an assignment is made, all of the parts owned are assigned.

An assignment is a total change in ownership and, as such, terminates the right of the employee or annuitant to change the beneficiary and cancels prior designations. The insured cannot change his or her mind. Once the assignment is made, the statutory order of precedence mandates payment to the beneficiary designated by the assignee.

Parties negotiating a divorce settlement may wish to agree on the assignment of FEGLI rights to a former spouse or a child and may include terms to that effect in their settlement agreement. However, the settlement agreement is insufficient. It is only effective if the insured files the appropriate assignment form. OPM cannot enforce a court order directing an assignment of FEGLI coverage or incorporating a settlement agreement mandating an assignment. The law merely allows the employee to make an assignment of FEGLI coverage voluntarily. It is the responsibility of the assignee to take steps to enforce the agreement, including through contempt or other state law remedies.

Once the assignment becomes effective, only the assignee has the right to designate a beneficiary. When the insured dies, benefits are paid to the assignee's beneficiary. If the assignee does not designate a beneficiary, benefits are paid to the assignee. If the assignee predeceases the insured, the policy passes to the assignee's heir, who becomes the owner of the policy.

After the assignment, the *assignee* has the right to

- cancel or reduce insurance;
- change the Basic post-65 reduction election to a 75 percent Reduction;
- change the Option B post-65 reduction election from No Reduction to Full Reduction;
- designate and change beneficiaries;
- convert to a private policy when FEGLI terminates; and
- reassign the insurance.[7]

After assignment, the insured still has the right to

- elect a post-65 reduction for Basic, Option B, and Option C at the time of retirement;
- elect more insurance, if an active employee, in which case all of the additional insurance, except Option C, will come under the existing assignment; and
- continue Option C coverage.

---

6. 5 U.S.C. § 8706(e): Termination of Insurance; Assignment of Ownership Insurance; Assignment of Ownership. Under regulations prescribed by the Office, each policy purchased under this chapter shall provide that an insured employee or former employee may make an irrevocable assignment of the employee's or former employee's incidents of ownership in the policy.

7. FEGLI Program Handbook, *supra* note 1.

Agency Contact Information

An annuitant can get the form to assign his or her FEGLI insurance from and submit it to

OPM Retirement Operations Center
PO Box 45
Boyers, PA 16017-0045

12.3.2 Court Order to Maintain FEGLI Life Insurance

Courts in some jurisdictions have authority to order that a divorcing spouse maintain life insurance for the benefit of a former spouse or a child.[8] Even in jurisdictions where courts have no such authority, it is common for parties to a settlement to agree that a spouse will maintain life insurance coverage for a financially dependent spouse or a child after divorce and to specify who will be the beneficiary. Such an agreement may be incorporated in the judgment of divorce.

This option does not result in a change of ownership of the policy; it merely specifies that the employee will maintain coverage and determine who will be the beneficiary. The employee or retiree would retain the right to name a different beneficiary if the former spouse-beneficiary died.

If an employee previously waived participation in FEGLI, he or she may cancel the waiver upon the occurrence of a Life Event, such as a divorce, in order to comport with a court order. Qualifying life events are marriage, divorce, death of a spouse, or acquiring an eligible child. The election must be filed with the employing office (Life Insurance Election Form SF 2817), along with proof of the event, within 31 to 60 days of the event. A divorcing couple negotiating a settlement where the federal employee previously waived FEGLI coverage may wish to seek reinstatement as one of the terms of settlement.

OFEGLI will honor a court order mandating that a federal employee designate a spouse or child as the beneficiary or incorporating a settlement agreement that provides for the former spouse to be the beneficiary, even if the insured did not execute an appropriate designation form, but only if a certified copy of the order is served on the employing *agency* before the death of the insured individual or, if the insured is a retiree, on OPM.[9] Anyone can submit the court order, including the ex-spouse or attorney. Annuitants must send the court order to OPM at Retirement Operations Center, Retirement and Correspondence Branch, P.O. Box 45, Boyers, PA 16017-0045.

The court order supersedes any prior designations. If the agency does not receive a certified copy of the court order, it will pay out according to the order of precedence.

---

8. *See* McBean v. McBean, 371 S.W.2d 930 (Tex. App. 1963) (court can order a spouse to maintain and make payments on life insurance policy for former spouse); Cal. Fam. Code § 4360 (court can order spouse to maintain life insurance to secure support to ex-spouse); Davis v. Davis, 184 N.J. Super. 430, 440 (App. Div. 1982) (court can order spouse to maintain life insurance to secure child support or alimony payments); Lee v. Lee, 18 A.D.3d 508, 512 (N.Y. App. Div. 2005) (court can order spouse to maintain life insurance as part of support obligation for former spouse or child or as guarantee for support payments); S.C. Code Ann. § 20-3-130 (court can order spouse to secure alimony or child support with life insurance policy); S.C. Code Ann. § 20-3-160; Wooten v. Wooten, 364 S.C. 532 (2005) (court may order life insurance after evaluating facts and determining that "special circumstances" warrant order for life insurance).

9. FEGLI Program Handbook, *supra* note 1.

Chapter Thirteen

Workers' Compensation Benefits for Federal Government Employees

13.1 Overview

Workers' compensation benefits are available to the federal government employee or to the employee's family if the employee is injured or killed on the job. In the case of injury, workers' compensation benefits can be paid in the form of periodic monthly payments (referred to as a scheduled award), a lump sum, or both.

Workers' compensation may be paid to the employee in the form of a scheduled award for a permanent impairment to certain members or functions of the body. It is possible for an employee to qualify for both workers' compensation benefits and disability retirement benefits. Generally, workers' compensation benefits and federal retirement benefits are not payable at the same time; therefore, the employee, or the employee's survivors, must choose between the two benefits.[1] Benefits available under workers' compensation are generally greater, so most employees choose it over disability retirement.

If the employee dies, the employee's surviving spouse and dependents may qualify for monthly workers' compensation benefits. However, the employee's surviving spouse must be living with, or dependent for support on, the employee at the time of the employee's death or must have been living apart from the employee for reasonable cause or because of the employee's desertion.

1. OPM Publ'n: Work Related Injuries and Fatalities, What You and Your Family Need to Know about Your Benefits, RI 84-2 (rev. Dec. 2008).

13.2 Workers' Compensation Death Benefits

The employee's surviving spouse and dependent children qualify for compensation death benefits from the Department of Labor if the employee dies because of a job-related injury or disease. Although they may also be eligible for survivor annuity benefits from CSRS, the two benefits are not payable at the same time. The employee's survivor must elect which of the two benefits he or she wishes to receive. Most survivors will choose workers' compensation benefits instead of a survivor annuity because workers' compensation usually pays a higher amount. If the survivor elects workers' compensation benefits, he or she may also elect to receive a lump-sum refund of the employee's contributions to the pension plan.

13.3 Death Gratuity Payment

A survivor of a federal employee who dies from a line-of-duty injury may be eligible for one or more of the following payments:[2]

(1) up to $800 payable by the Department of Labor to a surviving spouse or children for funeral expenses;
(2) $200 payable by the Department of Labor for reimbursement of the costs of termination of the deceased employee's status as a federal employee; and
(3) any amount paid under 5 U.S.C. § 8134 to the representative of any employee of any department or agency with appropriations from a Department of the Interior and Related Agencies Appropriations Act who is killed in the line of duty.

A discretionary payment may be made to the personal representative of a federal employee who dies from an injury sustained in the line of duty up to $10,000. The gratuity, when combined with the above payments, may not exceed $10,000.

13.4 Public Safety Officer Benefits

The Public Safety Officers' Benefits Act of 1976 authorizes payment of a benefit to survivors of public safety officers who died as the "direct and proximate result of a personal injury, traumatic injury involving external force sustained in the line of duty, and to claimant public safety officers found to have been permanently and totally disabled as the direct result of a catastrophic injury sustained in the line of duty."[3] The death benefit is payable in a lump sum to the spouse and eligible children of the deceased public safety officer. One-half of the benefit is payable to the spouse and one-half, in equal amounts, to the eligible children.

The death benefit is payable to a qualified survivor of a federal employee in addition to death benefits payable to the survivor resulting from FERS, CSRS, or workers' compensation benefits.

A public safety officer who is permanently and totally disabled as the direct result of a catastrophic injury sustained in the line of duty is entitled to the payment in the same amount as would be paid to survivors if he or she is permanently unable to perform any gainful employment.

---

2. Omnibus Consolidated Appropriations Act, Pub. L. No. 104-208, § 651 (1997).
3. 42 U.S.C. § 3796 *et seq.*

13.5 Workers' Compensation and Divorce

Compensation benefits are not payable to a former spouse.[4] Workers' compensation benefits are not divisible in divorce as property. However, in most jurisdictions, workers' compensation benefits can be treated as income for purposes of calculating child support or spousal support and can also be garnished for nonpayment of child support.

The lawyer for the spouse should include a provision in a marital settlement agreement and in the COAP that the employee cannot elect to receive a refund of employee contributions to his or her pension.[5] If the employee receives workers' compensation in lieu of a disability annuity, the spouse may still receive a survivor annuity, but only if the employee does not take a refund of contributions. Similarly, if the workers' compensation benefit decreases or ends, and if the employee has not taken a refund of contributions, the employee will be able to receive an annuity if the employee is otherwise entitled and that the spouse will share, if provided in a COAP.[6] For sample language, see Section 2.8.

4. See subchapter I of chapter 81 of title 5, United States Code.
5. 5 C.F.R. § 844.105.
6. *Id.*

Chapter Fourteen

Other Federal Employee Benefits

Chapter 14 gives an overview of the various other employee benefits available, some of which extend to the spouse and children and some of which do not. Some of these benefits can be used to factor into income for purposes of determining spousal or child support or may reduce the marital or child expenses. Visiting the agency's employee careers or benefits page may yield important information about these benefits.

14.1 Overview of Healthcare and Dependent Care Accounts

The federal government offers several types of Flexible Spending Accounts (FSAs) under its *Federal Flexible Spending Account Program (FSAFEDS)*. These programs are available only for active employees, not retirees. An FSA is an account that the employee can use to pay qualifying expenses, using pretax dollars, for the employee, the employee's spouse, qualifying children, and qualifying relatives. FSA funds are deducted from the employee's pay on a per-paycheck basis and deposited to the account for later use. Check the employee's pay statement for deductions.

PRACTICE TIP

Parties negotiating a settlement may wish to lay out how they will use an FSA to pay for certain expenses for the minor children.

14.1.1 Healthcare FSA

The Healthcare FSA (HCFSA) is a pretax account that the employee can use for qualified medical, dental, and vision expenses that are not covered by insurance. Funds are deposited to the HCFSA directly from each paycheck in pretax dollars. An employee can contribute up to a maximum of $2,750 per calendar year (as of 2020); however, he or she can use the full amount elected for the calendar year on the first day of the year. The contributed funds must be used in the year of contribution, except that the employee can roll over up to $500 per year to the following year.[1] All other unused funds are forfeited.

The employee can use his or her HCFSA to pay for qualified out-of-pocket healthcare expenses, such as[2]

- eligible medical, dental, and vision care expenses;
- professional services: physical therapy, chiropractic, and acupuncture;
- copays, coinsurance, and deductibles;
- prescription drugs, insulin, and prescribed over-the-counter medicine; and
- certain over-the-counter healthcare items.

The funds can also be used by the employee to reimburse him- or herself for these expenditures and, if the employee is enrolled in certain Federal Employees Health Benefits (FEHB) or Federal Employees Dental and Vision Insurance Program (FEDVIP) plans, can have the reimbursement processed automatically. The Office of Personnel Management (OPM) provides a list of the participating plans on the FSAFEDS website.[3]

Divorcing parties can agree to transfer funds from a participant's HCFSA to the spouse's Health Savings Account and still maintain the pretax nature of the funds. Similarly, the parties could agree to a payment scheme for the children's unreimbursed medical expenses that involves the use of HCFSA funds first prior to either party spending post-tax dollars.

14.1.2 HCFSAs in Divorce

Existing funds in an HCFSA may constitute an asset in a divorce and may be part of the marital estate under applicable state law. As such, the spouse's lawyer should look for an HCFSA on a federal employee's financial disclosures. If parties agree to or the court orders an award of HCFSA funds to the spouse of the participant, the spouse will have to

1. *Health Care FSA*, FSAFEDS, www.fsafeds.com/explore/hcfsa (last visited Nov. 18, 2020). FSAFEDS is sponsored by OPM.

2. *Id.*

3. *Reimbursement and Payments*, FSAFEDS, https://www.fsafeds.com/support/reimbursementsandpayments.

open his or her own HCFSA into which the participant will make the required transfer or rollover. The spouse will receive the funds tax-free if he or she follows applicable rules for transfer or rollover under the Internal Revenue Code and the terms of the plans.

The federal employee may continue to participate in his or her HCFSA after divorce. Parties may agree or a court may order a parent to pay future eligible healthcare expenses of a child or may award the nonparticipant spouse the right to use HCFSA funds for these expenses. The particulars as to how a nonparticipant may access these funds depend on the specific terms of each agency's plan.

A child whose parents are divorced, separated, or living apart is typically considered to be a dependent of both parents. This means that either parent can claim a child's expenses under his or her own HCFSA, as long as both parents don't claim the same expense for the child.

14.1.3 Dependent Care FSA

The Dependent Care FSA (DCFSA) is a pretax account that the employee can use to pay for eligible dependent care services, such as preschool, summer day camp, before- or after-school programs, and child or adult daycare for a dependent adult, such as a disabled parent.

Eligible daycare expenses for a qualified child under 13 include the following:[4]

- Before- and after-school care
- Babysitting and nanny expenses
- Daycare, nursery school, and preschool
- Summer day camp

The employee may also use his or her DCFSA to care for a spouse or a relative who is physically or mentally incapable of self-care and lives in the employee's home.[5]

The employee can contribute up to a maximum of

- $2,500 per year if he or she is married and files a separate tax return, or
- $5,000 per year if he or she is married and files a joint tax return.

The contribution amount is set by statute and is not adjusted for inflation, as is the HCFSA.[6]

Unlike the HCFSA, the employee may use the funds in the DCFSA only as they become available after being deducted from pay and deposited in the account. The employee must use the funds for a given year by March 15 of the following year, or they are forfeited.

14.1.4 DCFSAs in Divorce

Existing funds in a DCFSA may constitute an asset in a divorce under applicable state law. The lawyer for the spouse will need to review the plan to see if it allows for a rollover to effect a division upon a change in the marital status of the parents.

The employee may continue to participate in his or her DCFSA after divorce. An agreement may award use of DCFSA funds to the nonparticipant spouse to pay for eligible expenses for the children.

---

4. *Dependent Care FSA*, FSAFEDS, www.fsafeds.com/explore/dcfsa (last visited Nov. 18, 2020).
5. *Id.*
6. I.R.S. Publ'n 503, Cat. No. 15004M (Jan. 30, 2020).

PRACTICE TIP

In order for a parent who is a federal employee to pay an expense from his or her DCFSA, the child must have lived with the employee for at least half the year.

A child can benefit from only one DCFSA at a time. If both parents have such an account, including where one parent is a federal employee and the other is in the private sector, only the custodial parent with primary physical custody can use his or her account to pay these expenses.[7] If the parents have equal custody, only the parent with the higher adjusted gross income can use his or her DCFSA.[8]

14.2 Unused Annual Leave Payments and Unused Sick Leave

Federal employees are eligible for various types of leaves, including annual, sick, home, shore, funeral, emergency, and leave under the Family and Medical Leave Act (FMLA).[9] When a federal employee separates from service, he or she is entitled to a lump-sum payment for accumulated unused annual leave (i.e., vacation).[10] Unlike annual leave, unused sick leave days can be credited toward the days of employment used to calculate the retirement annuity, but the employee does not get a lump-sum payment for unused sick leave.[11] The lawyer representing a party should inquire about unused leave.

The rate of annual leave accrual is four hours per pay period for the first three years of federal service and six hours per pay period for years three to 15 of federal service, and if the employee serves more than 15 years, then the employee earns eight hours of leave per pay period.[12] Some exceptions to the accrual rates apply.

Parties may divorce at a point when a federal employee with unused annual leave accrued during the marriage is not close to retirement and has no plans to leave the job. The unused annual leave may be worth money in the future; however, the employee may elect to use the leave. Whether he or she will do so may be speculative. Similarly, such an employee may have unused sick leave accrued during the marriage that he or she may or may not use.

How a court in a contested proceeding may treat unused leave is a matter of state, not federal, law. Most state courts that have encountered the issue in a divorce proceeding

7. I.R.C. § 152(e)(4)(A).

8. Treas. Reg. § 1.152-4(d).

9. 5 C.F.R. § 630 *et seq.*

10. *See* 5 U.S.C. § 5551.

11. *Frequently Asked Questions: Retirement: Will I Get Paid for Unused Sick Leave in Retirement?*, Off. of Personnel Mgmt., https://www.opm.gov/faqs/QA.aspx?fid=735eda40-61a8-45df-b6ad-47185f4c91a5&pid=ffd788aa-037f-49fb-840d-2997aa4856d6 (last visited Nov. 18, 2020).

12. *Pay & Leave: Fact Sheet: Annual Leave (General Information)*, Off. of Personnel Mgmt., https://www.opm.gov/policy-data-oversight/pay-leave/leave-administration/fact-sheets/annual-leave/ (last visited Nov. 18, 2020).

have treated the lump-sum payment of accrued annual leave as marital property to be divided between spouses upon divorce.[13] Courts in a few states have not treated accrued annual or sick leave as marital property.[14]

14.3 Long-Term Care Insurance for a Former Spouse

Employees and retirees are eligible to participate in the Federal Long-Term Care Insurance Program (FLTCIP), sponsored by OPM, and such coverage is provided by John Hancock Life Insurance Company as of December 2019. Employees are able to take the coverage with them if they leave federal employment, so long as they keep paying the premiums. A current spouse and other family members may also participate.

There are various packages available at varying costs and levels of coverage. Coverage includes costs of nursing-home care, assisted living and hospice expenses, home care and adult daycare, services of a caregiver, respite services, and similar expenses.

If an employee is enrolled at the time he or she separates from employment with the federal government, the coverage will continue so long as the employee continues to make timely premium payments. The former employee can have payments deducted from the retirement annuity, or if the former employee has deferred the annuity, he or she must make the premium payments directly. If the employee is not enrolled at the time of separation from employment with the federal government, he or she may apply for enrollment at any time thereafter.

An employee and eligible family members, i.e., a qualified relative of an employee or retiree, including a spouse,[15] may apply for long-term care coverage at any time; they do not have to wait for Open Season. When a couple is divorcing, it may often make sense for the spouse of the employee to apply for coverage before divorce, if he or she is not yet enrolled and is interested.

A former spouse is not entitled to apply for FLTCIP coverage because he or she is not a qualified relative. However, if he or she was enrolled in FLTCIP coverage prior to the divorce, he or she may continue the coverage as long as the premiums are timely paid. Premium rates do not change after divorce.

---

13. Schober v. Schober, 692 P.2d 267 (Alaska 1984) (400 hours of unused leave that husband earned during marriage was marital asset; value should be considered when dividing parties' property); Arnold v. Arnold, 134 N.M. 381 (Ct. App. 2003) (husband's accrued sick and vacation leave is community property subject to division upon divorce); Wiech v. Wiech, 23 Neb. App. 370 (2015) (husband's unused sick leave is marital property, the value of which is subject to division at divorce, and wife gets equitable share of value); *In re* Marriage of Cardona, 316 P.3d 626 (2014) (accrued leave is marital property only when employee-spouse has enforceable right to payout; if value can be reasonably estimated, it must be equitably divided; if value cannot be ascertained, it is a factor the court should consider); Dye v. Dye, 17 So. 3d 1278 (Fla. 2nd Dist. Ct. App. 2009) (cash value of husband's unused sick and vacation leave is marital asset subject to equitable distribution; where husband's employment contract specifies method for ascertaining value, contract's valuation should be used); Grund v. Grund, 573 N.Y.S.2d 840 (Sup. Ct. 1993); Nuss v. Nuss, 65 Wash. App. 334 (1992).

14. *In re* Marriage of Abrell, 236 Ill. 2d 249 (2010) (value of accrued sick leave can be speculative when employee has not separated; it is not marital property subject to division; however, if accrued sick leave has already been converted to cash prior to divorce, cash value is part of the marital estate subject to division); Akers v. Akers, 729 N.E.2d 1029 (Ind. Ct. App. 2000) (husband's accumulated sick leave is not marital property, since he does not have vested interest at the time of divorce).

15. 5 U.S.C. § 9001.

PRACTICE TIP

If you represent the spouse and he or she does not have long-term care coverage, advise him or her to investigate the cost of FLTCIP and determine whether to apply for it before the divorce.

14.4 Federal Employees Dental and Vision Insurance Program

The Federal Employee Dental and Vision Benefits Enhancement Act of 2004[16] allowed OPM to establish dental and vision insurance benefits through the Federal Employees Dental and Vision Insurance Program (FEDVIP). Dental and vision benefits are available to eligible federal and Postal Service employees, retirees, and their eligible family members on an enrollee-pay-all basis. This program allows employees to purchase dental insurance and vision insurance on a group basis; premiums are competitive, and there are no preexisting condition limitations. Premiums for enrolled federal and Postal Service employees are withheld from salary on a pretax basis. The employee must be eligible for the FEHB program in order to be eligible to enroll in FEDVIP but need not actually be enrolled in FEHB.[17]

A former spouse eligible for FEHB coverage is not entitled to continue FEDVIP coverage after divorce. Accordingly, OPM will not honor a court order that purports to award FEDVIP coverage to a former spouse. Participation is limited to annuitants, employees, dependents, and family members.[18] Parties may nevertheless negotiate for continued coverage for a child, and, to the extent state law permits, a court may order continued coverage for a child.

A surviving current spouse of a deceased retiree may enroll in FEDVIP if the surviving spouse is eligible for a survivor annuity. A former spouse of a retired employee is not eligible to enroll even if he or she is eligible for a survivor annuity.

14.5 Benefits for Federal Employees Stationed Overseas

As of December 31, 2019, there were nearly 90,000 federal employees stationed overseas in more than 140 countries.[19] An attorney must navigate numerous legal, logistical, financial, cultural, and practical challenges when advising a separating or divorcing federal employee, or a spouse or domestic partner, who is residing or working in a foreign nation.

Although the federal government considers divorce to be a private family matter, each federal agency has made efforts through its employee assistance program to assist

---

16. 5 U.S.C. § 8952 (dental); 5 U.S.C. § 8982 (vision); 5 C.F.R. part 894: Federal Employees Dental and Vision Insurance Program.

17. *Dental & Vision*, Off. of Personnel Mgmt., https://www.opm.gov/healthcare-insurance/dental-vision/ (last visited Nov. 18, 2020).

18. *See* 5 U.S.C.A. § 8951.

19. *See Federal Overseas Jobs*, Fed. Gov't Jobs, www.federaljobs.net/overseas (last visited Nov. 18, 2020).

its employees and their families in transition. The employee and his or her spouse should seek out the various free and confidential services and resources provided, which often include counseling, legal consultations, and referrals.

More than 40 years ago, the Department of State recognized the challenges of its employees posted overseas and established the Family Liaison Office (FLO), which advocates for employees and families under Chief of Mission authority. FLO has grown to provide worldwide support and services not only for employees and family members from the Department of State but also for other agencies with personnel abroad, including the U.S. Agency for International Development, the Foreign Commercial Service, the Justice Department, and the Peace Corps. FLO developed a helpful guide entitled *Divorce and the Foreign Service,* which provides a comprehensive description of the rights and obligations of Foreign Service employees and their families, as well as a wonderful compendium of resources, checklists, and guidance.[20] Although FLO's advice is specific to Department of State employees, the handbook is helpful for employees of other federal agencies as well.

PRACTICE TIP

If your client is stationed overseas, advise him or her to make contact with the Family Liaison Office for additional help beyond what you may be able to provide. The Family Liaison Office can provide help with the following:

- Relocation
- Obtaining property
- Immigration issues
- Dispute resolution
- Domestic violence

One of the biggest issues facing overseas employees is physically separating and departing from the post. Although there are no Department of State regulations that require the post to provide separate housing for a spouse or domestic partner pending a marital separation or divorce, FLO advises that when a post has a vacancy in the housing pool, it may offer temporary housing to a spouse or partner who is still married and on the employee's travel orders. Temporary housing can be helpful when getting organized to leave post or when there are just a few months left in a school year and parents are trying to minimize disruption to their child's education. FLO recommends reaching out to the Family Advocacy Team at post, who can help play a role in advocating for such services.

In a situation where a spouse needs or wants to return to the United States prior to the end of the federal employee's tour of duty, the spouse can apply for advance travel at the government's expense and receive one-way transportation to the employee's service separation address or to any other location in the United States on a cost-constructive basis

20. *See Divorce and the Foreign Service*, Fam. Liaison Off., U.S. Dep't of State, https://www.state.gov/family-liaison-office/foreign-service-life/divorce-and-separation/divorce-and-the-foreign-service/ (last visited Nov. 18, 2020).

from the employee's post of origin to his or her separation address.[21] The U.S. Department of State's Foreign Affairs manual provides:

> Return travel of an employee's spouse or domestic partner as defined in 3 FAM 1610 may be authorized to the employee's service separation address in the United States (see definition of "United States" in 14 FAM 511.3) or any other location in the United States on a cost-constructive basis from the employee's post of origin to the employee's separation address when a permanent marital separation or divorce is intended, or a statement of dissolution of domestic partnership has been submitted. Generally, a separation agreement should exist, but in the absence of an agreement, the chief of mission or head of agency's establishment abroad may determine that such travel is warranted and may initiate authorization action. The circumstances upon which this determination is based should be summarized in writing and retained at post in accordance with 5 FAH-4, Records Management Handbook.[22]

A parent may apply for advance travel of a dependent child, but such travel will be authorized by the post only if the parties have a legal custody agreement in place or the employee agrees in writing to permit the child to leave post permanently with the spouse. In a circumstance where an employee has asked the spouse or partner to leave post but has refused to permit a child to leave post, the spouse may need to seek a court order authorizing the child to leave post.

An advance travel order will also provide for the shipment of personal belongings (referred to as HHE, household effects). The employee must request the shipment of HHE on behalf of his or her family members. For State Department employees, the request is sent from post to the Bureau of Human Resources Career Development and Assignments (HR/CDA); for employees of other agencies, the request is sent to the appropriate bureau of their agency. If the advance travel order includes the HHE addressed to the spouse or partner, this is typically sufficient for the HHE to be released to the spouse or partner. An extra layer of protection can be provided to the spouse or partner by the employee executing a notarized statement or authorization allowing him or her to receive HHE shipped from post. A Joint Property Statement is also helpful to identify items in storage that the spouse may retrieve. The parties may also be required by post leadership to execute various forms and/or agreements confirming their understanding about the rules and regulations regarding travel.

If the employee does not consent or refuses to cooperate by executing documents and authorizations, the spouse or partner may need to seek a court order authorizing the release of the property. FLO also has a Crisis Management and Support Officer dedicated to helping families navigate these types of situations.

FLO recommends that, regardless of whether the spouse is asked to leave post or decides to leave post, the spouse should not leave post until the parties have signed a simple statement indicating that their separation is by mutual consent and that the departing spouse is not abandoning or deserting his or her spouse or partner and/or family. Whether an employee or spouse/partner should sign such a statement, and the specific contents of the statement, depends upon a host of factors, including the law of the state where a party intends to file for divorce.

---

21. Cost-constructive basis involves the comparison of the following: (1) the cost to the U.S. government for travel or sending goods as prescribed in the travel authorization, and (2) the cost for the employee to travel or send goods in a way that is dictated by personal preference. If the second cost is more than the first, the employee pays the difference personally.

22. 14 Dep't of State, Foreign Affairs Manual § 532.8(a), *available at* https://fam.state.gov/FAM/14FAM/14FAM0530.html (last visited Nov. 18, 2020).

Each branch of the federal government, executive department, or individual agency may have issued specific notices or directives regarding the rights and obligations of its employees and the employees' families. For example, the State Department issued a cable notifying Foreign Service employees of responsibilities and resources when going through a separation or divorce, including a reminder of each employee's duty to cooperate and provide support for his or her family:

> The failure of an employee to arrange adequately for a spouse/domestic partner or children's transition from post can adversely affect the Department's ability to conduct business and can thus reflect adversely upon the employee as well as the U.S. government.
>
> . . .
>
> While dissolution of a relationship, itself, is a civil matter, the Chief of Mission and the Department have a legitimate concern for the safety and welfare of family members who accompany employees to post and for maintaining overall morale at post, as well as for protecting the integrity of Department operations.
>
> . . .
>
> If a family is unable to resolve its issues, the parties involved may decide that the spouse/domestic partner and family will leave post. In this case, employees have a responsibility to facilitate the return of the spouse or partner (and children, if any) to the United States or to another location the family may choose (as outlined in 14 FAM 532.8). Employees should reach an agreement with respect to disposition of household effects (HHE) before the spouse or partner departs. Employees should also reach an agreement with the spouse or same sex domestic partner to ensure adequate financial resources for the spouse or partner and family to establish themselves in the United States or other location.
>
> . . .
>
> If there are no arrangements in place prior to spouse/domestic partner/child departure from post to ensure that they have adequate financial resources and HHE to furnish a home—at least until they are financially stable and/or a final property agreement is made—employees in some circumstances, such as where employee behavior has an adverse impact on the operations of post, may be subject to curtailment from post in order to make such arrangements. . . .[23]

If a federal government employee does not know whom to contact for help at his or her agency, OPM maintains a database of each agency's work-life coordinator(s), and this list can be a helpful resource when seeking agency-specific contacts for benefits and services.[24]

Keep in mind there will be several issues that arise if the spouse is foreign-born and not a U.S. citizen. Department of State family members may be eligible for expeditious naturalization under section 319(b) of the Immigration and Nationality Act, which exempts certain spouses of U.S. government employees from the otherwise-applicable residence and physical presence requirements of naturalization. In such cases, FLO can typically help with expeditious naturalization.[25] Before contemplating a separation, the family law attorney should consult with an immigration attorney to be aware of how a separation will impact immigration issues for the entire family.

---

23. *Separation and Divorce: Responsibilities and Resources*, Dep't of State, 18 STATE 2234 (Jan. 9, 2018).

24. *See Work-Life Agency Coordinators*, Off. of Personnel Mgmt., https://www.opm.gov/CCLContact/ (last visited Nov. 18, 2020).

25. 8 U.S.C. § 1430.

PRACTICE TIP

In cases involving a foreign-born spouse, the client should contact an immigration lawyer and FLO before moving forward with a separation to learn about the immigration implications and options before it is too late.

14.6 Student Loan Repayment and Forgiveness

A party's debt may be relevant to the determination of alimony, child support, or division of property. As such, it makes sense to be aware if a party to a divorce is in the process of obtaining loan forgiveness or is receiving the benefit of loan repayment.

Some federal employees with student loans are entitled to agency contribution to the loan repayment. Each agency has discretionary authority to repay certain types of federally made, insured, or guaranteed student loans as a recruitment or retention incentive for highly qualified candidates or current employees.[26]

In order to receive loan repayment, the employee must sign a service agreement. The agreement will specify the amount of the loan to be repaid and the period of time the employee must remain working in order to receive the benefit, along with other terms. A service requirement must be set for a period of time not less than three years.[27] The service agreement may also specify any other employment conditions the agency considers to be appropriate, including the employee's (or job candidate's) position and the duties he or she is expected to perform, his or her work schedule, his or her level of performance, and the geographic location of his or her position.[28]

PRACTICE TIP

Request the Student Loan Repayment Service Agreement in discovery.

The agency makes student loan payments directly to the financial institution, not to the employee. For any one individual, an agency may agree to provide student loan repayment benefits of up to $10,000 per calendar year, subject to a cumulative maximum of $60,000 per employee. The amount of the loan paid by the government is taxable as income in the year the payment is made and will be reported as wages on the employee's income tax return. The employing agency will adjust the employee's tax withholding to take account of the tax liability on these payments.

26. 5 U.S.C. § 5379.
27. 5 U.S.C. § 5379(c)(1)(A).
28. *See* 5 C.F.R. §§ 537.108, 537.109.

Each agency must establish a plan that designates the official who is authorized to review and approve an offer of student loan repayment benefits.[29] The agency may use approval delegations similar to those used for other recruitment, relocation, and retention incentives.

An employee who is the borrower on a PLUS[30] loan for his or her child may qualify for repayment. However, if the employee's parent is the borrower on a PLUS loan for the benefit of the employee, the employee is not eligible for loan repayment benefits.

An employee who does not satisfy the terms of the service agreement is required to reimburse the government for all loan payments made on his or her behalf.[31] If an employee voluntarily separates from federal service before completing the period of service required in the applicable service agreement, or violates any other condition that specifically triggers a reimbursement requirement under the agreement, he or she will be obligated to reimburse the paying agency for the full amount of the loan repayment benefits provided (gross before any tax deductions from the loan payment). For example, if an employee's agreement states that he or she will receive $10,000 per year for three years, and the employee leaves with six months remaining on the service agreement after receiving $25,000 in loan repayment benefits, the employee must reimburse the paying agency the entire $25,000.[32]

Loan forgiveness can occur for federal employees under the Public Service Loan Forgiveness program under certain circumstances, generally as follows: the employee must work full time, have direct loans, have made 120 qualifying timely payments on his or her loans, and be making repayment under an income-driven repayment plan.[33] The forgiven amount is not subject to tax.

14.7 Miscellaneous Benefits

Various government agencies offer other benefits. The lawyer should visit the careers section of the agency website for more information. Such benefits include childcare. There are also various pretax commuter benefits and transit subsidies that include reimbursement of expenses or payment by the employee on a pretax basis of subway or bus fare, parking, and bicycle expenses (purchase of a bike, maintenance, repairs, and storage). Some agencies have free exercise facilities. Some of these nonmonetary benefits may factor into payor or payee income, financial need in a child-support or alimony scenario, or claimed expenses on an expense worksheet.

29. 5 C.F.R. § 537.103.

30. Federal loans that graduate or professional students and their parents can use to pay for higher education expenses.

31. *See* 5 U.S.C. § 5379(c)(3); 5 C.F.R. § 537.109(e).

32. *Pay & Leave: Student Loan Repayment*, Off. of Personnel Mgmt., https://www.opm.gov/policy-data-oversight/pay-leave/student-loan-repayment/#url=FAQs (last visited Nov. 18, 2020).

33. 34 C.F.R. § 685.219.

Part IV

Litigation Considerations

Chapter Fifteen

How to Determine Income of a Federal Employee

Federal government pay scales and their relevant locality pay increases are public information and published online.

15.1 U.S. Government Pay Scales

The Office of Personnel Management (OPM) sets the salary scale for most federal civilian positions on the General Schedule (GS Scale). Each individual agency determines the base Grade and Step on the GS Scale for each position. Other pay scales exist for positions that are not on the GS Scale. For example, Foreign Service officer positions are not on the GS Scale; the Department of State has a separate pay structure for Foreign Service officers.

The GS Scale is a table of Grades 1–15, and within each Grade, there are ten Steps. OPM reports that it takes approximately 18 years to progress from Step 1 to Step 10 within a single grade, with a maximum increase of one step per year; however, an employee can progress faster with outstanding performance reviews[1] or by changing positions to a higher Grade or Step. The GS Scale as of January 2018 is shown in Appendix A.

The GS Scale is the base salary for the federal civilian positions that it covers. Many areas of the United States are subject to locality pay that increases the GS Scale by a certain percentage. Currently, there are 46 geographic areas with locality pay. Locality pay is based on a comparison of the GS Scale and nonfederal pay within each area.[2] For 2018, locality pay rates were highest in the San Jose–San Francisco–Oakland, CA, locality with an increase of 39.28 percent. Any area outside of a delineated metropolitan region or the

1. *Pay Systems: General Schedule*, Off. of Personnel Mgmt., https://www.opm.gov/policy-data-oversight/pay-leave/pay-systems/general-schedule/ (last visited Nov. 18, 2020).

2. *Salaries & Wages: Locality Pay Areas*, Off. of Personnel Mgmt., https://www.opm.gov/policy-data-oversight/pay-leave/salaries-wages/fact-sheets/#url=Locality-Pay-Areas (last visited Nov. 18, 2020).

states of Alaska and Hawaii falls into the "Rest of the United States" category and receives a locality increase of 15.37 percent.[3]

Within the GS Scale, there are many subcategories of positions, which have different classifications and receive different compensation. OPM refers to these classifications as pay plan codes.[4]

In addition to regular GS Scale employees, there are GM employees, who are also covered by the Performance Management and Recognition System termination provisions; GL employees, law enforcement officers who receive special base rates at GS Grades 3–10; and GP and GR employees, who are physicians and dentists who receive market pay instead of locality pay. There are other pay plan codes that can be found on the OPM website, including senior and executive-level positions.

Higher levels of managerial, supervisory, and policy positions fall within the Senior Executive Service (SES), which consists of positions classified as over the GS-15 level. Employees in these positions can be political appointees or career employees who are promoted above the GS Scale. The salary is at minimum 120 percent of GS Grade 15, Step 1. The SES employee may also receive performance awards/bonuses for his or her regular review periods, as well as other cash awards for "special acts or services, suggestions, inventions, superior accomplishments or productivity gains not linked to a" performance review.[5]

Some federal agencies use different types of pay scales for positions that are not covered by the GS Scale. Foreign Service officers are paid on the FS Scale and can receive locality pay based on the region in the United States in which they are stationed. Foreign Service officers serving abroad can receive a multitude of forms of compensation in addition to their base salary as listed on the FS Scale, including the following:[6]

- Post (Hardship) Differential (compensation for serving where the conditions are substantially different than the conditions in the United States as a form of recruitment and retention incentive);
- Post (Cost-of-Living) Allowance;
- Living Quarters Allowance (to reimburse the employee for adequate living quarters at a location where the government does not provide housing, to include rent, utilities, taxes, and similar fees);[7]
- Education Allowance (to allow a child accompanying the Foreign Service officer to receive education comparable to a public education in the United States);[8]

---

3. *See 2018 GS Scale and Locality Pay Tables*, Off. of Personnel Mgmt., https://www.opm.gov/policy-data-oversight/pay-leave/salaries-wages/salary-tables/pdf/2018/GS.pdf (last visited Dec. 1, 2020).

4. *Pay Administration: Fact Sheet: Pay Plans*, Off. of Personnel Mgmt., https://www.opm.gov/policy-data-oversight/pay-leave/pay-administration/fact-sheets/pay-plans/ (last visited Nov. 18, 2020).

5. *Senior Executive Service, Compensation*, Off. of Personnel Mgmt., https://www.opm.gov/policy-data-oversight/senior-executive-service/compensation/ (last visited Nov. 18, 2020).

6. *Allowances for Transitions*, Dep't of State, https://www.state.gov/m/fsi/tc/31361.htm (last visited Nov. 18, 2020); *Post Hardship Differential*, Dep't of State, https://aoprals.state.gov/content.asp?content_id=377&menu_id=75 (last visited Nov. 18, 2020).

7. *Frequently Asked Questions: Living Quarters Allowance*, Dep't of State, https://aoprals.state.gov/content.asp?content_id=165&menu_id=75#01 (last visited Nov. 18, 2020).

8. *Allowances for Transitions*, Dep't of State, https://www.state.gov/m/dghr/flo/c21944.htm (last visited Nov. 18, 2020).

- Danger Pay Allowance (for service at certain locations where civil insurrection, terrorism, or war conditions threaten harm or danger to U.S. government employees);[9]
- Foreign Per Diem (reimbursement for lodging, meals, and incidental expenses);[10] and
- Service Needs Differential (positions that are identified by the head of an agency to warrant additional retention or recruitment compensation).[11]

The Foreign Service Base Salary Table effective as of January 2018 is shown in Appendix B. Other agencies use pay bands, which specify a certain salary range for each position and allow each employee's salary to vary within that band based on performance and experience. Agencies using the pay band scheme may also offer locality pay and/or cost-of-living allowances based on the location of the position. An example of the Federal Aviation Administration pay tables with the pay bands system as of December 2019 is shown in Appendix C.

An agency can also offer a variety of other forms of compensation. For example, the Central Intelligence Agency offers Foreign Language Incentives.[12] The incentive programs include maintenance programs, so that employees can keep up their language proficiency, and bonuses for having to use a language proficiency on a regular basis.

15.2 Reading a Government Pay Stub

The pay stub for federal government employees is called the Statement of Earnings and Leave. It shows all forms of compensation received by the employee, leave taken, and the total amount of leave the employee has available. The lawyer for the federal employee should have his or her client provide a recent Statement of Earnings and Leave, and the lawyer for the spouse should request it in discovery. See the image in Appendix D.

Box 1 shows the last day of the pay period for which the employee earned the compensation shown.

Box 2 shows the date on which payment was made (if direct deposit) for the pay period in Box 1.

Box 3 identifies the employee by name.

Box 4 denotes the pay plan and the Grade and Step within that pay plan. This employee is a Grade 14, Step 1 on the GS Scale.

Box 7 shows that the employee's base annual salary is $89,370; the basic GS Scale effective January 2018 for Grade 14, Step 1 also reads $89,370.

Box 7 also shows that this employee works in an area with locality pay. The locality pay is $25,220 per year, as shown in Box 9, or 28.22 percent of the employee's base salary. So this employee's actual annual salary is $114,590 as reported in Box 7.

---

9. *Frequently Asked Questions: Danger Pay*, DEP'T OF STATE, https://aoprals.state.gov/content.asp?content_id=177&menu_id=75#01 (last visited Nov. 18, 2020).

10. *Foreign Per Diem Rates*, DEP'T OF STATE, https://aoprals.state.gov/content.asp?content_id=184&&menu_id=75&menu_id=75 (last visited Nov. 18, 2020).

11. *Frequently Asked Questions: Service Needs Differential*, DEP'T OF STATE, https://aoprals.state.gov/content.asp?content_id=155&menu_id=75 (last visited Nov. 18, 2020).

12. *Careers & Internships: Foreign Language Incentive Program*, CENT. INTELLIGENCE AGENCY, https://www.cia.gov/careers/foreign-language/foreign-language-incentive-program.html (last visited Nov. 18, 2020).

Box 5 breaks down the employee's annual pay into an hourly or daily rate. This employee's salary breaks down to $54.91 per hour. It is the same information as presented in Box 7, just in a different form. If the employee receives a different rate of pay for any overtime worked, then that rate will appear in Box 6.

Box 10 indicates whether the employee is covered by the minimum wage and overtime provisions in the Fair Labor Standards Act (FLSA). An E, as shown in this Earnings and Leave Statement, means that the employee is exempt, or not covered. An N means that the employee is not exempt and is covered by the standards in the FLSA.[13]

Box 11 shows the employee's Service Computation Date (SCD). Among other things, this is the date used to determine the employee's leave accrual rate.[14] See Section 14.2 for discussion of leave.

PRACTICE TIP

The employee's SCD can be found on every Statement of Earnings and Leave. If the employee contends that part of the Federal Employees' Retirement System (FERS) or Civil Service Retirement System (CSRS) pension is from before the marriage, the SCD may confirm or refute the assertion. However, the SCD is not always the same as the date the employee started to work for the federal government, as he or she may have worked in a position, such as intern, that did not afford participation in a pension. Moreover, the employee may have military service that counts toward calculation of the pension.

Statements from other agencies may look different from the statement included in Appendix D, but all the information described herein will be included regardless of the format.

The lawyer may be able to glean other valuable information from the Earnings and Leave Statement, including bank account information, whether a military deposit has been paid, the pension system that the employee is in, health and life insurance enrollment, and more.

---

13. *Terms Used on the Leave and Earnings Statement*, Nat'l Insts. of Health, https://hr.nih.gov/sites/default/files/public/documents/benefits/pay/pdf/lesterms.pdf (last visited Nov. 18, 2020).

14. *Id.*

Chapter Sixteen

Process to Collect Support Payments from a Federal Employee's Salary or Pension

16.1 Earnings Withholding Orders to Collect Spousal or Child Support

Amendments to the Social Security Act of 1935 established that U.S. government agencies and the District of Columbia will enforce their employees' legal obligations to pay child support and alimony.[1] Therefore, the pay of a federal employee who has an obligation of child support or alimony may be garnished to enforce the obligation. Each agency has identified a professional to accept service of garnishment orders. Check with the employing agency to determine this person and the contact address.

The designated agent can receive legal process documents by certified or registered mail, return receipt requested, or by personal service. However, a garnishment order for child support or alimony does not need to be made by certified or registered mail, return receipt requested, or by personal service. It can be sent by regular mail.

In response to proper service, the agent will send written notice to the employee-obligor as soon as possible, but not later than 15 calendar days after receipt.

The amount that can be withheld from the employee's pay is a percentage of his or her Aggregate Disposable Earnings. Aggregate Disposable Earnings means the employee's pay that is subject to garnishment, as defined below, and after certain exclusions. The employee's pay subject to garnishment consists of compensation such as wages, salary, commission, and bonus pay and includes[2]

1. 42 U.S.C. § 659.
2. 5 C.F.R. § 582.102(5), Definition of Pay; *see also* 5 C.F.R. § 581.103, Moneys Which Are Subject to Garnishment.

(1) payments made pursuant to provisions of the Federal Tort Claims Act, 28 U.S.C. §§ 1346(b) and 2671 *et seq.*;

(2) refunds and other payments made in connection with overpayment or erroneous payment of income tax and other taxes levied under the Internal Revenue Code (26 U.S.C.);

(3) grants;

(4) fellowships;

(5) contracts, except where the contractor recipient performed personal services and received payments in his or her capacity as an employee of a government entity; and

(6) reimbursement for expenses incurred by an individual in connection with his or her employment or allowances in lieu of reimbursement and other payments, including—
   (a) uniform allowances,
   (b) travel and transportation expenses including mileage allowances,
   (c) relocation expenses,
   (d) storage expenses,
   (e) post differentials,
   (f) foreign areas allowances,
   (g) education allowances for dependents,
   (h) separate maintenance allowances,
   (i) post allowances and supplementary post allowances,
   (j) home service transfer allowances,
   (k) quarters allowances,
   (l) cost-of-living allowances when applicable to an employee in a foreign area or an employee stationed outside the continental United States or in Alaska;
   (m) remote worksite allowances, and
   (n) per diem allowances.

Where to Find the Law

Requirements to garnish and limits on garnishment are detailed in

(a) Title 42, United States Code (U.S.C.) section 659, "Consent by the United States to income withholding, garnishment, and similar proceedings for enforcement of child support and alimony obligations";
(b) 42 U.S.C. § 666, "Requirement of statutorily prescribed procedures to improve effectiveness of child support enforcement";
(c) 15 U.S.C. § 1673, "Consumer Credit Protection Act";
(d) 5 U.S.C. § 5520a, "Garnishment of Pay";
(e) 5 Code of Federal Regulations (C.F.R.) § 581, "Processing Garnishment Orders for Child Support and/or Alimony"; and
(f) 5 C.F.R. 582, "Commercial Garnishment of Federal Employees' Pay."

Certain monies are excluded and are not subject to garnishment. The Aggregate Disposable Earnings means the employee's pay after the following exclusions:[3]

1. withholdings required by law (e.g., Social Security and Medicare taxes);
2. federal, state, or local income tax withholdings authorized or required by law, if the amounts withheld are not greater than would be withheld if the employee claimed all dependents to which he or she was entitled;[4]
3. health insurance premium withholdings;
4. normal retirement contributions, except deductions for supplemental coverage;[5]
5. normal life insurance premium withholdings such as Basic Life Federal Employees' Group Life Insurance premiums (not including deductions for Optional Federal Employees' Group Life Insurance premiums and other life insurance premiums paid for by allotment); and
6. debts that the employee owes to the United States, except a levy for income tax under 26 U.S.C. § 6331 will not be excluded if a garnishment for child support was served before the date of the levy.

The percentage of Aggregate Disposable Earnings that can be withheld by garnishment is subject to a cap pursuant to the Consumer Credit Protection Act, unless a lower maximum garnishment is set by state or local law.[6]

16.1.1 Federal Interception Programs to Collect Child Support Arrears

The U.S. Department of Health and Human Services (DHHS) is home to the Administration for Children and Families (ACF). Within the ACF is the Office of Child Support Enforcement (OCSE), which coordinates federal programs with state, tribal, and local child support agencies.[7] The OCSE oversees the Federal Collections and Enforcement Program, which has authority to intercept payments from the federal government and other agencies or private companies directed to a person owing more than $2,500 in child support arrears and redirect the funds to the parent who is entitled to receive the child support payments.[8] The authority also extends to denial or interception of passports.[9]

---

3. Exclusions from garnishment are listed in 5 C.F.R. §§ 581.105, 582.103.

4. *See* 26 U.S.C. § 3402(i) (withholding of additional amounts may be permitted only when the employee presents supporting evidence of a tax obligation).

5. Amounts contributed under 5 U.S.C. § 8351 for the Civil Service Retirement System and 5 U.S.C. § 8432(a) for the Federal Employees Retirement System to the Thrift Savings Plan are normal retirement contributions. Amounts voluntarily contributed toward additional civil service annuity benefits are supplemental.

6. 15 U.S.C. § 1673(b)(2)(A), (B).

7. *About the Office of Child Support Enforcement*, Dep't of Health & Human Servs., https://www.acf.hhs.gov/css/about (last visited Nov. 18, 2020).

8. *Overview of the Federal Collections and Enforcement Program: Remedies*, Dep't of Health & Human Servs. (Feb. 1, 2020), https://www.acf.hhs.gov/css/resource/overview-of-the-federal-collections-and-enforcement-program#fop.

9. *Id.*

16.2 Garnishment of Federal Government Pensions and Thrift Savings Plan Accounts

Where to Find the Law

The Office of Personnel Management's (OPM's) regulations on garnishment of federal retirement benefits may be found in parts 581 and 582 of title 5, Code of Federal Regulations.

Civil Service Retirement System (CSRS) and Federal Employees' Retirement System (FERS) pensions are generally nonassignable and not subject to attachment or garnishment except as specifically permitted by law.[10] In addition to an order dividing retirement benefits as a disposition of property rights at divorce, a court may issue legal process to enforce a retired employee's spousal or child support obligation through garnishment of the pension.[11] Similarly, the employee's Thrift Savings Plan (TSP) account is generally inalienable, may not be assigned, and is not attachable except in certain limited circumstances, including to collect child support and alimony.[12] Child support and alimony are defined in 42 U.S. Code § 659(i):

> (2) Child support
>
> The term "child support", when used in reference to the legal obligations of an individual to provide such support, means amounts required to be paid under a judgment, decree, or order, whether temporary, final, or subject to modification, issued by a court or an administrative agency of competent jurisdiction, for the support and maintenance of a child, including a child who has attained the age of majority under the law of the issuing State, or a child and the parent with whom the child is living, which provides for monetary support, health care, arrearages or reimbursement, and which may include other related costs and fees, interest and penalties, income withholding, attorney's fees, and other relief.
>
> (3) Alimony (A) In general
>
> The term "alimony", when used in reference to the legal obligations of an individual to provide the same, means periodic payments of funds for the support and maintenance of the spouse (or former spouse) of the individual, and (subject to and in accordance with State law) includes separate maintenance, alimony *pendente lite*, maintenance, and spousal support, and includes attorney's fees, interest, and court costs when and to the extent that the same are expressly made recoverable as such pursuant to a decree, order, or judgment issued in accordance with applicable State law by a court of competent jurisdiction . . .

10. CSRS: 5 U.S.C. § 8346(a); FERS: 5 U.S.C. § 8470(a).

11. Other exceptions, not pertinent here, permit garnishment of a federal pension. OPM will honor an attachment of an annuity by a trustee in bankruptcy. If the employee owes a debt to the U.S. government, OPM can withhold money from the annuity to settle the debt, if the employee was a party to the debt (for example, as cosigner of a Federal Housing Administration loan or student loan or in the case of a joint tax return).

12. 5 U.S.C. § 8437.

Section 659(i) provides that if OPM is served with an appropriate child support or alimony enforcement order, it must respond within 15 days and comply with the terms within 30 days.

16.2.1 How to Garnish a TSP Account for Spousal Support or Child Support

A TSP account can be garnished with a legal process, such as a writ, order, summons, or other similar court order in the nature of a garnishment that is brought to enforce a participant's child support or alimony obligation. The TSP will honor orders to collect only arrears, not ongoing or future payments. The legal process must comply with the requirements of 5 U.S.C. § 8437(e)(3) and 5 C.F.R. part 1653, subpart B. It must contain the dollar amount to be garnished (not a percentage) and may not provide for a series of payments. If the payee is the spouse or former spouse, the amount paid out will be taxable to the payee. If the payee is a dependent child, the amount paid will be taxable to the payor-employee.[13] If the payments are to a state child support enforcement agency, the amount will be taxable to the participant.

The process for submitting such a garnishment order is similar to that for a Court Order Acceptable for Processing (COAP). The legal process for these purposes must also provide (or be accompanied by a document that provides)

(1) the participant's account number or Social Security number (SSN);
(2) the name and last known mailing address of each payee covered under the order; and
(3) the SSN and state of legal residence of the payee if he or she is the current or former spouse of the participant.

The process to review and approve the order and distribute the funds is similar to that of a COAP.

Once the order is approved, if the payment is made to the spouse or former spouse, the taxable portion of the payment is reported to the IRS as gross income to the spouse or former spouse, unless the funds are transferred to the spouse's traditional IRA, Roth IRA, or his or her employer-sponsored plan. This is the case even if the funds are being collected to satisfy an obligation that would otherwise have been nontaxable to the spouse, such as child support. However, if the payment is made to someone other than a spouse or former spouse, such as to a child support enforcement agency, the taxable portion is reported to the IRS as taxable income to the employee. In either case, the early withdrawal penalty does not apply.

Payment will typically be disbursed to a support agency within 31 days of the order having been approved by TSP. Payment will not be made prior to the expiration of 31 days after the decision letter is rendered.

PRACTICE TIP

Request attorney's fees to be included in the garnishment order when seeking arrears for alimony or child support if the state court made a fee award.

13. Thrift Savings Plan Tax Notice, TSP-582 (July 2019).

A TSP participant cannot take a loan or withdrawal so long as there is a garnishment order against the account to enforce a spousal or child support order.

The definitions of "alimony" and "child support" have been expanded to include attorney's fees and court costs, but only if included in the court order that requires the payment of the arrears.[14] The order must specify a specific dollar amount as the attorney fee award—it cannot be for a percentage or fraction of the account.

16.2.2 Garnishment for Child Abuse

A FERS or CSRS pension may be garnished to satisfy an obligation arising out of child abuse. A child abuse creditor is an individual who applies for benefits under CSRS or FERS based on a child abuse judgment enforcement order.[15] A child abuse judgment enforcement order means a court or administrative order requiring OPM to pay a portion of an employee annuity or a refund of employee contributions to a child abuse judgment creditor as a means of collection of a "judgment rendered for physically, sexually, or emotionally abusing a child."[16]

Likewise, a TSP account may be garnished. The creditor must obtain a perfected enforceable judgment arising out of physical, sexual, or emotional abuse of a child.[17]

A court order related to a TSP account should be sent to the following:

If by fax:	If by overnight delivery:
(703) 592-0151	ATTN: TSP Legal
Mailing address:	Processing Unit
TSP Legal Processing Unit	12210 Fairfax Town Center
P.O. Box 4390	Unit 906
Fairfax, VA 22038-4390	Fairfax, VA 22033

16.2.3 Protection from Other Garnishment

Pension or TSP funds may be garnished only to satisfy child support, alimony, or an award for child abuse, as described above. A spouse entitled to a property award under a court order or incorporated settlement agreement may not garnish a pension or a TSP account to satisfy the judgment or to enforce the contractual obligation.

Pension and TSP funds that are exempt from garnishment remain exempt even after paid to the annuitant and deposited into the annuitant's bank account. A retiree may take steps to stop garnishment of his or her bank account to the extent of the exempt funds by demonstrating to a court that funds in the account were derived from retirement funds. Such a process varies from state to state but would most likely involve a hearing and the retiree showing proof of the source of deposits. If the retiree can show that funds in the account are exempt, the creditor is barred from obtaining the exempt portion of the funds through garnishment.[18]

14. 5 C.F.R. § 1653.11.
15. 5 C.F.R. part 838.
16. 5 U.S.C. §§ 8345(j)(3)(B), 8467(c)(2).
17. 5 C.F.R. part 1653, subpart C, Child Abuse Court Orders.
18. 31 C.F.R. part 212.6.

Chapter Seventeen

Obtaining Documents and Information from the Federal Government

17.1 Overview

In many divorces, parties will cooperate to provide documents available to them regarding federal government employment, including account statements for the Thrift Savings Plan (TSP) and documents and downloadable material regarding their pension benefits and other federal benefits. Some information about the TSP is readily available to a spouse of an employee.[1] When the employee does not cooperate to produce necessary documents, or documents are otherwise not readily available, the lawyer has several options to obtain needed documents directly from the U.S. government:

- By an informal request
- Under the Freedom of Information Act (FOIA)
- By subpoena

17.2 Access to Employee Information—Informal Request

With limited exceptions, every federal employee has an Official Personnel Folder (OPF) subject to Office of Personnel Management (OPM) record-keeping requirements set forth in 5 C.F.R. part 293. OPM publishes a Guide to Personnel Recordkeeping from time to time, with the most recent version having been published July 1, 2011.

Each agency has housekeeping regulations, known as Touhy regulations, by which the agency decides the procedures under which a member of the public can request

1. *See* Section 10.7.

documents or witness testimony from the agency and how the agency will respond to subpoenas or other requests for information.[2]

Certain information about former and present federal employees is available to the public pursuant to OPM regulations (5 C.F.R. § 293.311), which provide:

(a) The following information from both the Official Personnel Folder and employee performance file system folders, their automated equivalent records, and from other personnel record files that constitute an agency record are considered available to the public:

1 Name;
2 Present and past position titles and occupational series;
3 Present and past grades;
4 Present and past annual salary rates (including performance awards, merit pay amount, Meritorious or Distinguished Executive Ranks, and allowances and differentials);
5 Present and past duty stations (includes room numbers, office designations, or other identifying information regarding buildings or places of employment); and
6 Position descriptions, identification of job elements, and those performance standards (but not actual performance appraisals), the release of which would not interfere with law enforcement programs or severely inhibit agency effectiveness. Performance elements and standards (or work expectations) may be withheld when they are so intertwined with performance appraisals that their disclosure would reveal an individual's performance appraisal.

(b) The Office or agency will generally not disclose information where the data sought is a list of names, present or past position titles, grades, salaries, performance standards, and/or duty stations of Federal employees which, as determined by the official responsible for custody of the information:

1 Is selected in such a way that would reveal more about the employee on whom information is sought than the six enumerated items, the disclosure of which would constitute a clearly unwarranted invasion of personal privacy; or
2 Would otherwise be protected from mandatory disclosure under an exemption of the FOIA.

(c) In addition to the information described in paragraph (a) of this section, a Government official may provide other information from these records (or automated equivalents) of an employee, to others outside of the agency, under a summons, warrant, subpoena, or other legal process; as provided by the Privacy Act (5 U.S.C. 552a(b)(4) through (b)(11)), under those Privacy Act routine uses promulgated by the Office, and as required by the FOIA.

---

2. *Touhy v. Ragen*, 340 U.S. 462 (1951), held that the head of a federal agency may make the determination on his or her sole authority to produce documents and authorize an employee's testimony in response to a subpoena or other demand for information.

Requests for such information can be made to the following:

Agency	Address
Department of State	Office of Information Resource Management Programs and Services (A/RPS/IPS) SA-2, Room 6001 Washington, DC 20522-6001
USAID	M/AS/IRD USAID RRB/ITC Room 2.7C Washington, DC 20523-2701 202-712-5027
For a former employee	National Personnel Records Center 1411 Boulder Blvd Valmeyer, IL 62295
Administrative Office of the U.S. Courts	Administrative Office of the U.S. Courts Human Resources Division 1 Columbus Circle, NE Washington, DC 20544
Army and Air Force Exchange Service	(Nonappropriated Fund employees) Army and Air Force Exchange Service HA-AAFES, ATTN:PE-P P.O. Box 660202 Dallas, TX 75266-0202
Department of Agriculture	Animal and Plant Health Inspection Service (Foreign Service employees) Chief, Resource Management Support Staff International Services Animal and Plant Health Inspection Service U.S. Department of Agriculture 4700 River Road, Unit 65 Riverdale, MD 20737 Foreign Agriculture Service (Foreign Service employees) Personnel Officer Foreign Agriculture Service U.S. Department of Agriculture 14th & Independence Avenue Washington, DC 20250
Department of Air Force (Civilian)	(Defense Civilian Intelligence Personnel Management System employees) Department of the Air Force HQ USAF/DPCE 1040 Air Force Pentagon Washington, DC 20330-1040 (Nonappropriated Fund employees) Department of the Air Force HQ AFMWRSA/MWXHC 550 C Street W, Suite 56 Randolph AFB, TX 78150-4758
Department of Army	(Defense Civilian Intelligence Personnel Management System employees) HQDA, ODCS, G-2 Attn: DAMI-CP 1000 Army Pentagon Washington, DC 20310-1000 (Nonappropriated Fund employees) Department of Army NAF Personnel Division Human Resources, HQDA (CFSC-HR-P), Room IN39, Hoffman 2 200 Stovall Street Alexandria, VA 22331-0532
Department of Commerce	(Foreign Service employees) Department of Commerce Office of Foreign Service Personnel, Room 3226 14th and Constitution Avenue, NW Washington, DC 20230

Agency	Address
Department of Navy	(Defense Civilian Intelligence Personnel Management System employees) Department of Navy Civilian Intelligence Personnel 4251 Suitland Road, Room 2A101 Washington, DC 20395-5720 (Nonappropriated Fund employees) Bureau of Personnel Department of Navy MWR Human Resource Division Naval Support Memphis (PERS-653) 7800 3rd Avenue, Bldg 457 Millington, TN 38054-5054 Navy Exchange Command NEXCOM Human Resource Principal Associate Director 3280 Virginia Beach Blvd. Virginia Beach, VA 23452 Other Department of Navy activities Department of Navy Office of Civilian Personnel Management Director for NAF Human Resources Code 02N, BTC#1, Room 1205 800 North Quincy Street Arlington, VA 22203-1998
Department of State	(Foreign Service employees) Chief, Personnel Records Branch Bureau of Personnel PER/EX/ADM/RM, Room 1609NS U.S. Department of State Washington, DC 20520
Department of Veterans Affairs	(Medical positions filled under title 38, United States Code) Department of Veterans Affairs Shared Service Center 3401 SW 21st Street Topeka, KS 66604
Federal Judicial Center	Federal Judicial Center Personnel Office, Room 6190 Thurgood Marshall Federal Judiciary Building One Columbus Circle, NE Washington, DC 20002-8003
General Accounting Office	General Accounting Office Director of Personnel Washington, DC 20548
Library of Congress	For amendment requests: General Counsel Library of Congress Personnel Operations Office Washington, DC 20540 For access requests: Library of Congress Personnel Office 101 Independence Avenue, SE Washington, DC 20540
Marine Corps	(Nonappropriated Fund employees) MWR Human Resource Branch HQ US Marine Corps 3044 Catlin Avenue Quantico, VA 22134-5099
National Security Agency	National Security Agency Civilian Personnel Ft. George G. Meade, MD 20755

Agency	Address
Peace Corps	(Foreign Service employees) Peace Corps Director of Personnel 1990 K Street, NW Washington, DC 20526
U.S. Postal Service	For amendment requests: Manager Corporate Personnel Operations Room 1813 475 L'Enfant Plaza, SW Washington, DC 20260-4261 For access requests: Last employing office
White House—Executive Office of the President	Director of Human Resources Division Office of Administration Executive Office of the President 725 17th Street, NW Washington, DC 20503

17.3 Freedom of Information Act (FOIA) Request

The Freedom of Information Act,[3] or FOIA, establishes the public's right to information contained in federal government records. Agencies are authorized to respond to a request for information from a member of the public as to the content of an employee's OPF. A FOIA request may seek salary information, disciplinary information, benefits, disability retirement, life insurance, beneficiary designation forms, survivor annuity designation history, retirement application, and communications between federal employees. The written request must specify the data the requesting person seeks. The agency will respond with existing documents but will not create documents or analyze data. Detailed information on how to make a FOIA request can be found at https://www.foia.gov/how-to.html, which includes instructive YouTube videos.

17.4 Subpoenas

A litigant can issue a subpoena to the employing agency to obtain information about a current employee's pension. The agency can provide a statement of retirement system coverage (Civil Service Retirement System (CSRS) or Federal Employees' Retirement System (FERS)), the amount of money withheld by that agency to credit to the employee's pension, and an annuity estimate using the employee's service history to date. The exact requirements for obtaining information vary among agencies.

For a retiree or former employee, OPM will be the source of pension information. In response to a subpoena, OPM will provide a statement of retirement system coverage (CSRS, FERS, or other pension system), the amount of pay withheld by that agency to credit to his or her pension, and annuity rate information. A subpoena should be sent to Chief, Plans and Policies Division, Office of Personnel Management, 1900 E Street, NW, Washington, DC 20415.

3. 5 U.S.C. § 552 (1996) as amended.

A subpoena to OPM is governed by 5 C.F.R. § 294.111:

> § 294.111 Custody of records; subpoenas.
>
> (a) The Chief, Plans and Policies Division, Administration Group, OPM, has official custody of OPM records. A subpoena or other judicial order for an official record from OPM should be served on the—
>
> Chief, Plans and Policies Division, Office of Personnel Management, 1900 E Street NW., Washington, DC 20415
>
> (b) See 5 CFR part 297, Subpart D—Disclosure of Records, of this title, for the steps other officials should take on receipt of a subpoena or other judicial order for an Office record.

A party intending to issue a subpoena must also comply with the employing agency's Touhy regulations.[4]

Before issuing a subpoena, the requesting party must submit a written request to OPM that complies with 5 C.F.R. § 295.203 and must contain the following information:

> (1) The caption of the legal proceeding, docket number, and name and address of the court or other authority involved
> (2) A copy of the complaint or equivalent document setting forth the assertions in the case and any other pleading or document necessary to show relevance
> (3) A list of categories of records sought, a detailed description of how the information sought is relevant to the issues in the legal proceeding, and a specific description of the substance of the testimony or records sought
> (4) A statement as to how the need for the information outweighs the need to maintain any confidentiality of the information and outweighs the burden on OPM to produce the records or provide testimony
> (5) A statement indicating that the information sought is not available from another source, from other persons or entities, or from the testimony of someone other than an OPM employee, such as a retained expert
> (6) If testimony is requested, the intended use of the testimony, a general summary of the desired testimony, and a showing that no document could be provided and used in lieu of testimony
> (7) A description of all prior decisions, orders, or pending motions in the case that bear upon the relevance of the requested records or testimony
> (8) The name, address, and telephone number of counsel to each party in the case
> (9) An estimate of the amount of time that the requester and other parties will require with each OPM employee for time spent by the employee to prepare for testimony, in travel, and for attendance in the legal proceeding

4. *Touhy,* 340 U.S. 462.

The party seeking documents or testimony must submit the written request before serving a subpoena. OPM will not respond to a subpoena if the serving party does not first submit a written request, as described above.

If OPM denies the written request, the party may then serve a subpoena. The location to send the written request or to serve the subpoena follows:

Chief
Plans and Policies Division
U.S. Office of Personnel Management
1900 E Street, NW
Washington, DC 20415

A party seeking records can request "records" or "official records and information" with respect to the employee or retiree who is a party to the divorce, defined as follows:

(1) All documents and materials which are OPM agency records under the Freedom of Information Act, 5 U.S.C. 552;
(2) All other documents and materials contained in OPM files; and
(3) All other information or materials acquired by an OPM employee in the performance of his or her official duties or because of his or her official status.[5]

5. 5 C.F.R. § 295.103.

Chapter Eighteen

Domestic Violence

18.1 Security Clearances and Domestic Violence

All U.S. government civilian and military personnel, consultants, contractors, employees of contractors, licensees, certificate holders or grantees, and their employees and other individuals who require access to classified information are required to obtain a security clearance. Each individual agency will determine which employees are required to obtain a security clearance. An individual can receive Confidential, Secret, or Top Secret clearance. The determination is made by each individual agency regarding its employees. Obtaining and maintaining a clearance may be a requirement for a specific job.

In cases involving an allegation of domestic violence against a federal employee, potential loss of a security clearance can be a concern to both the employee and the spouse. A perpetrator may threaten that reporting an assault will result in loss of clearance, and thereby loss of employment and income to the family, which may discourage the victim from reporting domestic violence.

Prior to 2010, on Standard Form 86, the government's questionnaire for security clearances, the section devoted to criminal history did not inquire about domestic violence history. The form was updated in 2010 and now requires applicants to disclose any prior arrest involving an allegation of domestic violence and whether a domestic violence protective order has ever been entered against him or her.[1]

1. Caitlin Gibson, *For Domestic Violence Victims, Abusers' Security Clearances Add an Extra Layer of Fear*, Wash. Post, May 17, 2014.

32 C.F.R. § 147.2 lays out the criteria for the adjudicative process regarding a person's eligibility for a security clearance:

> (a) The adjudicative process is an examination of a sufficient period of a person's life to make an affirmative determination that the person is eligible for a security clearance. Eligibility for access to classified information is predicated upon the individual meeting these personnel security guidelines. The adjudicative process is the careful weighing of a number of variables known as the whole person concept. Available, reliable information about the person, past and present, favorable and unfavorable, should be considered in reaching a determination. In evaluating the relevance of an individual's conduct, the adjudicator should consider the following actors:
>
> (1) The nature, extent, and seriousness of the conduct;
> (2) The circumstances surrounding the conduct, to include knowledgeable participation;
> (3) The frequency and recency of the conduct;
> (4) The individual's age and maturity at the time of the conduct;
> (5) The voluntariness of participation;
> (6) The presence or absence of rehabilitation and other pertinent behavioral changes;
> (7) The motivation for the conduct;
> (8) The potential for pressure, coercion, exploitation, or duress;
> (9) The likelihood of continuation of recurrence.
>
> (b) Each case must be judged on its own merits, and final determination remains the responsibility of the specific department or agency. Any doubt as to whether access to classified information is clearly consistent with national security will be resolved in favor of the national security.
>
> (c) The ultimate determination of whether the granting or continuing of eligibility for a security clearance is clearly consistent with the interests of national security must be an overall common sense determination based upon careful consideration of the following, each of which is to be evaluated in the context of the whole person, as explained further below:
>
> (1) Guideline A: Allegiance to the United States.
> (2) Guideline B: Foreign influence.
> (3) Guideline C: Foreign preference.
> (4) Guideline D: Sexual behavior.
> (5) Guideline E: Personal conduct.
> (6) Guideline F: Financial considerations.
> (7) Guideline G: Alcohol consumption.
> (8) Guideline H: Drug involvement.
> (9) Guideline I: Emotional, mental, and personality disorders.
> (10) Guideline J: Criminal conduct.
> (11) Guideline K: Security violations.
> (12) Guideline L: Outside activities.
> (13) Guideline M: Misuse of Information Technology Systems.
>
> (d) Although adverse information concerning a single criterion may not be sufficient for an unfavorable determination, the individual may be disqualified if available information reflects a recent or recurring pattern of questionable judgment, irresponsibility, or emotionally unstable behavior. Notwithstanding, the whole person concept, pursuit of further investigations may be terminated by an appropriate adjudicative agency in the face of reliable, significant, disqualifying, adverse information.
>
> (e) When information of security concern becomes known about an individual who is currently eligible for access to classified information, the adjudicator should consider whether the person:

(1) Voluntarily reported the information;
(2) Was truthful and complete in responding to questions;
(3) Sought assistance and followed professional guidance, where appropriate;
(4) Resolved or appears likely to favorably resolve the security concern;
(5) Has demonstrated positive changes in behavior and employment;
(6) Should have his or her access temporarily suspended pending final adjudication of the information.

(f) If after evaluating information of security concern, the adjudicator decides that the information is not serious enough to warrant a recommendation of disapproval or revocation of the security clearance, it may be appropriate to recommend approval with a warning that future incidents of a similar nature may result in revocation of access.

While none of the guidelines in subsection (c) specifically refer to domestic violence, there is an implication in Guideline J: Criminal Conduct that a domestic violence protective order could fall under this purview. Guideline J specifically states, "Conditions that could raise a security concern and may be disqualifying include: (1) Allegations or admissions of criminal conduct, *regardless of whether the person was formally charged*" (emphasis added). Conditions that could mitigate the security concerns include the following:

> (1) The criminal behavior was not recent; (2) The crime was an isolated incident; (3) The person was pressured or coerced into committing the act and those pressures are no longer present in that person's life; (4) The person did not voluntarily commit the act and/or the factors leading to the violation are not likely to recur; (5) Acquittal; (6) There is clear evidence of successful rehabilitation.[2]

There is no clear-cut answer as to whether or not a domestic violence protective order issued against a federal employee will affect a security clearance. It will depend on the specific facts of a given case. It is certainly something that is considered and examined during the course of a security clearance investigation. If the issue arises during a security clearance investigation, the employee can have an administrative hearing where he or she has the opportunity to give an explanation of what happened. Each agency has its own adjudication arm; for example, the Department of Defense has the Defense Office of Hearings and Appeals. There are attorneys who specialize in the area of security clearance issues. These attorneys help with the beginning stages of the application process, including specifically what to write in an initial application all the way through representing clients at these hearings. If there is an issue of domestic violence, it is a good practice to consult with or refer the client to one of these attorneys for representation during a security clearance investigation and/or revocation investigation.

18.2 Policy to Protect Domestic Violence Victims

Domestic violence, sexual assault, and sexual harassment have always been present, but until recent years, they were rarely talked about. Individual agencies have dealt with these issues to varying degrees for several years, with little consistency. There were no streamlined guidelines or policies until recently.

In 2012, President Obama issued a presidential memorandum mandating that each federal agency institute internal policies for addressing domestic violence in the federal

---

2. 32 C.F.R. § 147.12.

workforce, stating, "As the Nation's largest employer, the Federal Government should act as a model in responding to the effects of domestic violence on its workforce."[3]

The goal of this initiative is that every federal agency develop internal policies and procedures to include

(1) early intervention in and prevention of domestic violence committed against or by employees;
(2) guidelines for assisting employee victims and leave policies relating to domestic violence situations;
(3) general guidelines on when it may be appropriate to take disciplinary action against employees who commit or threaten acts of domestic violence; and
(4) measures to improve workplace safety related to domestic violence.

As a result of the presidential memorandum, OPM issued Guidance for Agency-Specific Domestic Violence, Sexual Assault, and Stalking Policies regarding establishing individual agency policies. Each agency was required to submit its proposed policies for review and approval by OPM.

The OPM guidance required agencies to develop reporting procedures "that provide an effective, confidential, and accessible way for employees to report incidents and concerns" and to develop incident response plans.[4] Each agency policy is required to include the following components: Workplace Flexibilities, Disciplinary Actions and Legal Implications, Training, Awareness, Employee Assistance Programs, and Building Safety and Security,[5] discussed further below.

Any federal employee who is a victim of domestic violence, sexual assault, or stalking, whether inside or outside of the workplace, is encouraged to speak with his or her supervisor or go directly to the agency's Employee Assistance Program (EAP) coordinator to discuss the resources the agency can provide, including a workplace safety plan, appropriate leave accommodations, outside referrals, resources, counseling, and reporting a perpetrator who works within the same agency.

18.3 Workplace Flexibilities

Various types of workplace flexibilities are available to an employee when the employee and/or the employee's family member(s) are victims of domestic violence, sexual assault, or stalking. To the greatest extent possible, agencies should work in collaboration with the employee to provide leave and/or other workplace flexibilities to help the employee remain safe and maintain his or her work performance. All possible leave options should be considered for an employee in this situation.[6]

The leave options available to an employee who is a current victim of domestic violence, sexual assault, or stalking or who is suffering from trauma related to a past situation are annual leave; advanced annual leave; sick leave; advanced sick leave; leave without pay; excused absence (administrative leave); Family and Medical Leave Act (entitles an employee to up to 12 weeks of unpaid leave); voluntary leave transfer and bank programs;

3. Presidential Memorandum—Establishing Policies for Addressing Domestic Violence in the Federal Workforce (Apr. 18, 2012).

4. *Guidance for Agency-Specific Domestic Violence, Sexual Assault, and Stalking Policies*, Off. of Personnel Mgmt. (Feb. 2013), https://www.opm.gov/policy-data-oversight/worklife/reference-materials/guidance-for-agency-specific-dvsas-policies.pdf.

5. *Id.*

6. *Id.*

telework and flexible work schedule including credit hours; and compensatory time off and compensatory time off for travel. If an employee is AWOL (absent without leave/ prior permission) as a result of domestic violence, sexual assault, or stalking, the employee may substitute a form of approved paid or unpaid leave upon return to work and with supervisor approval.

18.4 Disciplinary Actions and Legal Implications

18.4.1 Employee as Perpetrator

A disciplinary action can be taken against an employee for misconduct committed either inside or outside of work. When taking adverse action against an employee, an agency must be able to show that there is a clear and direct relationship between the grounds for the adverse action and the employee's ability to perform his or her duties or some other legitimate governmental interest promoting the "efficiency of the service."[7] When misconduct happens in the workplace or during duty hours, a nexus may be presumed. The standard of proof is preponderance of the evidence. The penalty can include removal from federal government service.

18.4.2 Employee as Victim

It is important for agencies to work to make sure that workplace policies do not revictimize victims to the extent possible, while maintaining appropriate workplace standards. Agencies should not discriminate against victims of domestic violence, sexual assault, or stalking in hiring, staffing, discipline, or other terms and conditions of employment. Such treatment revictimizes the victim. Upon becoming aware of domestic violence, sexual assault, or stalking, the supervisor is to refer the victimized employee to the resources within the agency for support and assistance. Every agency has an EAP, discussed below, which is often the agency's best resource for the victim. Agencies are mandated to recognize and respect a victim's right to privacy and the need for confidentiality and autonomy.

18.4.3 Employees in the Same Workplace

When the victim and the perpetrator, or alleged perpetrator, are employed in the same agency, the agency should consider options to maintain safety, such as switching tours of duty, changing work locations, granting telework, and issuing a cease-and-desist order. Each employee's supervisor may deliver a directive to avoid contact in the form of a Memorandum of Instruction.

18.5 Training, Awareness, and Employee Assistance Programs (EAPs)

An Employee Assistance Program (EAP) is a voluntary, confidential program that helps employees (including management) work through various life challenges that may adversely affect job performance, health, and personal well-being to optimize an organization's success. EAP services include assessments, counseling, and referrals for additional services to employees with personal or work-related concerns, such as stress, financial

7. 5 U.S.C. § 7513(a).

issues, legal issues, family problems, office conflicts, and alcohol and substance use disorders.[8] OPM has created a Domestic Violence, Sexual Assault, and Stalking Resource List.[9] Each EAP has access to this resource list as well as additional resources depending on the agency and the geographic location. EAP counselors can also assist the victim with developing a safety plan at work.[10] Each agency has a work-life agency coordinator and/or EAP administrator. The OPM website provides the contact person for each agency.[11]

In addition to providing support and resources for victims, each agency is required to engage in workplace awareness and outreach and trainings for employees, as well as more specific training for supervisors, human resources professionals, and EAP providers. Agencies may use one or several of the following ways to provide training regarding domestic violence, sexual assault, and stalking in the workplace: new employee orientation or new manager training; in-person training or workshops; web-based training; videoconferencing; and supplementing training with policy and resource content in employee handbooks, management guidebooks, or other written policy and procedural materials.

18.6 Building Safety and Security

Each agency is required to have one or more multidisciplinary Domestic Violence, Sexual Assault, and Stalking Response Teams to assess incidents of domestic violence, sexual assault, and stalking impacting the workplace. These teams are required to be trained on addressing the needs of victims of domestic violence, sexual assault, and stalking. The team should include representatives from the agency's security, human resources, employee assistance, and other appropriate offices. The team should be tasked with developing recommendations for the specific threat reported to the team and working with the victim and management to implement the safety plan.

PRACTICE TIP

When an employee is the victim of domestic violence, consider involving the federal workplace's Domestic Violence Response Team in your safety planning.

A safety plan may involve a temporary change, such as moving the employee to a more secure location or instituting an adjustment to the employee's work schedule to make the employee less vulnerable to attack. The agency's security office should keep a copy of a restraining order and photos of the perpetrator at all appropriate guard stations

8. *Work-Life: Employee Assistance Programs*, Off. of Personnel Mgmt., https://www.opm.gov/policy-data-oversight/worklife/employee-assistance-programs (last visited Nov. 19, 2020).

9. Included in the downloadable resources provided with this book, available at https://ambar.org/RepFed.

10. *Work-Life: Responding to Domestic Violence: Where Employees Can Find Help*, Off. of Personnel Mgmt., https://www.opm.gov/policy-data-oversight/worklife/reference-materials/responding-to-domestic-violence-where-federal-employees-can-find-help (last visited Nov. 19, 2020).

11. *Work-Life Agency Coordinators*, Off. of Personnel Mgmt., https://www.opm.gov/cclcontact (last visited Nov. 19, 2020).

when available and deemed appropriate. It is critical to involve the security office when the victim and perpetrator work in the same physical location. Other aspects of the safety plan can include changing the employee's phone extension, having phone calls screened, removing the employee's contact information from the agency's internal and public websites, installing a panic alarm at the employee's work station, creating a safe layout of the employee's work station, and, if possible, having a security officer walk the employee to his or her car or public transportation. If an employee chooses to disclose the existence of a protection or restraining order, an agency, wherever possible, should assist the employee to enforce his or her order.

With respect to an employee who is the perpetrator, if he or she is convicted of a qualifying misdemeanor crime of domestic violence, he or she may not possess a firearm even for official use, such as during duty as a law enforcement officer.

Glossary

Agency/Service Automatic (1 Percent) Contribution—The contribution equal to 1 percent of basic pay each pay period, contributed to a FERS participant's TSP account by his or her agency or service. CSRS participants do not receive automatic contributions.

Agency/Service Matching Contribution—The contribution made by the agency or service to the TSP account of FERS participants who contribute their own money to the TSP. CSRS participants do not receive matching contributions.

Annuitant—A former employee entitled to an annuity under a retirement system established for employees.

Annuity—A fixed sum of money paid to a former employee on a monthly basis, usually referring to a defined benefit pension. When referring to a TSP, the guaranteed monthly income for the life of the TSP participant who has elected to annuitize the TSP after separating from federal service.

Basic Employee Death Benefit—The payment to the current spouse of a deceased employee, equal to $15,000 as adjusted with COLAs (this total sum is $32,423.56 as of December 1, 2016), plus one-half of the employee's final salary (or average salary, if higher). 5 U.S.C. § 8462.

Beneficiary Participant Account—An inherited TSP account established in the name of a spouse-beneficiary of a deceased TSP participant.

Catch-Up Contributions—Contributions that are made via payroll deductions by a participant age 50 or older to a TSP account and are permitted to exceed the Internal Revenue Code elective deferral limit.

Catch-Up Contribution Limit—An annual dollar limit, established under IRC § 414(v), on the amount of catch-up contributions that a participant age 50 or older can make to employer-sponsored plans like the TSP. It is separate from the elective deferral limit imposed on regular employee contributions.

Civil Service Retirement System (CSRS)—The retirement system for federal employees hired on or before December 31, 1983, usually referred to as the old system. *See* 5 C.F.R. § 838.103.

Composite Retirement Annuity—The annuity computed when a phased retiree attains full retirement status. *See* 5 C.F.R. § 838.103.

Contribution—A deposit made to the TSP by a participant through payroll deduction or on behalf of the participant by his or her agency or service.

Contribution Allocation—A participant's choice that tells the TSP how contributions, rollovers, and loan repayments that are going into his or her account should be invested among the TSP funds.

Contribution Election—A request by a participant to start contributing to the TSP, to change the amount of his or her contribution to the TSP each pay period, or to terminate contributions to the TSP.

Cost-of-Living Adjustment (COLA)—An increase in pay or in an annuity amount based on inflation as measured by the Consumer Price Index.

Court Order—As defined by OPM, any judgment issued, or property settlement approved, by any court of any state; the District of Columbia; the Commonwealth of Puerto Rico, Guam, the Northern Mariana Islands, or the Virgin Islands; and any Native American tribal court in connection with, or incident to, the divorce, annulment of marriage, or legal separation of a federal employee or retiree.

Court Order Acceptable for Processing (COAP)—A court order that allocates federal retirement benefits pursuant to 5 C.F.R. § 838.103 and can affect an employee annuity, a refund of employee contributions, and a former spouse survivor annuity. If a court order is prepared properly, OPM will deem it a Court Order Acceptable for Processing and will therefore implement it according to its terms. Synonymous with Qualifying Court Order and Retirement Benefits Court Order.

Deferred Annuity—The future annuity of an employee who separated from federal service before he or she was eligible to retire and who may later become eligible to receive an annuity. *See also* **Retirement, Deferred**.

Dental Supplemental Benefit Plan or Dental Plan—A dental benefits plan participating in the Federal Employees Dental and Vision Insurance Program (FEDVIP) established under 5 U.S.C. chapter 89A.

Dependent Care Flexible Spending Arrangement (DCFSA or Day Care FSA)—An account established by the employer for designated allotments made by the employee for reimbursement of eligible dependent care expenses.

Designation of Beneficiary—The participant's formal indication of who should receive the monies payable upon his or her death, such as his or her TSP account, refund of employee contributions to a federal pension program, or FEGLI life insurance.

Disabled Child—For purposes of a FERS benefit, an unmarried dependent child whom the Social Security Administration finds is eligible for continued Social Security child's benefit because the child is incapable of self-support.

Eligible Employer Plan—A plan qualified under IRC § 401(a), including a § 401(k) plan, profit-sharing plan, defined benefits plan, stock bonus plan, and money purchase plan; an IRC § 403(a) annuity plan; an IRC § 403(b) tax-sheltered annuity; and an eligible IRC § 457(b) plan maintained by a government employer.

Employee Annuity—The recurring payments under CSRS or FERS made to a retiree, the recurring phased retirement annuity payments under CSRS or FERS made to a phased retiree in phased retirement status, and recurring composite retirement annuity payments under CSRS or FERS made to a phased retiree when he or she attains full retirement status. The employee annuity does not include payments of accrued and unpaid annuity after the death of a retiree or phased retiree under 5 U.S.C. §§ 8342(g) or 8424(h). *See* 5 C.F.R. § 838.103.

ERISA—The Employees Retirement Income Security Act, 29 U.S.C. § 1001 *et seq*. (*See* 5 C.F.R. § 838.103.)

Federal Employees Health Benefits Program (FEHB)—The federal employee group health insurance program, which encompasses over 200 plans, described in 5 U.S.C. § 8901 *et seq.*

Federal Employees' Retirement System (FERS)—The retirement system for federal civilian employees who were hired on or after January 1, 1984.

Federal Flexible Benefits Plan (FEDFLEX)—OPM's cafeteria plan. In order to offer pretax benefits, OPM was required to create a plan document in accordance with IRS regulations that outlines the benefits and employee choices under that plan. The HCFSA, DCFSA, and LEX HCFSA fall under this plan.

Federal Flexible Spending Account Program (FSAFEDS)—Sponsored by OPM and currently administered by WageWorks, Inc. *See* www.fsafeds.com.

Foreign Service Pension System (FSPS)—The new Foreign Service pension system for hires on or after January 1, 1984. Participants pay into Social Security and receive TSP matching funds.

Foreign Service Retirement and Disability System (FSRDS)—The old Foreign Service pension system for Foreign Service employees hired before December 31, 1983. Participants do not participate in Social Security.

Former Spouse under CSRS/FERS—(1) In connection with a court order affecting an employee annuity or a refund of employee contributions, a living person whose marriage to an employee has been subject to a divorce, annulment of marriage, or legal separation resulting in a court order, or (2) in connection with a court order awarding a former spouse survivor annuity, a living person who was married for at least nine months to an employee or retiree who performed at least 18 months of civilian service covered by CSRS or who performed at least 18 months of civilian service creditable under FERS and whose marriage to the employee or retiree was terminated prior to the death of the employee or retiree.

Former Spouse under FSRDS/FSPS—A former wife or husband of a participant or former participant who was married to such participant for not less than ten years during the participant's creditable service under the FSRDS or FSPS and whose divorce from such participant occurred on or after February 15, 1981.

Former Spouse Survivor Annuity—A recurring benefit under CSRS or FERS that is payable to a former spouse after the employee's or retiree's death. *See* 5 C.F.R. § 838.103.

Full Annuity under FSRDS/FSPS—The full, unreduced annuity of a participant in one of the Foreign Service pensions who retires and does not provide a survivor annuity to a spouse, former spouse, or designated beneficiary. A full annuity means an annuity computed without any reduction to provide a survivor annuity. Also referred to as gross annuity.

Full Retirement Status—A phased retiree has ceased employment and is entitled, upon application, to a composite retirement annuity, as provided under subpart Q of 5 C.F.R. part 831 or 5 C.F.R. part 848.

Full Withdrawal—A post–separation from service withdrawal of a participant's entire TSP account through an annuity, a single payment, or TSP monthly payments (or a combination of these three options).

Government Pension Offset—The provision of the Social Security Act that affects CSRS retirees who are also entitled to a Social Security spousal benefit, sometimes referred to as the Public Pension Offset. The Social Security spousal benefit is reduced, or offset, in accordance with a formula.

Gross Annuity under FERS/CSRS—The amount of monthly annuity payable to a retiree or phased retiree after reducing the self-only annuity to provide survivor annuity benefits but before any other deduction. Gross annuity also includes any lump-sum payments made to the retiree under 5 U.S.C. §§ 8343a or 8420a. (*See* 5 C.F.R. § 838.103.)

Gross Annuity under Foreign Service Pension—Same meaning as the term "full annuity" under FSRDS/FSPS.

Health Care Flexible Spending Arrangement (HCFSA)—An account established by the employer for designated allotments made by the employee for reimbursement of eligible health care expenses.

High-3 Average Pay (high-3)—The highest average basic pay earned during any three consecutive years of service. The basic pay is the basic salary earned for a position. It includes increases to salary for which retirement deductions are withheld, such as shift rates. It does not include payments for overtime or bonuses.

HR/RET—FSRDS/FSPS Department of State's Office of Retirement. Mailing address: Room H-620, SA-1, Washington, DC 20522-0108.

In-Service Withdrawal—A disbursement made from a participant's TSP account, available only to a participant who is still employed by the federal government.

Insurable Interest—A person who is financially dependent on the employee and could reasonably expect to derive financial benefit from his or her continued life. Blood relatives and adopted relatives (but not relatives by marriage) who are closer than first cousins are presumed to have an insurable interest.

IRC Catch-Up Contribution Limit—An annual dollar limit, established under IRC § 414(v), on the amount of catch-up traditional and Roth employee contributions that a participant age 50 or older can make to an employer-sponsored plan like the TSP. It is separate from the elective deferral limit and the annual additions limit.

IRC Elective Deferral Limit—An annual dollar limit, established under IRC § 402(g), on the amount of traditional and Roth employee contributions that a participant can make to an employer-sponsored plan like the TSP.

Joint Life Annuity (Federal Reserve System Plan)—An annuity that provides monthly payments to the employee while he or she and the person with whom he or she chooses to share the annuity (joint annuitant) are alive. When one party dies, monthly annuity payments will be made to the survivor for his or her lifetime. The amount of the payment made while both are alive and the amount of the payment to the survivor depend on the percentage of the survivor annuity elected.

Lump-Sum Credit—The unrefunded amount of an employee's pension consisting of retirement deductions made from the employee's basic pay, amounts deposited by an employee such as a military buyback, and the interest thereon. 5 U.S.C. § 8401(19).

Maximum Survivor Benefit—The maximum amount of an employee's annuity that can be provided to his or her surviving spouse; 55 percent of the employee's self-only annuity in CSRS and FSRDS and 50 percent of the employee's self-only annuity in FERS and FSPS. *See* 5 C.F.R. § 838.103.

Minimum Retirement Age (MRA)—The earliest age at which a FERS participant may retire voluntarily or elect to receive benefits if separated from federal service after at least ten years of service. The MRA varies according to the year in which the employee was born.

Net Annuity—The amount of monthly annuity payable to a retiree or phased retiree after deducting from the gross annuity any amounts that are

(1) Owed by the retiree to the United States;

(2) Deducted for health benefits premiums under 5 U.S.C. §8906 and 5 CFR 891.401 and 891.402;

(3) Deducted for life insurance premiums under 5 U.S.C. § 8714a(d);

(4) Deducted for Medicare premiums;

(5) Properly withheld for Federal income tax purposes, if the amounts withheld are not greater than they would be if the retiree claimed all dependents he or she was entitled to claim;

(6) Properly withheld for State income tax purposes, if the amounts withheld are not greater than they would be if the retiree claimed all dependents he or she was entitled to claim; or

(7) Already payable to another person based on a court order acceptable for processing or a child abuse judgment enforcement order.

Unless the court order expressly provides otherwise, net annuity also includes any lump-sum payments made to the retiree under 5 U.S.C. §§ 8343a or 8420a. (*See* 5 C.F.R. § 838.103.)

Nonpay Status—Actively employed by the federal government but not receiving regular pay because of furlough, suspension, or leave without pay (including leave without pay to perform military service) or pending resolution of a grievance or appeal.

Office of Personnel Management (OPM)—An independent agency of the United States federal government that manages the government's civilian workforce. The agency provides federal human resources policy, oversight, and support and tends to healthcare, insurance, and retirement benefits and services for federal government employees.

Open Season—The annual period between mid-November and mid-December in which federal employees can make changes to their health insurance coverage enrollment. Typically, federal employees cannot make a change to their health insurance coverage during the year; it must be made during the Open Season, unless the employee experiences a Qualifying Life Event.

Pay Status—Term of art. An annuitant is in pay status once he or she starts to receive regular payments from his or her pension.

Phased Employment—The less-than-full-time employment of a phased retiree, as provided under 5 C.F.R. part 831, subpart Q, or part 848. (*See* 5 C.F.R. § 838.103.)

Phased Retiree—A retirement-eligible employee who (1) with the concurrence of an authorized agency official enters phased retirement status in accordance with 5 C.F.R. part 831, subpart Q, or part 848; and (2) has not entered full retirement status.

Phased Retirement Annuity—The annuity payable under 5 U.S.C. § 8336a or 8412a and 5 C.F.R. part 831, subpart Q, or part 848, before full retirement. *See* 5 C.F.R. § 838.103.

Phased Retirement Status—A phased retiree is concurrently employed in phased employment and eligible to receive a phased retirement annuity. *See* 5 C.F.R. § 838.103.

Postponed Retirement—An employee eligible for an immediate retirement at separation from federal service who postpones receipt of his or her annuity to avoid the reduction based on age.

Present Value—The current value of a sum of money or stream of cash to be received in the future, such as a pension, given a specified rate of return. Future cash flows are discounted at the discount rate, and the higher the discount rate, the lower the present value of the future cash flows (https://www.investopedia.com/terms/p/presentvalue.asp).

Previous Spouse under FSRDS or FSPS—Any person formerly married to a participant or former participant, whether or not such person qualifies under the definition of a "former spouse."

Principal—A participant or former participant whose service forms the basis for a benefit under FSRDS or FSPS for a spouse, previous spouse, former spouse, or child of a participant.

Pro Rata Share—One-half of the fraction whose numerator is the number of months of federal civilian service (and combined military service) that the employee performed during the marriage and whose denominator is the total number of months of federal civilian and military service performed by the employee through the day before the effective date of phased retirement or separation for retirement, as applicable to the annuity calculation. In the computation of the division of phased retirement annuity and a composite retirement annuity, a pro rata share will be computed through the day before the effective date of an employee's phased retirement for the computation of the division of a phased retirement annuity and then recomputed for division of the composite retirement annuity under §§ 831.1742 and 848.502. With respect to the allocation of survivor annuity benefits, pro rata share is defined at 5 C.F.R. § 838.922(a)—"'Prorata share' means the fraction of the maximum survivor annuity allowable under § 831.614 or § 842.613 of this chapter whose numerator is the number of months of Federal civilian and military service that the employee performed during the marriage and whose denominator is the total number of months of Federal civilian and military service performed by the employee."

Qualified Earnings—Earnings on Roth contributions that are eligible to be paid out tax-free at withdrawal. Earnings are considered qualified as long as the following two requirements are met: (1) it has been five years since January 1 of the calendar year the participant made the first Roth TSP contribution AND (2) the participant is at least age 59½ and permanently disabled (or deceased).

Qualifying Court Order—A court order or judgment approved by any court of any state that is "in connection with, or incident to, the divorce, annulment of marriage, or legal separation of a Federal employee or retiree" that awards a portion of a future annuity or a survivor annuity to a former spouse and is determined by OPM, CIA, or the Foreign Service, as appropriate, to meet the requirement of a qualifying court order. 5 C.F.R. § 838.1004. Synonymous with COAP.

Qualifying Life Event—An event that allows an employee to change his or her enrollment coverage only between self-only, self plus one, and family enrollments. Most Qualifying Life Events do not allow the federal employee to change the plan in which he or she is enrolled. Such events include divorce, marriage, or birth of a child.

Reamortize—Adjust the terms of a loan to change the loan payment amount or to shorten or lengthen the repayment period.

Refund of Employee Contributions—A pension participant may elect a return of his or her contributions before going into pay status. If such an election is made, the employee is entitled to his or her contributions, plus interest. Taking a refund of contributions voids entitlement to an annuity. 5 C.F.R. § 838.103.

Required Minimum Distribution—The amount of money, based on a participant's age and previous year's TSP account balance, that the IRS requires to be distributed to a participant each year after the participant has reached age 70½ and is separated from service.

Residual Annuity—Under the Federal Reserve Board Plan, if the employee withdraws the value of the PCO as a lump sum, the difference between the value of the traditional formula pension benefit and the PCO lump-sum payment, payable as a residual annuity beginning as early as age 62.

Retiree—A former employee, including a phased retiree who has entered full retirement status, or a member of Congress who is receiving recurring payments under CSRS or FERS based on his or her service as an employee or member. "Retiree" does not include an employee receiving a phased retirement annuity or a person receiving an annuity only as a current spouse, former spouse, child, or person with an insurable interest. (*See* 5 C.F.R. § 838.103.)

Retirement, Deferred—Retirement under CSRS or FERS when the employee separates from service with at least five years of civilian service but before meeting the requirements for an immediate annuity. A deferred retirement under CSRS begins on the employee's 62nd birthday. Under FERS, the deferred retirement can begin as early as the employee's MRA if the employee had at least ten years of service. *See also* **Deferred Annuity**.

Retirement, Early, FERS—Retirement under FERS with at least ten but less than 30 years of service after reaching the MRA and receiving a reduced annuity. Not available under CSRS. Also called MRA + 10 benefit.

Retirement, Unreduced—Retirement under CSRS or FERS with full benefits after meeting appropriate age and length-of-service requirements. (Also called unreduced benefits.)

Roth Balance—The portion of a TSP account made up of Roth (after-tax) contributions and accrued earnings. Portions of this balance may have originated from tax-exempt pay.

Roth Contributions—Contributions from pay that have already been taxed (or from tax-exempt pay) and that have been deposited to a Roth balance. Earnings are tax-free at withdrawal, subject to certain requirements.

Roth IRA—An individual retirement account that is described in section 408A of the Internal Revenue Code. A Roth IRA provides tax-free earnings.

Self-Only Annuity—The single-life annuity under CSRS and FERS. Specifically, the recurring unreduced payments under CSRS or FERS to a retiree whose pension is not reduced to provide a survivor annuity payable to anyone. Self-only annuity also includes the recurring unreduced phased retirement annuity payments under CSRS or FERS to a phased retiree before any other deduction. This is the full, unreduced annuity. (*See* 5 C.F.R. § 838.103.)

Separated Employee—A former employee or member of Congress who has separated from a position in the federal government covered by CSRS and FERS, who is not currently employed in such a position, and who is not a retiree. (*See* 5 C.F.R. § 838.103.)

Single-Life Annuity—An annuity that provides monthly payments only to the retired employee as long as he or she lives with no survivor annuity payable after his or her death.

Supplementary Annuity—Monthly benefit payable in addition to a monthly survivor benefit to certain survivors of deceased retirees.

Survivor Annuitant—A surviving family member of a deceased federal employee or annuitant who is entitled to an annuity under a retirement system established for employees.

Survivor Annuity—A survivor annuity provides for an annuity to be paid to the survivor after the death of the former employee. The survivor could be a current spouse, a former spouse, or both, up to the plan-specific cap. The amount of the cost and the maximum benefit available depend on the pension system.

Temporary Continuation of Coverage (TCC)—Medical coverage that may be available to a participant who leaves federal service, a dependent or former spouse who loses coverage because he or she no longer qualifies as an eligible family member, or a child who turns age 26 and loses coverage.

Traditional Contributions (TSP)—Traditional contributions are tax deferred.

Taxes are paid on contributions and earnings when withdrawn. Also referred to as tax-deferred, pre tax, or non-Roth contributions.

TSP Beneficiary Participant Account— An account inherited by the spouse-beneficiary of a deceased TSP participant.

TSP Monthly Payments—Payments that the participant elects to receive each month from his or her TSP account after separating from service. Money remains in the TSP account and is paid out directly from the account.

Vesting (FERS)—The time in service that an employee must have upon separation from service in order to be entitled to keep Agency/Service Automatic (1 percent) Contributions and associated earnings. Most FERS participants are vested in these automatic contributions after completing three years of service. Congressional pension participants become vested after two years of service.

Windfall Elimination Provision—The provision of the Social Security law that reduces Social Security benefits for federal government employees who have less than 30 years of substantial coverage under Social Security and get a pension from employment not covered by Social Security (for example, a CSRS benefit).

Forms

COLA

2005 OPM COLA Letter

CSRS and FERS Forms

2011 Retirement Poster
Form 20-64A Electing Survivor Annuity for Former Spouse 2011
Form 2801 CSRS Immediate Retirement 2013
Form 2804 CSRS Voluntary Contributions 2006
Form 3107 FERS Immediate Retirement 2014
Form 3112 Disabled Retirement Documentation 2011
Form RI 25-15 Change in Student Status 2013
Form RI 30-10 Disabled Dependent Questionnaire 2010
Form RI 92-19 FERS Deferred or Postponed Retirement 2012
RI 20-7 Representative Payee Application
RI 20-120 Request for Change to Unreduced Annuity
RI 30-1 Disability Annuity Questionnaire
RI 38-122 Alternative Annuity and Rollover Election
RI 38-124 Voluntary Contributions Election
SF 2808 CSRS Designation of Beneficiary
SF 3102 FERS Designation of Beneficiary

FEGLI Forms

Form RI 76-10 FEGLI Assignment
SF 2817 FEGLI Election
SF 2823 FEGLI Designation of Beneficiary

FEHB Forms

Form 2810 FEHB Notice of Change in Enrollment
Form RI 79-9 FEHB Cancellation and Suspension Form 2014
OPM 2809 Health Benefits Election FEHB

Foreign Service Forms

DS5002 Designation of Beneficiary FSRDS and FSPS
DS5004 Application for Retirement for Foreign Service
DS5008 Election of Less Than Maximum Survivor Benefit
DS5012 Disability Retirement FSRDS
DS5013 Disability for FSPS Part 2
DS5026 Annuity Supplement Information Request
DS5028 Disability for FSPS
DS5034 FSRDS Offset Retirement
Form W-4P Withholding Certificate for Pension and Annuity
FSPS Annuity Supplement Eligibility
JF0037 Election of Annuity Benefits for FSRDS and FSPS

Military Buyback Forms

Estimated Earnings Instructions
Form 3108 2013 Deposit FERS Military Application to Make Service Credit Payment
RI 20-97 2013 Estimated Earnings Form

OPM

OPM Deductions Key

TSP Forms

Form 2008 TSP-9 Change in Address for Separated Participant
Form 2012 TSP-20 Loan Application
Form 2012 TSP-60 Roth Transfer
Form 2012 TSP-79 Change from Monthly to Final Payment
Form 2012 TSP Loan Payment Coupon
Form 2015 TSP-75 Age-Based In-Service Withdrawal Request
Form 2017 TSP-3 Designation of Beneficiary
Form 2018 TSP-92 Court Order Division
Form 2018 TSP-U1 Election
Form 2018 TSP-92b Specialist Authorization Form
Form TSP-3 Designation of Beneficiary
Form TSP-15 2010 Change in Name for Separated Participant
Form TSP-16 2011 Exception to Spousal Requirements
Form TSP-25 2018 Automatic Enrollment Refund Request
Form TSP-60 2012 Request for a Transfer into the TSP
Form TSP-65 2012 Request to Combine Civilian and Uniformed Services TSP Accounts
Form TSP-70 2018 Request for Full Withdrawal
Form TSP-76 2018 Financial Hardship In-Service Withdrawal Request
Form TSP-77 2018 Request for Partial Withdrawal When Separated
Form TSP-92 Court Order Form
Form TSP-92D 2018 Request for Participant Account
Form W-4P 2017 Withholding Certificate

Samples

Divorce Cable DOS
FERS COAP $1
FERS COAP Book
FERS Letter
FERS Statement
TSP COAP Book
TSP Determination Letter
TSP Garnishment
TSP Letter—Denial of Order
TSP Letter
TSP Loan Statements
TSP Statement

Quick Reference Guides

CSRS Eligibility for Retirement Pay Status

There are five categories of benefits under the Civil Service Retirement System (CSRS). Eligibility is based on the employee's age and the number of years of creditable service and any other special requirements. In addition, the employee must have served in a position subject to CSRS coverage for one of the last two years before retirement. If the employee meets one of the following sets of requirements, he or she may be eligible for an immediate retirement benefit. An immediate annuity is one that begins within 30 days after separation from employment.

Optional: If the employee leaves federal service before meeting the age and service requirements for an immediate retirement benefit, he or she may be eligible for deferred retirement benefits. To be eligible, he or she must have at least five years of creditable civilian service and be age 62.

Age	Years of Service
62	5
60	20
55	30

Special/Early Optional: The employing agency must be undergoing a major reorganization, reduction in force, or transfer of function determined by the Office of Personnel Management (OPM). The employee's annuity is reduced if he or she is under age 55.

Age	Years of Service
50	20
Any Age	25

Special Provision Retirement: The employee must retire under special provisions for air traffic controllers or law enforcement and firefighter personnel, nuclear materials couriers, Supreme Court police, and Capitol police.

Age	Years of Service
50	20
Any Age*	25

*ONLY air traffic controllers can retire at any age with 25 years of service as an air traffic controller.

Discontinued Service: Separation is involuntary and not a removal for misconduct or delinquency.

Age	Years of Service
50	20
Any Age	25

Disability: Must be disabled for useful and efficient service in current position and any other vacant position at the same grade or pay level within commuting area and current agency for which he or she is qualified. Must have been disabled prior to retirement, and the disability should be expected to last for more than one year.

Age	Years of Service
Any Age	5

What Can and Can't Be Ordered by the Court (FERS/CSRS)[1]

A court order related to a divorce or separation can

1. divide a Civil Service Retirement System (CSRS) or Federal Employees' Retirement System (FERS) annuity (see Section 2.2);
2. divide or prohibit a refund of CSRS or FERS employee contributions to his or her pension (see Section 2.5);
3. provide a survivor annuity payable upon the death of an employee or retiree (see Section 2.3.1);
4. shift the cost of the survivor annuity (see Sections 2.3.2 and 8.6);
5. allow a former spouse to continue coverage under the Federal Employees Health Benefits (FEHB) program by maintaining sufficient retirement benefits coverage (see Section 11.2);
6. require an employee to cover his or her children under the FEHB plan (see Section 11.5);
7. require an employee or retiree to assign his or her Federal Employees' Group Life Insurance (FEGLI) benefits to a former spouse or children (see Section 12.3);
8. require an employee to name his or her former spouse or children as beneficiaries under FEGLI (see Section 12.3.2); and
9. garnish retirement benefits for alimony or child support or for an award in a case involving child abuse.

A court order related to a divorce or separation cannot

1. make a former spouse of an employee or annuitant eligible for Federal Employees Dental and Vision Insurance Program (FEDVIP) benefits (see Section 14.4);
2. require an agency or retirement system to enroll an employee or annuitant in a FEDVIP plan to cover his or her children (see Section 14.4); or
3. make a former spouse a qualified relative eligible to enroll in the Federal Long-Term Care Insurance Program (see Section 14.3).

1. Adapted from OPM Publ'n: Court Ordered Benefits for Former Spouses, Civil Service Retirement System, Federal Employees Retirement System, Federal Employees Group Life Insurance, Federal Employees Health Benefits, RI 84-1 (rev. July 2014).

FERS Retirement Pay Status Eligibility[2]

Eligibility is determined by the employee's age and number of years of creditable service. In some cases, he or she must have reached the Minimum Retirement Age (MRA) to receive retirement benefits. Use the following chart to figure the MRA.

If the employee was born	The MRA is
Before 1948	55
In 1948	55 and 2 months
In 1949	55 and 4 months
In 1950	55 and 6 months
In 1951	55 and 8 months
In 1952	55 and 10 months
In 1953–1964	56
In 1965	56 and 2 months
In 1966	56 and 4 months
In 1967	56 and 6 months
In 1968	56 and 8 months
In 1969	56 and 10 months
In 1970 and after	57

Immediate Retirement: An immediate retirement benefit is one that starts within 30 days from the date an employee stops working. If an employee meets one of the following sets of age and service requirements, he or she is entitled to an immediate retirement benefit:

Age	Years of Service
62	5
60	20
MRA	30
MRA	10

If the employee retires at the MRA with at least ten but less than 30 years of service, the benefit will be reduced by 5 percent a year for each year he or she is under 62, unless the employee has 20 years of service and the benefit starts when he or she reaches age 60 or later.

2. *Retirement Services: Eligibility*, Off. of Personnel Mgmt., https://www.opm.gov/retirement-services/fers-information/eligibility/ (last visited Nov. 20, 2020).

Early Retirement: The early retirement benefit is available in certain involuntary separation cases and in cases of voluntary separation during a major reorganization or reduction in force. To be eligible, one must meet the following requirements:

Age	Years of Service
50	20
Any Age	25

Deferred Retirement: If an employee leaves federal service before meeting the age and service requirements for an immediate retirement benefit, he or she may be eligible for deferred retirement benefits. To be eligible, the employee must have completed at least five years of creditable civilian service. The employee may receive benefits when he or she reaches one of the following ages:

Age	Years of Service
62	5
MRA	30
MRA	10

If the employee retires at the MRA with at least ten but less than 30 years of service, the benefit will be reduced by 5 percent a year for each year under age 62, unless there were 20 years of service and the benefit starts after age 60.

Disability Retirement:

Age	Years of Service
Any Age	18 months

The employee must have become disabled, while employed in a position subject to FERS, because of a disease or injury, for useful and efficient service in the current position. The disability must be expected to last at least one year. The agency must certify that it is unable to accommodate the disabling medical condition in the present position and that it has considered the employee for any vacant position in the same agency at the same grade/pay level, within the same commuting area, for which he or she is qualified for reassignment.

CSRS and FERS Quick Comparison Guide[3]

<table>
<tr><th>Item</th><th>CSRS</th><th>FERS</th></tr>
<tr><td>A. Basic Benefit
1. Regular Annuity</td><td>Guaranteed annuity based on service under a single plan.</td><td>Guaranteed annuity based on service under the Basic Benefit Plan.</td></tr>
<tr><td>2. When benefits can be received.
a. Voluntary retirement benefits (unreduced)</td><td>Available at the following age and service combinations:
• Age 55 with at least 30 years of service
• Age 60 with at least 20 years of service.
• Age 62 with at least 5 years of service.</td><td>Available at the following age and service combinations:
• At least the Minimum Retirement Age (MRA)* with 30 years of service or more.
• At least age 60 with 20 years of service or more.
• At least age 62 with 5 years of service or more.
<table>
<tr><th>If the employee was born . . .</th><th>The employee's MRA is . . .</th></tr>
<tr><td>Before 1948</td><td>55</td></tr>
<tr><td>in 1948</td><td>55 and 2 months</td></tr>
<tr><td>in 1949</td><td>55 and 4 months</td></tr>
<tr><td>in 1950</td><td>55 and 6 months</td></tr>
<tr><td>in 1951</td><td>55 and 8 months</td></tr>
<tr><td>in 1952</td><td>55 and 10 months</td></tr>
<tr><td>In 1953-1964</td><td>56</td></tr>
<tr><td>in 1965</td><td>56 and 2 months</td></tr>
<tr><td>in 1966</td><td>56 and 4 months</td></tr>
<tr><td>in 1967</td><td>56 and 6 months</td></tr>
<tr><td>in 1968</td><td>56 and 8 months</td></tr>
<tr><td>in 1969</td><td>56 and 10 months</td></tr>
<tr><td>In 1970 and after</td><td>57</td></tr>
</table></td></tr>
<tr><td>b. Immediate reduced voluntary retirement benefits</td><td>None available.</td><td>Available at the MRA with at least 10 years of service. (Benefit is reduced 5 percent a year for each year payment begins before age 62. Receipt of benefits can be postponed until as late as age 62 to lessen or avoid the reduction.)</td></tr>
<tr><td>c. Immediate involuntary early retirement</td><td>Available at the following age and service combinations provided separation is not for cause or misconduct:
• Age 50 with at least 20 years of service.
• Any age with at least 25 years of service.
(Benefit reduced 2% a year for each year payment begins before age 55.)</td><td>Unreduced benefits available at the following age/service combinations:
• At age 50 with 20 years of service or more.
• At any age with 25 years of service or more.
(Special Retirement Supplement begins at MRA and continues until age 62.)</td></tr>
</table>

3. Copied from OPM Publ'n: FERS Federal Employees Retirement System Transfer Handbook, A Guide to Making Your Decision, RI 90-3 (rev. Dec. 2008).

<table>
<tr><th>Item</th><th>CSRS</th><th>FERS</th></tr>
<tr><td>d. Deferred retirement</td><td>Available at age 62 to former employees with at least 5 years of civilian service who did not withdraw their retirement contributions after separation from service. If the employee's death occurs after separation but prior to age 62, only a refund of deductions is paid</td><td>Unreduced benefit available at the following age/service combinations:
• At age 62 to those who had at least 5 years of civilian service and did not take a refund.
• At age 60 with 20 years of service or more.
• At MRA with 30 years of service or more.
Reduced benefit (at 5% per year under age 62) available at MRA with 10 years of service or more. Receipt of benefits can be postponed until as late as age 62 to lessen or avoid the reduction in annuity.</td></tr>
<tr><td>3. Basic annuity formula
a. Salary base</td><td>Average of highest 3 consecutive years of salary.</td><td>Average of highest 3 consecutive years of salary.</td></tr>
<tr><td>b. Benefit calculation formula (For CSRS Offset employees, the benefit is reduced at age 62 by the amount of their Social Security entitlement attributable to CSRS Offset service.)</td><td>General formula equal to:
[1] (1 1/2%) x (High-3) x (first 5 years service) +
[2] (1 3/4%) x (High-3) x (second 5 years service) +
[3] (2%) x (High-3) x (all service over 10 years).</td><td>1.00% x (High-3) x all years of service if retiring before age 62 with less than 20 years of service.
1.10% x (High-3) x all years of service if retiring at age 62 or older with at least 20 years of service.</td></tr>
<tr><td>4. Cost-of-Living adjustments (COLA's)</td><td>Paid annually to all annuitants beginning the year after retirement. CSRS COLA's equal the rate of inflation as measured by the Consumer Price Index (CPI).</td><td>Paid annually to retirees over 62 years of age, to those who have received disability payments for more than 1 year, and to those receiving survivor benefits
The following chart describes FERS COLAs:
<table>
<tr><th>Increase in CPI</th><th>Annual COLA Percentage</th></tr>
<tr><td>Up to 2%</td><td>Same as CPI</td></tr>
<tr><td>2% to 3%</td><td>2%</td></tr>
<tr><td>3% or more</td><td>CPI increase minus 1%</td></tr>
</table></td></tr>
<tr><td>5. Special Retirement Supplement</td><td>Not paid under CSRS.</td><td>An approximation of the portion of a full-career Social Security benefit earned while under FERS.
Paid to retirees receiving unreduced retirement benefits from Minimum Retirement Age until age 62. (Subject to Social Security Earnings Test.)</td></tr>
<tr><td>6. Cost to participate</td><td>In 2008, 7% of basic pay. CSRS Offset employees also pay 7%, divided between 6.2% to SSA and .80% to CSRS up to the SSA maximum taxable wage base, above tax base, entire 7% goes to CSRS.</td><td>In 2008, .80% of basic pay. (The cost of the FERS Basic Benefit plus Social Security taxes generally equals 7%.)</td></tr>
</table>

Item	CSRS	FERS
7. Refund options	May choose to withdraw contributions in lump sum when the employee leaves. Will receive no annuity credit unless contribution redeposited after reemployment. Exception: full credit for refunded service will be given without redeposit, subject to an actuarial reduction in annuity, if refunded service ended before October 1, 1990. Contributions refunded without interest if the employee has 5 years or more of service.	May choose to withdraw contributions in lump sum when the employee leaves. Will receive no annuity. Refunded contributions may not be redeposited. Refunds receive market rate interest.
8. Disability benefits a. Definition of disability	An employee must be unable to perform his or her duties and there must be no suitable vacancy in his or her own agency within the same commuting area and at the same grade or pay level as the current position.	Same as for CSRS.
b. Eligibility requirements	An employee must have 5 or more years of civilian service. CSRS Offset employee who applies for CSRS disability benefits must also apply for Social Security disability benefits or show that they are not eligible for them.	An employee must have 18 months or more of civilian service. Those who apply for FERS disability benefits must also apply for Social Security disability benefits or show that they are not eligible for them.
c. Disability benefit formula	Disability benefits are the **higher** of two computations: [1] the annuity computed using the employee's years of service and High-3 under the general formula; or [2] the **lesser** of the following: a) 40% of the High-3; or b) annuity computed according to the general formula after increasing the length of service as if the employee had worked to age 60. If the employee has at least 21 years and 11 months of service, or is age 60 or older, the annuity is computed under [1]. For CSRS Offset employees, the benefit is reduced by the amount of Social Security disability entitlement attributable to CSRS Offset service.	The formula used to determine FERS disability benefits differs depending on how many years an employee is disabled. During the first year of disability, FERS pays 60% of an employee's high-3 (average pay if less than 3 years service) minus 100 % of any Social Security benefits received. No COLA's are paid during this year. During the second and any additional years of disability until an employee reaches age 62, the employee will receive 40% of his or her high-3 average pay minus 60% of any Social Security benefits received. COLA's are paid for these years, at the same rate as noted under FERS in Item 4 above. FERS disability benefits are recomputed at age 62. The employee then receives a nondisability FERS retirement benefit that includes credit for years in receipt of disability annuity.
9. Survivor benefits a. Eligibility requirements	Survivor benefits are payable to eligible survivors of an employee who was contributing to the CSRS on the date of death with at least 18 months of civilian service.	Same as CSRS
b. Who may receive survivor benefits.	Under CSRS, survivor benefits can be paid under various conditions to current and former spouses and to children. Survivors must meet certain age and length of marriage requirements in order to qualify for benefits.	Same as CSRS. In addition, under FERS, a survivor's age can affect the amount of benefits he/she may receive.

Item	CSRS	FERS
c. Survivor benefit payments 1.) Spouses of deceased employees	An eligible spouse of an employee who dies while a Federal employee will receive 55% of the disability annuity that would have been payable if the employee had retired on the date of death. For CSRS Offset employees, the benefit is reduced by the amount of Social Security survivor benefit entitlement attributable to CSRS Offset service when the SSA benefit becomes payable.	FERS pays the eligible spouse of an employee who dies while a Federal employee a lump sum payment of $15,000, adjusted for inflation, plus 50% of the employee's final basic pay (or average pay, if higher). The $15,000 portion has increased to $28,093.53 with the 2008 COLA. In addition to the above lump sum, FERS pays the eligible spouse of an employee who has 10 years of service or more an annuity equal to 50 percent of the employee's accrued Basic Benefit.
2.) Spouses of deceased annuitants	An eligible spouse of a retiree will receive 55% of the retiree's unreduced annuity amount (or a lesser amount if jointly elected by the retiree and spouse).	FERS will pay the eligible spouse of a FERS retiree 50% of the retiree's annuity amount (or 25% if that lesser amount was jointly elected by the retiree and spouse), plus a Special Retirement Supplement if the spouse is younger than age 60 and not yet eligible for Social Security benefits.
3.) Spouses of employees who die after leaving Federal service, but before deferred annuity payments begin	A lump-sum death benefit consisting of the deceased's unrefunded retirement contributions is payable unless the deceased designated another person as beneficiary.	FERS will pay a benefit to the spouse of an employee who has 10 or more years of Federal service, leaves the Federal workforce, and dies before his or her annuity payments begins. The benefit is payable if the employee did not take a refund of his or her contributions. If the employee had not reached the MRA when separated, the survivor annuity will begin when the employee would have reached age 62 (age 60 if employee had 20–29 years of service; or employee's MRA if he/she had 30 or more years of service). The annuity can begin sooner if the spouse elects a reduced benefit. If the employee had attained the MRA when separated (and had at least 10 years of service), the spouse receives 1/2 of employee's accrued annuity beginning the day after death.
4.) Death benefits paid to children.	CSRS pays an annuity to the eligible children of employees or retirees who die. The annuity varies depending on the number of children and whether or not there is a surviving spouse or former spouse who is a parent of the children. The benefits of children of CSRS Offset employees are offset for Social Security benefits in the same way that spousal benefits are offset.	FERS pays the eligible children of employees or retirees who die an annuity that varies depending on the number of children and whether or not there is a surviving spouse or former spouse who is a parent of the children. The annuity is reduced by any Social Security benefits the children may be receiving.

<table>
<tr><th>Item</th><th>CSRS</th><th>FERS</th></tr>
<tr><td>a. Cost of survivor benefits for retired employees</td><td>Unless waived by the retiree and the spouse, the annuity is reduced in order to provide a survivor benefit. The first $3,600 of the retiree's annual benefit will be reduced by 2.5%. The remaining annuity benefit is reduced by 10%. For most career retirees, this amounts to a 7-8% reduction. Note: the 55% spouse's benefit is based on the amount of the annuity before this reduction is made.</td><td>Unless waived by the retiree and the spouse, the annuity is reduced to provide a survivor benefit. This reduction amounts to 10% (or 5% , if elected) of the annual benefit. Note: The 50% (or 25%) spouse's benefit is based on the amount of the annuity before this reduction is made.</td></tr>
<tr><td>b. Survivor benefits Cost-of-Living Adjustments (COLA's)</td><td>CSRS survivor benefits receive full CSRS COLA's equal to the rate of inflation.</td><td>FERS survivor benefits receive FERS COLA's at any age.</td></tr>
<tr><td>B. Thrift Savings Plan
1. Participation</td><td>CSRS employees may use this plan at their option.</td><td>FERS employees automatically have an amount equal to 1 percent of pay contributed to their Thrift Savings Plan account by the Federal Government. Additional contributions may be made at the option of the employee. If made, the Government increases its contributions, also.</td></tr>
<tr><td>2. Employee Contributions</td><td>CSRS employees may contribute up to the IRS Deferral Limit which is $15,500 for 2008.</td><td>FERS employees may contribute up to the IRS Deferral Limit which is $15,500 for 2008.</td></tr>
<tr><td>3. Government contributions</td><td>None available.</td><td>The Federal Government automatically contributes an amount equal to 1% of basic pay into each FERS employee's Thrift Savings Plan account each pay period. If employee makes contributions, the Government also provides matching.
<table>
<tr><th>If they save</th><th>Government will add</th><th>Total</th></tr>
<tr><td>0%</td><td>1%</td><td>1%</td></tr>
<tr><td>1%</td><td>2%</td><td>3%</td></tr>
<tr><td>2%</td><td>3%</td><td>5%</td></tr>
<tr><td>3%</td><td>4%</td><td>7%</td></tr>
<tr><td>4%</td><td>4.5%</td><td>8.5%</td></tr>
<tr><td>5%</td><td>5%</td><td>10%</td></tr>
<tr><td>6-10%</td><td>5% (max)</td><td>11-15%</td></tr>
</table>
</td></tr>
<tr><td>4. Catch-up Contributions</td><td>The limit on catch-up contributions for 2008 is $5,000. If the employee is at least age 50 (or will become age 50 during the calendar year) and if the employee has made or will make the maximum amount of employee contributions for the calendar year (e.g., $15,000 in 2008), the employee may also make catch-up contributions to the employee's TSP account.</td><td>Same as CSRS</td></tr>
</table>

Item	CSRS	FERS
5. Plan Options a. Investment choices	Employees may invest any portion of their Thrift Savings account in any of the six investment Funds: • G Fund—Government Securities Investment Fund • C Fund—Common Stock Index Investment Fund • F Fund—Fixed Income Index Investment Fund • S Fund—Small Capitalization Stock Index Investment Fund • I Fund—International Stock Index Investment Fund • L Fund—Lifecycle Funds	Same as CSRS.
b. Opportunities to change investment amounts and choices.	CSRS employees can start, change, stop or resume Thrift Savings Plan contributions at any time.	Same as CSRS.
C. Social Security Benefits **1. Applicability**	Not a part of the CSRS plan. For most CSRS employees, applies only if they have enough covered service outside the Federal Government. CSRS Offset employees, are however, covered by Social Security.	Employees covered by Social Security.

Appendix A

SALARY TABLE 2018-GS
INCORPORATING THE 1.4% GENERAL SCHEDULE INCREASE
EFFECTIVE JANUARY 2018

Annual Rates by Grade and Step

Grade	Step 1	Step 2	Step 3	Step 4	Step 5	Step 6	Step 7	Step 8	Step 9	Step 10	WITHIN GRADE AMOUNTS
1	$ 18,785	$ 19,414	$ 20,039	$ 20,660	$ 21,285	$ 21,650	$ 22,267	$ 22,891	$ 22,915	$ 23,502	VARIES
2	21,121	21,624	22,323	22,915	23,175	23,857	24,539	25,221	25,903	26,585	VARIES
3	23,045	23,813	24,581	25,349	26,117	26,885	27,653	28,421	29,189	29,957	768
4	25,871	26,733	27,595	28,457	29,319	30,181	31,043	31,905	32,767	33,629	862
5	28,945	29,910	30,875	31,840	32,805	33,770	34,735	35,700	36,665	37,630	965
6	32,264	33,339	34,414	35,489	36,564	37,639	38,714	39,789	40,864	41,939	1,075
7	35,854	37,049	38,244	39,439	40,634	41,829	43,024	44,219	45,414	46,609	1,195
8	39,707	41,031	42,355	43,679	45,003	46,327	47,651	48,975	50,299	51,623	1,324
9	43,857	45,319	46,781	48,243	49,705	51,167	52,629	54,091	55,553	57,015	1,462
10	48,297	49,907	51,517	53,127	54,737	56,347	57,957	59,567	61,177	62,787	1,610
11	53,062	54,831	56,600	58,369	60,138	61,907	63,676	65,445	67,214	68,983	1,769
12	63,600	65,720	67,840	69,960	72,080	74,200	76,320	78,440	80,560	82,680	2,120
13	75,628	78,149	80,670	83,191	85,712	88,233	90,754	93,275	95,796	98,317	2,521
14	89,370	92,349	95,328	98,307	101,286	104,265	107,244	110,223	113,202	116,181	2,979
15	105,123	108,627	112,131	115,635	119,139	122,643	126,147	129,651	133,155	136,659	3,504

Appendix B

United States Department of State
2018 Foreign Service (FS) Salary Table

Base Schedule

Authorized by Executive Order 13819

Effective January 7, 2018

Rates in U.S. Dollars

Class	Step 1	Step 2	Step 3	Step 4	Step 5	Step 6	Step 7	Step 8	Step 9	Step 10	Step 11	Step 12	Step 13	Step 14
1	105,123	108,277	111,525	114,871	118,317	121,866	125,522	129,288	133,167	136,659	136,659	136,659	136,659	136,659
2	85,181	87,736	90,369	93,080	95,872	98,748	101,711	104,762	107,905	111,142	114,476	117,910	121,448	125,091
3	69,022	71,093	73,225	75,422	77,685	80,015	82,416	84,888	87,435	90,058	92,760	95,543	98,409	101,361
4	55,929	57,607	59,335	61,115	62,949	64,837	66,782	68,786	70,849	72,975	75,164	77,419	79,741	82,134
5	45,319	46,679	48,079	49,521	51,007	52,537	54,113	55,737	57,409	59,131	60,905	62,732	64,614	66,552
6	40,514	41,729	42,981	44,271	45,599	46,967	48,376	49,827	51,322	52,862	54,447	56,081	57,763	59,496
7	36,218	37,305	38,424	39,576	40,764	41,987	43,246	44,544	45,880	47,256	48,674	50,134	51,638	53,187
8	32,378	33,349	34,350	35,380	36,442	37,535	38,661	39,821	41,015	42,246	43,513	44,819	46,163	47,548
9	28,945	29,813	30,708	31,629	32,578	33,555	34,562	35,599	36,667	37,767	38,900	40,067	41,269	42,507

Base Pay Cap = FS-01, Step 10, which is 136,659

EXECUTIVE SCHEDULE		SENIOR FOREIGN SERVICE (SFS) PAY RANGE		SFS PAY CAPS	
EX-I	210,700	Minimum	Maximum	OC	177,990
EX-II	189,600	126,148	189,600	MC	186,715
EX-III	174,500			CM	189,600
EX-IV	164,200				
EX-V	153,800				

Appendix C[1]

Conversion From FG to Core Compensation Plan
Pay Bands With Locality

Core Compensation Plan Pay Bands, effective January 5, 2020

Note: Pay rates for FAA employees, including locality pay, are capped by law at $197,300 — the rate for level II of the Executive Schedule (P.L. 104-264 paragraph 40122 c).

No Locality:									Percentage:				
Pay Band	A	B	C	D	E	F	G	H	I	J	K	L	M
Minimum	$19,306	$22,064	$24,933	$29,345	$35,820	$39,948	$46,321	$55,649	$66,936	$82,632	$97,163	$116,057	$136,686
Maximum	$28,022	$31,994	$37,398	$44,017	$53,730	$59,924	$71,803	$86,259	$103,741	$128,103	$150,552	$179,932	$184,566
Minimum w/loc													
Maximum w/loc													
Student		Level 1 FG-1/2	Level 2 FG-3/4	Level 3 FG-5-9									
Clerical Support			Level 1 FG-1-4	Level 2 FG-5/6	Level 3 FG-7/8								
						Mgr. 1	Mgr. 2						
Admin. Support				Level 1 FG-3-6	Level 2 FG-7/8	Level 3 FG-9/10							
							Mgr. 1 FG-8 & below	Mgr. 2 FG-9 & above					
Technical Support					Level 1 FG-5/6	Level 2 FG-7/8	Level 3 FG-9-11						
								Mgr. 1 FG-11 & below	Mgr. 2 FG-12 & above				
Para-Professional						Level 1 FG-7-9	Level 2 FG-10/11	Level 3 FG-12/13					
									Mgr. 1 FG-13 & below	Mgr. 2 FG-14 & above			
Professional						Level 1 FG-5-9	Level 2 FG-10/11	Level 3 FG-12	Level 4 FG-13	Level 5 FG-14/15			
									Mgr. 1 FG-13 & below	Mgr. 2 FG-14	Mgr. 3 FG 15 & above		
Technical							Level 1 FG-5-9	Level 2 FG-10-12	Level 3 FG-13	Level 4 FG-14	Level 5 FG-15		
										Mgr. 1 FG-14 & below	Mgr. 2 FG-15	Mgr. 3 None	
Engineering							Level 1 FG-5/7/9	Level 2 FG-11/12	Level 3 FG-13	Level 4 FG-14	Level 5 FG-15		
										Mgr. 1 FG-14 & below	Mgr. 2 FG-15	Mgr. 3 None	

AHB-300 core_salary_with_conversion (1).xlsx No Locality

1. *Pay & Benefits*, FED. AVIATION ADMIN., https://www.faa.gov/jobs/working_here/benefits/ (last visited Nov. 20, 2020)._Image of Core Compensation Pay Band is only a section from the FAA publication found at this link. Additional information on other agencies using the pay band structure includes *What Is TSA?*, FED. L. ENFORCEMENT, https://www.federallawenforcement.org/tsa/ (last visited Nov. 20, 2020).

Appendix D

CIVILIAN LEAVE AND EARNINGS STATEMENT

1. Pay Period End 06/23/18	2. Pay Date 06/29/18			
3. Name [redacted]	4. Pay Plan/Grade/Step GS 14 01	5. Hourly/Daily/Rate 54.91	6. Basic/OT Rate 54.91	7. Basic Pay + Locality Adj = Adjusted Basic Pay 89,370.00 25,220.00 114,590.00
8. Soc Sec No ***-**-2323	9. Locality % 28.22	10. FLSA Category E	11. SCD Leave [redacted]	12. Max Leave Carry Over 240 / 13. Leave Year End 01/05/19
14. Financial Institution - Net Pay [redacted]	15. Financial Institution - Allotment #1 [redacted]	16. Financial Institution - Allotment #2 [redacted]		

17.

Tax	Marital Status	Exemptions	Add'l
FED	S	3	0
MD	S	3	0

18. Tax / Marital Status / Exemptions / Add'l / Taxing Authority

19. Cumulative Retirement FERS: 6,058.71

20. Military Deposit

21.

	Current	Year to Date
GROSS PAY	4,392.80	59,145.00
TAXABLE WAGES	4,166.44	55,426.70
NONTAXABLE WAGES	226.36	2,930.57
TAX DEFERRED WAGES		787.73
DEDUCTIONS	1,860.28	25,809.76
AEIC		
NET PAY	2,532.52	33,335.24

22.

CURRENT EARNINGS

TYPE	HOURS/DAYS	AMOUNT	TYPE	HOURS/DAYS	AMOUNT	TYPE	HOURS/DAYS	AMOUNT
REGULAR PAY	80.00	4,392.80						

DEDUCTIONS

TYPE	CODE	CURRENT	YEAR TO DATE	TYPE	CODE	CURRENT	YEAR TO DATE
ALLOTMENT,SV	(2)	200.00	2,600.00	FEGLI	Z5	17.55	227.85
FEGLI OPTNL	ABC	12.80	166.20	FEHB	JN5	178.55	2,308.74
MEDICARE		60.41	815.11	OASDI		258.31	3,485.29
RETIRE, FERS	K	35.14	456.04	TAX, FEDERAL		631.23	8,759.40
TAX, STATE	MD	295.76	3,986.21	TSP LOANS	809001G	122.72	1,595.36
TSP SAVINGS		0.00	787.73	DENTAL		37.25	484.40
VISION		10.56	137.43				

LEAVE

TYPE	PRIOR YR BALANCE	ACCRUED PAY PD	ACCRUED YTD	USED PAY PD	USED YTD	DONATED/ RETURNED	CURRENT BALANCE	USE-LOSE/ TERM DATE
ANNUAL	167.00	6.00	72.00	0.00	8.00	0.00	231.00	79.00
SICK	705.75	4.00	48.00	0.00	2.00	0.00	751.75	
TIME OFF AWD	40.00	0.00	0.00	0.00	40.00	0.00	0.00	
HOLIDAY	0.00	0.00	0.00	0.00	24.00	0.00	0.00	

BENEFITS PAID BY GOVERNMENT FOR YOU

TYPE	CURRENT	YEAR TO DATE	TYPE	CURRENT	YEAR TO DATE
FEGLI	8.78	113.99	FEHB	521.58	6,757.37
MEDICARE	60.41	815.11	OASDI	258.31	3,485.29
RETIRE, FERS	601.81	7,810.05	TSP BASIC	43.93	570.10
TSP MATCHING	0.00	787.73			

REMARKS

YOUR PAYROLL OFFICE ID NUMBER IS [redacted] - DEPARTMENT OF HEALTH AND HUMAN SERVICES.
IT IS IMPORTANT TO REVIEW YOUR LEAVE AND EARNINGS
STATEMENT EACH PAY PERIOD. ANY QUESTIONS OR DISCREPANCIES
MUST BE REPORTED TO YOUR TIMEKEEPER AND/OR MANAGEMENT.
PRETAX FEHB EXCLUSION $ 178.55

THIS REPORT CONTAINS INFORMATION SUBJECT TO THE PRIVACY ACT OF 1974 AS AMENDED

Summary of OPM Publications Used

Introduction

Data, Analysis & Documentation, OFF. OF PERSONNEL MGMT. (Sept. 2017), https://www.opm.gov/policy-data-oversight/data-analysis-documentation/federal-employment-reports/reports-publications/federal-civilian-employment/#note1.

Retirement Statistics, OFF. OF PERSONNEL MGMT., https://www.opm.gov/retirement-services/retirement-statistics/ (last visited Nov. 11, 2020).

Part I: Pensions

Computation, OFF. OF PERSONNEL MGMT., https://www.opm.gov/retirement-services/fers-information/computation/ (last visited Nov. 11, 2020).

OPM PUBL'N: RETIREMENT FACTS 10, VOLUNTARY CONTRIBUTIONS UNDER THE CIVIL SERVICE RETIREMENT SYSTEM, RI 83-10 (Apr. 1998).

OPM PUBL'N: RETIREMENT FACTS 14, LAW ENFORCEMENT AND FIREFIGHTER CSRS RETIREMENT, RI 83-20 (Oct. 1997).

OPM PUBL'N: RETIREMENT FACTS 13, CSRS OFFSET RETIREMENT, RI 83-19 (Apr. 1998).

OPM BENEFITS ADMIN. LETTER No. 12-104 (Oct. 3, 2012).

OPM BENEFITS ADMIN. LETTER No. 14-201 (Jan. 30, 2014).

OPM PUBL'N: INFORMATION FOR FERS ANNUITANTS, RI 90-8 (May 2012).

OPM PUBL'N: RETIREMENT FACTS 9, REFUNDS UNDER THE CIVIL SERVICE RETIREMENT SYSTEM, RI 83-9 (Oct. 1997).

OPM PUBL'N: INFORMATION FOR ANNUITANTS: CIVIL SERVICE RETIREMENT SYSTEM (CSRS), RI 20-59 (June 2013).

OPM PUBL'N: INFORMATION ON ELECTING A SURVIVOR ANNUITY FOR YOUR FORMER SPOUSE, RI 20-64B (Sept. 2013).

OPM PUBL'N: A HANDBOOK FOR ATTORNEYS ON COURT-ORDERED RETIREMENT, HEALTH BENEFITS AND LIFE INSURANCE UNDER THE CIVIL SERVICE RETIREMENT BENEFITS, FEDERAL EMPLOYEES RETIREMENT BENEFITS, FEDERAL EMPLOYEES GROUP LIFE INSURANCE PROGRAM, RI 38-116 (rev. July 1997).

OPM PUBL'N: COURT ORDERED BENEFITS FOR FORMER SPOUSES, CIVIL SERVICE RETIREMENT SYSTEM, FEDERAL EMPLOYEES RETIREMENT SYSTEM, FEDERAL EMPLOYEES GROUP LIFE INSURANCE, FEDERAL EMPLOYEES HEALTH BENEFITS, RI 84-1 (July 2014).

OPM BENEFITS ADMIN. LETTER No. 14-208 (Oct. 7, 2014).

YOUR FEDERAL RESERVE RETIREMENT PLAN HANDBOOK INFORMATION FOR FEDERAL RESERVE BANK, BOARD AND BUREAU PARTICIPANTS (Federal Reserve Employee Benefits System 2019).

YOUR FEDERAL RESERVE RETIREMENT PLAN HANDBOOK INFORMATION FOR BOARD OR GOVERNORS AND CONSUMER FINANCIAL PROTECTION BUREAU PARTICIPANTS (Federal Reserve Employee Benefits System 2019).

Part II: Thrift Savings Plan

OPM PUBL'N: FEDERAL EMPLOYEE PARTICIPATION PATTERNS IN THE TSP 2008–2012 (June 2015).

OPM PUBL'N: SUMMARY OF THE THRIFT SAVINGS PLAN, TSPBK09 (Oct. 2020).

OPM PUBL'N: TSP AFTER SERVICE WITHDRAWAL, TSPBK12 (Sept. 2019).

OPM Publ'n: Managing Your Account for Civilian Federal Employees, TSPBK30 (Jan. 2018).
OPM Publ'n: Court Orders and Powers of Attorney (Sept. 2014).

Part III: Other Federal Government Employee Benefits

Insurance: FastFacts, Off. of Personnel Mgmt., https://www.opm.gov/healthcare-insurance/fastfacts/ (last visited Nov. 17, 2020).
Healthcare Reference Materials: Former Spouses, Off. of Personnel Mgmt., https://www.opm.gov/healthcare-insurance/healthcare/reference-materials/reference/former-spouses/ (last visited Nov. 17, 2020).
Healthcare Reference Materials: Termination, Conversion, and Temporary Continuation of Coverage, Off. of Personnel Mgmt., https://www.opm.gov/healthcare-insurance/healthcare/reference-materials/reference/termination-conversion-and-temporary-continuation-of-coverage/ (last visited Nov. 17, 2020).
FEGLI Calculator, Off. of Personnel Mgmt., https://www.opm.gov/retirement-services/calculators/fegli-calculator/ (last visited Nov. 20, 2020).
Federal Employees' Group Life Insurance (FEGLI) Program Handbook, Off. of Personnel Mgmt. (Apr. 2014), https://www.opm.gov/healthcare-insurance/life-insurance/reference-materials/handbook.pdf.
OPM Publ'n: Work Related Injuries and Fatalities, What You and Your Family Need to Know about Your Benefits, RI 84-2 (Dec. 2008).
Frequently Asked Questions: Retirement: Will I Get Paid for Unused Sick Leave in Retirement?, Off. of Personnel Mgmt., https://www.opm.gov/faqs/QA.aspx?fid=735eda40-61a8-45df-b6ad-47185f4c91a5&pid=ffd788aa-037f-49fb-840d-2997aa4856d6 (last visited Nov. 18, 2020).
Pay & Leave: Fact Sheet: Annual Leave (General Information), Off. of Personnel Mgmt., https://www.opm.gov/policy-data-oversight/pay-leave/leave-administration/fact-sheets/annual-leave/ (last visited Nov. 18, 2020).
Work-Life Agency Coordinators, Off. of Personnel Mgmt., https://www.opm.gov/CCLContact/ (last visited Nov. 18, 2020).
Pay & Leave: Student Loan Repayment, Off. of Personnel Mgmt., https://www.opm.gov/policy-data-oversight/pay-leave/student-loan-repayment/#url=FAQs (last visited Nov. 18, 2020).

Part IV: Litigation Considerations

Pay Systems: General Schedule, Off. of Personnel Mgmt., https://www.opm.gov/policy-data-oversight/pay-leave/pay-systems/general-schedule/ (last visited Nov. 18, 2020).
Salaries & Wages: Locality Pay Areas, Off. of Personnel Mgmt., https://www.opm.gov/policy-data-oversight/pay-leave/salaries-wages/fact-sheets/#url=Locality-Pay-Areas (last visited Nov. 18, 2020).
Pay Administration: Fact Sheet: Pay Plans, Off. of Personnel Mgmt., https://www.opm.gov/policy-data-oversight/pay-leave/pay-administration/fact-sheets/pay-plans/ (last visited Nov. 18, 2020).
Guidance for Agency-Specific Domestic Violence, Sexual Assault, and Stalking Policies, Off. of Personnel Mgmt. (Feb. 2013), https://www.opm.gov/policy-data-oversight/worklife/reference-materials/guidance-for-agency-specific-dvsas-policies.pdf.
Work-Life: Employee Assistance Programs, Off. of Personnel Mgmt., https://www.opm.gov/policy-data-oversight/worklife/employee-assistance-programs (last visited Nov. 19, 2020).
Work-Life: Responding to Domestic Violence: Where Employees Can Find Help, Off. of Personnel Mgmt., https://www.opm.gov/policy-data-oversight/worklife/reference-materials/responding-to-domestic-violence-where-federal-employees-can-find-help (last visited Nov. 19, 2020).
Work-Life Agency Coordinators, Off. of Personnel Mgmt., https://www.opm.gov/cclcontact (last visited Nov. 19, 2020).

Index